THE KARAGIOZIS
HEROIC PERFORMANCE
IN GREEK SHADOW
THEATER

UNIVERSITY PRESS OF NEW ENGLAND

HANOVER AND LONDON

THE KARAGIOZIS
HEROIC PERFORMANCE
IN GREEK SHADOW
THEATER

TRANSLATION BY KOSTAS MYRSIADES
TEXT BY LINDA S. MYRSIADES

UNIVERSITY PRESS OF NEW ENGLAND

BRANDEIS UNIVERSITY

BROWN UNIVERSITY

CLARK UNIVERSITY

-UNIVERSITY OF CONNECTICUT

DARTMOUTH COLLEGE

UNIVERSITY OF NEW HAMPSHIRE

UNIVERSITY OF RHODE ISLAND

TUFTS UNIVERSITY

UNIVERSITY OF VERMONT

© 1988 by University Press of New England

Illustration on title page: Heroic figures by the Karagiozis player Sotiris Spatharis.

Printed in the United States of America

∞

LIBRARY OF CONGRESS CATALOGING-IN-PUBLICATION DATA
Myrsiades, Linda S.
The Karagiozis heroic performance in Greek shadow theater.
Includes index.
1. Karagöz. 2. Shadow pantomimes and plays—Greece.
I. Myrsiades, Kostas. II. Title.
PN1979.S5M97   1988   791.5   87-40508
ISBN 0-87451-429-0

5 4 3 2 1

CONTENTS

Illustrations follow page 62

PREFACE

This volume fills a distinct need in modern Greek studies for it provides, for the first time in English, texts of two performances from the Karagiozis shadow puppet theater, a form whose importance over the last century and a half in Greek folklore and Greek theater is well recognized. Though much has been written about Karagiozis over the last half century in Greece, little in English has been available to students of Greek folklore and oral traditional culture. The texts themselves, only partially available in Greek,[1] are unavailable in English, with the exception of a translation of one comedy published by these translators in 1977. The history of the performance has been largely speculative,[2] and textual criticism is limited in any language.[3] This edition attempts, at least partially, to rectify the neglect into which this rich source of Greek folk ideas and art has fallen. It is designed to satisfy the needs of both the serious student of Greek culture and a more general readership.

The work is divided into four parts: (1) a history of the Karagiozis performance, including the origins of the performance in Greece, its subsequent development, and the historical context in which it survived; (2) critically annotated translations of two classic heroic texts, that is, texts that distinguish the performance as a uniquely Greek expression; (3) an analysis of each text, examining its sources and structure and comparing variants of the texts performed by different Karagiozis players; and (4) an appendix that provides data on characters in the performance, production aspects (including the stage, puppet figures, scenery, properties, and sound and light effects), and the print texts (explaining the history of published texts and their relationship to the oral performance).

Kostas Manos's *Katsandonis* and Markos Ksanthos's *Alexander,* the two texts translated and studied in this work, were selected from a body of 160 texts and represent not only two different forms of heroic plays but the two most important heroic performances of the Greek Karagiozis tradition. The heroic performance was the dominant contribution made by the Greek players to this derivatively Turkish folk form, and those translated here were performed by two of the tradition's most important players during the height of the popularity of the form (1910–1940). The *Katsandonis* text, which represents the historical cycle text that took three nights to perform, provides the most completely developed ideological statement made by the Karagiozis performance. Moreover, our research has uncovered and we have thus resurrected here a major lost text variant by one of the great practitioners of the form. As a complement to *Katsandonis*, the *Alexander* text represents the single most widely popular Karagiozis text, a text that most completely expresses the Greek folk culture's sense of its identity. The *Alexander* variant presented here represents the earliest performed version of the text and was performed by a master player trained in the tradition of the great master of the Greek performance, Mimaros of Patras.

In spite of the difficulties of translating Karagiozis texts, we have attempted in these translations to render the puns, allusions, idioms, and regional dialects with sensitivity to the values of the source culture and its folklore as well as to the performance qualities of the source texts. Please note, however, that because we are dealing with a product of the oral tradition, we have had to negotiate the constraints inherent in using a print text to represent an oral performance (see Appendix C).[4]

The study that makes up the first part of this work provides a history of the Karagiozis performance from its Turkish origins in the sixteenth century through its nineteenth-century assimilation into Greek culture. The history was constructed by examining an extensive range of historical materials, thereby documenting as definitively as possible the growth of the form. This history not only updates but supersedes previous attempts to document the history of the form. Moreover, it adds a new dimension to the history of the form by tying it to historical forces that shaped the social and political life of nineteenth-century Greece.

The critical notes and annotation that support both the study and translation sections of the work present the English-speaking audience with references to the widest possible body of critical materials, including textual and performance commentary by players, text variants, relevant folklore materials, and the scholarly literature. Annotations to the translations in particular make it possible to compare historical and folk tradition testimony on the lives of the heroes, as well as the literature and folklore that has grown up around them, and to examine critical material and commentary on the performances from the perspective of the players themselves.

The breadth of original, authenticated player performances and testimony used to research this work represents an attempt to provide wider access to study materials in a field in which access to such materials has been lean at best. The base of 160 texts in print and on tape is supplemented by commentary by and interviews with thirty-six players in print and on tape.

This work is designed to reach two different audiences, the scholarly and the popular, and has relevance for audiences in such fields as oral literature, theater and drama, folklore, comparative literature, Greek studies, Turkish studies, and Balkan studies. The texts are of interest not only to students of the form but to Greek communities in America, Canada, and Australia, many of whose children will find their only access to this rich form of Greek culture and folklore through these English translations.

This work, finally, provides for the first time in any language other than Greek two major heroic texts of the Greek Karagiozis performance (and in Greek it makes accessible for the first time a major lost work), thereby allowing cross-cultural comparisons with traditional heroic texts in Serbo-Croatian and Turkish as well as with those in other European, Middle Eastern, and Balkan languages. Such study makes it possible not only to determine cross-cultural connections with other traditions but to appreciate more fully the quintessentially Greek attributes of the Karagiozis texts themselves.

This translation was advanced by a grant from the Hellenic-American League, for which we wish to express our gratitude. A subsequent grant from the National Endowment for the Humanities made it possible to explore the Mario Rinovolucri and Cedric Whitman tape collections at the Center for the Study of Oral Literature, Harvard University. We are greatly indebted to the kindness and support of Albert B. Lord and, earlier, David Bynum, curators of the center. A series of grants provided by West Chester University for released time and the purchase of tape materials was exremely helpful, as was the cooperation of the library staffs of both Widener and West Chester universities, particularly the help of Widener University's interlibrary loan librarian, Elizabeth W. Twarog, for which we are very grateful. We are indebted, as well, to Kimon Friar, the dean of modern Greek translators, and to Willis Barnstone, professor of comparative literature at Indiana University, whose skills as teachers and translators we hope is reflected here. Peter Bien's careful reading of this work was of incomparable help as was his continuing and committed support for the study of Karagiozis. We thank, as well, Minas Savvas for his helpful comments on the text, which resulted in several useful changes. Finally, we wish to thank Walter J. Meserve, Director of the Institute for Amer-

ican Theatre Studies at Indiana University, for his long-term involvement in this project, particularly for his thoughtful and penetrating
comments on earlier versions of this manuscript.

Newtown Square, Pennsylvania   K.M.
November 1987   L.S.M.

CHAPTER 1

HISTORY OF THE KARAGIOZIS PERFORMANCE

Karagiozis, or Greek shadow puppet theater, has been referred to in contemporary Greek criticism as "theatre of the Greek people" and "the national theatre of Greece." [1] It has been seen, equally, as the most representative of national Greek dramatic arts since old comedy and Aristophanes. [2] A popular form utilizing stock characters, scenes of daily life, a variety of national and regional costumes, dialects, and manners, its greatest single resource is, indeed, the life of the Greek people. As a political expression reflecting the aspirations and sentiments of the common people, its delimitations are certainly those of the common man.

As an expression of the common world of the Greek folk, Karagiozis establishes and maintains indelible ties to popular folk culture. [3] The popular sense of history and the popular heroes that appear in songs of the folk are its historical understanding and its heroes. Folk characters and types from plays and tales [4]—the quack doctor, old man, old woman, devil, Jew, Vlah, Moor, gypsy, swaggering soldier, old rustic, jesting servant, trickster, parasite, stuttering child, ogre, kindly giant, dragon, baldchin, and great beauty—are its types as well. Popular and folk dances, regional songs, and heroic poetry and ballads appear throughout Karagiozis performances. The loose plots, anecdotal materials, and oral techniques typical of folk tradition belong to it, too. The influence, it appears, was mutual: in Gonusa, Corinth, the marriage of Karagiozis has been interpolated into an old ritual performance.[5] With such easy access to the cultural life of the people, Karagiozis was as certain to prosper among the common people as more cultivated theatrical performances, requiring substantial equipment, regular audiences, highly populated centers, greater sophistication, and literary tastes, were certain in their initial phases to fail.

The Karagiozis form was, nevertheless, not native to Greece. Rather, it appeared first as an Ottoman entertainment and was only much later disseminated to the Greek territories of the Ottoman Empire. Moreover, the Greek people were themselves, during the period of Ottoman rule, part of a culture coextensive with that of the Balkans and Anatolia, a pluralistic culture out of which national cultures would not develop until much later. Thus, Karagiozis remained true to its Ottoman origins well into the nineteenth century, ultimately to break away from its progenitor when it developed heroic texts in the last quarter of that century. These heroic texts integrated Romaic or ethnically mixed (heterotropic) popular, cultural attitudes of native Greeks of the Ottoman period, adding an overlay of Hellenic or ethnically singular (homotropic), middle- and upper-class cultural attitudes of foreign Greeks (heterochthons) of the eighteenth and nineteenth centuries. Developed to naturalize the Karagiozis performance more completely in its Greek home, these texts were intended to minimize hostile reactions of both the Orthodox Church and the new Greek state to the great popularity of the performance in Greece.

Karagoz was one among a number of shadow theater performances played by Turkish mimes of the Ottoman Empire from perhaps as early as the fourteenth century, although the earliest historical references do not appear until the seventeenth century.[6] An instructive form, Turkish shadow puppetry was designed both to entertain and to achieve religious experience, based on the Sufi Islam doctrine that man is but a shadow manipulated by his Creator.[7] Shades or shadows, used earlier in Central Asia in conjunction with ancestor worship or funeral rites, influenced Turkish shadow performances, but it was the arrival of shadow puppet theater from Egypt, apparently at the end of the thirteenth century, that consolidated mime, Sufi, and theatrical influences to create the stable form that developed into Karagoz.[8]

From the classical through the Byzantine to the Ottoman periods, the mime tradition merged with a larger stream of popular entertainments and gradually minimized the religious aspect of shadow puppetry in Turkey.[9] Having included puppetry as one of their specialties at least as early as the fifth century B.C.,[10] mimes exerted a particularly conducive influence on Turkish shadow puppet development. Certainly, the bald-headed, hunch-backed, phallophoric Karagoz fool-hero is curiously similar to the shaven-headed classical and Byzantine mime fools.[11] Mime plots, themes, types, and structures, as well, appear in Turkish Karagoz, some modified by folk literature (like the thieving slave, the haglike old woman, and the cowardly warrior), others adopted more directly (like the obscenity, invective, ridicule of contemporary types and live figures, physical blows, variety of foreign costumes and dialects, and arbitrary plot construction). Indeed, like its counterpart Commedia dell'Arte, Karagoz has been referred to by some as the heir of classical and Byzantine mime.[12]

More importantly, however, as a Turkish-occupied territory, Greece enjoyed entertainments general to the Ottoman Empire. One could speak of Greek and Turkish lands in many ways as coextensive in the entertainments they enjoyed. Le Fevre, in his *Théâtre de la Turquie*, offers typical testimony to the entertainments that were performed during the Moslem holy month, Ramadan.[13] Performed by Greeks, Armenians, and Jews, they consisted of masquerades, buffoonery, and parades of tradesmen with decorated wagons.

Ottoman court festivities, held to celebrate events of religious, political, or military importance, were likely sites for Christian populations to enjoy Moslem entertainments.[14] The international character of the elaborate pageantry made them, after the fourteenth-century Ottoman assumption of power, the most likely heirs of earlier Byzantine pomp and ceremony. As indicated by Murad III's *Surname*,[15] a festival book prepared for the summer 1585 circumcision of Mehmed, the Sultan's son, Ottoman entertainments spanned a wide range of types, from sacred dances, circus acts, and puppetry—often mixed with live actors—to pageant carts, processions, and tournaments. These amusements were performed by troupes of professional performers that enjoyed the status of trade guilds.

Commercial fairs held throughout the empire offered the freest intercourse between Turkish and Greek populations. Here itinerant performers who traveled throughout the provinces offered entertainment.[16] The Moslem traveler Evliya Chelebi's *Narrative Travels in Europe, Asia, and Africa*, 1670, reports on a typical commercial fair in Doliani[17] at which appeared rope artists, tumblers, jugglers, dancers, animal trainers, singers, clowns, athletes, story tellers, musicians, players with fire and sword, and shadow puppet players.

The Karagoz performance does not clearly emerge from this welter of religious and secular, popular, and spectacular entertainments until the seventeenth century. Previously, the term "Karagoz" had been used to mean "black eyes" (that is, a "Turk"). We find such a use in an inscription on what is purported to be the original fourteenth-century tombstone of Sheih Kusteri: "How many karagozes were extinguished from the screen of life." [18] In the popular tradition, Kusteri is taken as the father of the Turkish Karagoz performance. A seventeenth-century *gazel* (the traditional dedicatory poem that opens a Turkish shadow puppet performance) by the Turkish poet Birri notes Kusteri as the patron of shadow puppet players, but nowhere mentions Karagoz. [19] Chelebi merely refers to Kusteri as the inventor of a rudimentary musical instrument, but links Hasan Zadeh, chief mime in the reign of Murad IV (1623–1640), to Karagoz. Referred to as a player and composer of at least three hundred plays of "Chinese shades," Hasan Zadeh is described further in the following terms: "Being extremely fond of women, he invented all the famous scenes of the Karagoz, which are known by the name of the 'Young Man and Nigar Play,' 'Huveyya Play,' 'The Dumb Men's Play,' 'Arab Beggar's and Albanian Play,' 'Bekri Mustafa, the Drunkard and Blind Beggar Play,' 'Spendthrift Gentleman Play,' 'Strolling Gentleman Play,' 'Three Brigand Play,' 'The Public Bath Play,' and 'Serbetcizade Play,' being the father of Hacivad." [20] Here Chelebi provides the first clear identification of Karagoz as a performance. Chelebi goes on to provide specific information on the supposed origin of the two heroes of the performance, Karagoz and Haciavad. Presumed to have been based on a real life figure, Karagoz is identified by Chelebi as a gypsy court messenger to the last Greek emperor, Constantine (the fifteenth-century Constantine Paleologus), while Haciavad is described as court messenger to Ala-ud-din, Prince of the Seljouks (thus placing him in the thirteenth century). The famous battle of wits in which the two figures supposedly engaged, according to Chelebi, would have been difficult given the incompatibility of the dates Chelebi suggests. A more coherent version is expressed in a popular variant to Chelebi's account that places both figures in the reign of the Ottoman ruler, Orhan, in the mid-fourteenth century, contemporaneous with Sheih Kusteri. Kusteri could thus be identified as the creator of the performance that immortalized the comic combatants. It appears that attempts to associate the origin of the Karagoz performance with some illustrious figure (yet another variant places both figures at the court of Suleiman the Magnificent in the early sixteenth century) have prevailed over both historical perspective and veracity.

In any case, the establishment of the Karagoz performance in Turkey is not likely to have occurred earlier than its generic type, "shadow puppet theater," which was not clearly separated from other puppet performances by its own term in Turkish (*hayal-i-zill*) until the sixteenth century.[21] We find the 1585 *Surname*, for example, referring to shadow puppetry as a novelty, here performed by Arabs, in which a cat ate a mouse, young lovers courted a beautiful girl, and a dragon swallowed people[22]—scenes that reappear in later Karagoz and Greek Karagiozis performances throughout the nineteenth century. Moreover, it was not, as previously noted, until the seventeenth century in Turkey that the term "Karagoz" began to refer to a specific type of shadow puppet performance. Certainly the first historical record of the performance does not appear until the seventeenth century, in Chelebi.

By the seventeenth century, at any rate, Karagoz was an entertainment sufficiently well established not only to have been transported to those Middle Eastern nations ultimately taken in by the boundaries of the Ottoman Empire, but to survive there with a distinctly Turkish identity. Thus, it had established itself by the seventeenth century in Egypt, Syria, Persia, Tunisia, and Algeria.[23] Indeed, by the first half of the nineteenth century, considerable evidence exists that this firmly implanted Turkish interloper had become a preferred means of making stinging attacks on political and social abuses in its host countries.[24]

Some commentators accept the presence of Karagoz in the Balkans from the time those countries were subdued by the Turks, assuming the same pattern found in the Arabic countries. Walter Puchner in his work on Karagoz in the Balkans[25] argues that the Balkans was the most plausible of two possible routes of entry for Karagoz into Greece. The first was from the south after the Revolution of 1821, brought by players coming directly from Constantinople.[26] The second was from the north before the revolution, brought by itinerant players of the Ottoman Empire performing in the Balkans.[27] Puchner argues that the second route led to the appearance of the first historically documented performance in Greece (observed in Ioannina at a cafe by the English traveler John Hobhouse in 1809, see p. 19). He does not, however, note an earlier account by de Pouqueville (in 1799) who was farther south, in Tripolitza, which, if it does not conclusively demonstrate an actual Karagoz performance, does indicate knowledge of the performance (see p. 14).

In making his argument, Puchner insists on the following points: that Karagoz was a court entertainment in the Balkans; that it was known to upper-class Greeks (or Fanariotes)[28] in the Balkans who imitated the powerful of Byzantium by holding Ottoman entertainments at their courts; and that these entertainments were thus familiar to upper-class Greeks in the Turkish form (although performed in Greek and Rumanian as well as in Turkish) in the eighteenth century and possibly as far back as the seventeenth century.

What is most important to Puchner is not where Karagoz first appeared in Greece or whether it was performed in Turkish or Greek, but whether it was known during the Turkish occupation by the secret Greek revolutionary society, the Filiki Eteria, and its members, the Fanariotes. In making his argument, Puchner states that upper-class court performances appeared earlier than performances in cafes for lower-class audiences. While discussing evidence of the latter performances in Greece in the mid-nineteenth century, he makes it clear that he believes the performance had, by this time, lost the exotic attraction it had retained in good society until the 1830s.

The implications of Puchner's argument regarding the Fanariotes makes the Greek Karagiozis performance a natural receptacle for Hellenic influences, for it would have been effectively introduced to Greece by heterocthon Greeks from the Balkans, having been familiar to them possibly as long as a century before it was known to lower-class audiences in Greece. The problem with Puchner's argument is his sources, as Puchner himself admits. Sources in Greece, in particular, are sparse, and those in the Balkans, uneven across the centuries. Moreover, Ottoman sources suggest that the Turkish performance cannot be identified as largely an upper-class entertainment. Whereas the performance's appearance at royal circumcisions and Ottoman court festivities makes it clear that upper-class court entertainments played a role in the development of the performance, Karagoz remained across the extent of the empire a performance that appealed to and expressed its common audience, that is, it was more compatible with attitudes of the common class. It is certainly true, moreover, that reports of Karagoz in Greece consistently refer to cafe performances, lower-class audiences, and oriental attitudes, a situation that would not have obtained had Karagoz been brought to Greece or been sponsored in Greece by Fanariote interests. To substantiate Puchner's argument, one would have to account for the integration of this tradition with that of Fanariote, court-sponsored Karagoz performances in the Balkans. Puchner cites a single source to this effect, Vellianitis in *Estia Ikonografimeni*, 1893, who writes of the interest displayed in Athens by foreign ambassadors and the upper classes in these "strange performances"; he notes that the Austrian Ambassador Prokesch-Osten took the performance from a cafe into his own home. The ambassador does not, however, mention the event in his own writings.[29]

Puchner's argument that the Balkans was the entry route into Greece for Karagoz is germane to the debate over the Romaic nature of the performance. If Greek Karagiozis can be identified as continuous with Balkan performances, it strengthens the argument that the performance was endemic to those same Byzantine lands that, swallowed by the Ottoman Empire, had once been coterminous lands that shared an indigenous and pluralistic culture, a culture whose origin was Byzantine while its time frame was that of a vaguely distant past that stood for all time.

One must at the outset, however, admit that the extensive evidence Puchner marshalls is not entirely satisfactory. His evidence as far back as the seventeenth century, for example, speaks almost exclusively of marionettes,[30] plays,[31] and shadow theater,[32] but not of Karagoz. He does note, however, an important piece of information from 1695 demonstrating that Turkish travelers near Ottoman-held Belgrade saw Karagoz figures (together with candles to light the performance) at a commercial fair.[33]

Puchner's eighteenth-century evidence suffers from much the same problem. Although the evidence refers to vulgar dialogues, farces, and comedies performed by army sergeants (both Turkish and Armenian soldiers playing in Rumanian, Greek, and Turkish), as well as shadow theater and story-telling (Meddah), nowhere does it identify the Karagoz performance. The performances cited, moreover, appear in cafes, village squares (*platias*), and fairs as well as at the courts of princes and pashas; in many instances the performances are played by amateurs rather than itinerant, professional performers. Though we do find a healthy and diverse number of performances, we do not find a coherent playing tradition. The testimony speaks of live performances of vulgar comedies in the style of or like "the famous puppet theater," and it refers to shadow theater, but it does not distinguish live from puppet theater, puppet theater from shadow theater, or shadow theater from Karagoz. Moreover, the one reference to Karagoz that does appear in the eighteenth century (a note in Prince Kantemir's history of Ottoman rule) merely refers again to Karagoz as a term meaning "black eyes."[34]

In brief, the evidence can be highlighted as follows. In 1715, the Venetian Del Chiaro cited vulgar farces performed by an obscene and scandalous troupe of buffoons at Prince Nicholas Mavrogordato's court at Bucharest. It then performed for the Chiefs of Bogiaron and later at market town cafes and in the villages.[35] In 1780, the Swiss Franz Sulzer, serving as an Austrian army captain, witnessed two types of performances presented by Turkish army sergeants at the court of the Fanariote, Prince Alexander Ipsilanti, in Bucharest. They performed first an improvised comedy in the style of the "famous puppet theater" in Romanian, Greek, and Turkish. The second performance was referred to as what the Greeks call an "opera" and as "Turkish spectacle," but was clearly shadow puppet theater. Performed in Greek and Romanian, this performance used a screen, table, cardboard puppets—said to be like Hanswurst—and lights.[36] A few years after 1776, Turkish travelers on the Dalmatian coast reported Armenians among the Turkish sergeants, playing Turkish comedies with vulgar jokes; they also played various stories at cafes.[37] The second performance viewed by Sulzer and the first witnessed by the Turkish travelers is understood by Puchner to be Orta Oyunu (a live Turkish mime form), and the second viewed by the Turkish travelers as the Turkish art of story-telling, or Meddah.[38] In 1786 in Dubrovnik, Josep Skuventa organized a performance with "Chinese shades" with which he was familiar from Ottoman-held Bosnia.[39] In Raicevic in 1788, a diplomat from the Dalmatian coast noted that Armenian actors performed farces in the courts of the Fanariotes.[40] Yet another shadow theater performance was performed in 1798 in a square (platia) in Orlandum.[41] At some time in the eighteenth century, a foreign traveler at the court of the Paradunian prince viewed a vulgar dialogue using two protagonists, which lasted as long as a theatrical performance.[42]

We thus find ourselves at the threshold of the nineteenth century and the first reference (in 1809) to a Karagoz performance (in a cafe) in a Greek territory (in northern Greece). Puchner suggests several possible, transitional pieces of evidence that might seal the Balkan origin of the Greek Karagiozis performance. Among them is the only direct reference to Karagoz—testimony discovered by Veludis of an amateur theater in 1817 in Odessa, which presented lewd and indecent things such as Karagoz in Constantinople.[43] Puchner acknowledges that even this testimony probably does not refer to an actual Karagoz performance in Odessa.

In sum, the evidence suggests that there existed in the Balkans a tradition of shadow theater performances that shared themes, characters, and jokes not only with Karagoz, but with Orta Oyunu (live mime comedy) and Meddah (story-telling). The performances in the Balkans seem to have been mixed forms, reflecting the same type of performances found in the Ottoman Empire just prior to the separation of the Karagoz form as a distinct type in the seventeenth century. Out of this mixed, Ottoman tradition of comedies and shadow theater, a distinctive Karagoz form emerged whose early popularity permitted players to distinguish themselves specifically as professional Karagoz players. When performed in the provinces, where Karagoz was less well known, it is likely that players reverted to mime and farce in a variety of languages possibly more appealing to their provincial audiences. That Karagoz performances were known of seems to be beyond question (certainly the term "Karagoz" was known, with a variety of meanings in a number of Balkan languages, as Puchner demonstrates).[44] What is more difficult to demonstrate is that there was a sufficient tradition of Karagoz performances in the Balkans to insure that this route would be the chosen means by which the performance would enter Greece.

Puchner goes on to argue that, with the banishment of the Fanariotes in 1821, the court performances of Karagoz moved into the cafes of the cities and the market towns. He argues thus in spite of evidence of cafe and market town performances as early as Chelebi's reference to performances at a fair in Doliani in 1660[45] and Del Chiaro's references to performances at cafes in Bucharest in 1715.[46] Moreover, references to Fanariote princes in particular as hosts of general performances at court (let alone references to Karagoz performances, of which there are none) are infrequent, making it unlikely that, as a group, the Fanariotes had adopted the Karagoz performance, brought it to Greece, and turned it into a Hellenized performance for upper-class audiences.

Although the argument favoring Karagoz as an upper-class entertainment does not appear to be demonstrable, and even though a clear tradition of Karagoz performances in the Balkans cannot be accepted as an established fact, it is apparent that a rich body of theatrical entertainments as well as knowledge of the Karagoz performance did exist in the Balkans. The existence of such performances demonstrates the presence of a pluralistic culture consistent with that of Byzantine times, a culture rooted in the indigenous population and, at the same time, sharing values similar to the Romaic values of the native population of the Greek territories.

One final question is raised by the existence of several significant notices of nineteenth-century Karagoz performances in the Balkans, coincident with the growth of performance notices of Greek Karagiozis.[47] In spite of the fact that the initial reference (in 1695) to Karagoz in the Balkans[48] (of Karagoz figures and candles to light the performance, carried to Belgrade by Turkish merchants) is 114 years earlier than the first notice of a Karagoz performance in Greece, the real flourishing of these performances appears to have occurred in both the Balkans and Greece at about the same time: in the latter part of the nineteenth century. One could argue that the coincidental flowering of the performance in both places at the same time supports once again the notion of a continuing, coextensive culture across Greek and Balkan lands. This culture retained its diversity of theatrical performances out of which Karagiozis emerged, flourishing when the popular climate finally became fully receptive to it in the nineteenth century.

In Greece itself, until the late eighteenth century (the earliest century fully documented by foreign travelers), the evidence for the presence of Karagoz is inconclusive. A tradition of popular entertainments existed continuously in Greek lands from the Byzantine through the Ottoman period.[49] Saints' holidays and fairs provided opportunities for the native population to view numerous itinerant performers who traveled throughout the mainland. Indeed, as the English traveler John Cam Hobhouse remarked in 1809, "This oppressed people would find life too long and burthensome, were it not for their religious festivals. . . ."[50] Guys, a French traveler to Turkish-occupied Crete in 1750, testifies: "Les Grecs aiment encore les fêtes, les jeux, les spectacles, le luxe; mais le gouvernment leur impose une constrainte qui le décourage."[51]

Travelers' memoirs show that popular entertainments among the Greeks included dramatic dances, folk plays, fool shows, mumming, and story-telling, performances that could have established a receptive dramatic climate for shadow theater.[52] The dramatic instinct of the Greek common class appears not to have required formal theatrical performances; certainly we find that live theater had difficulty establishing itself in Greece, not making any headway until well after the Greek Revolution of 1821.[53] The dramatic instinct was apparently well satisfied by the elaborate masquerading and the traditional folk plays that appeared at carnival, by the mumming at May Day, and by the dramatic rituals and processionals provided during weddings, funerals, and on religious holidays, particularly Easter. Moreover, masquerades, mumming, and folk plays had not only the merit of being closely associated with a native religious occasion, but expressed continuity with vintage festivals from preclassical times.

The taste for the free-form buffoonery of the Ottoman mimes was transferred to the shadow theater and to its specialized offshoot, Karagoz. Buffoonery does not appear to have persisted in Greek popular entertainment to the same degree as among the Turks, other than in those performances played during the Carnival season, which served as an excuse for easing restrictions and tolerating popular social and political excesses. The body of entertainments available in Greece included few fool shows and little buffoonery, entertainments whose presence in any numbers would have indicated a taste among Greeks for an entertainment such as Karagoz.

Judging from surviving accounts, a broad and intimate diffusion of amateur entertainments among the Greek people was provided by singers of klephtic songs, native dancers, and local tale-tellers in the villages themselves. It seems to have provided the Greek folk with accessible, periodic entertainments to supplement, together with periodic commercial fairs, those rather numerous religious festivals that fill the Orthodox church calendar and the folk rituals that punctuate the year. Indeed, during the Byzantine period, church prohibitions against mimes and theater seem to have had a more prevalent effect on the conservative, provincial Greek mainland than on the more international world of court life in Constantinople, which formed tastes like those outlined here that, once developed, were later difficult to change.

A distinct separation between Greek entertainments and those of the Ottoman peoples in Greece did not, however, exist.[54] Other than during the riotous evenings of Ramadan and during private palace entertainments, the populations of occupied Greece mingled freely. Common Greeks were not considered by foreign travelers either culturally superior to or more moral than their Turkish counterparts, indeed, they were sometimes described as despised and mean creatures who had lost all contact with their glorious, classical predecessors.[55] Ottomans in Greece were frequently given credit for greater sensibility and stronger religious values, a comment that may, however, have had more to do with their role as the conquering class than to a necessarily superior character. But, in general, common Greeks were closely identified with oriental cultures, more so than with the Western sentiments and manners of Greeks of the diaspora who, with the success of the Revolution of 1821, would soon rule in Greece. The likelihood, therefore, existed that Karagoz would not find an inhospitable climate in Greece, even if it had not yet found a favorable opportunity to be introduced to the general population there.

It is possible, on the other hand, that performances of Karagoz occurred at pashas' palaces in such places as Tripolitza in the Peloponnesos and Tepellene in Epirus, centers of activity for Turkish culture in Greece. But we find no evidence from seventeenth- and eighteenth-century visitors of such entertainments; rather, they speak of attending hunting parties, promenades, and musical evenings at which appeared dancing dervishes, minstrels, story-tellers, and fools. Karagoz performances could, however, have appeared in the palaces or harems of pashas throughout Greece without being called to the attention of either foreign visitors or Greeks. The latter would have had little opportunity to visit the private recesses of the serai. Similarly, while foreign travelers in Constantinople saw Karagoz performances played in cafes,[56] they were not invited to those performed for members of the ruling class's inner circle. Harsh and moralistic European reaction to common Karagoz performances possibly discouraged upper-class Turks from tendering such invitations. Foreign visits were, moreover, formal occasions treated with some delicacy by officials and wealthy Turks, who preserved a reputation of cultured men rich in sensibility. Finally, the Karagoz performance was reserved in Turkish lands for those special occasions, such as Ramadan evenings and royal circumcisions, when restrictions were eased and the political and social satire of the performance was tolerated—a situation much like what prevailed at Greek Carnival and such European holidays as All Fools Day. Indeed, as one educated Turk informed a Western visitor in 1844,[57] Karagoz was, in one quarter, not only tolerated but encouraged in its excessive grossness to serve as an antidote to antisocial behavior. Ubicini in 1855 claims, as well, that during Ramadan "saturnales de l'islamisme" all abuse was protected.[58] Thus, that Karagoz would have been performed whenever it pleased a pasha in Greece, while possible, is not entirely likely. More unlikely is the possibility that foreign visitors would have been present to record such entertainments. The only foreign visitor who does note such performances in a serai in Greece (de Pouqueville during Ramadan in Tripolitza, 1799) apparently did not himself see the performance.[59] A subsequent eyewitness account of a Ramadan performance in Greece (Hobhouse in Epirus, 1809) places the performance not at the serai in Tepellene but at a cafe in a poor section of nearby Ioannina.[60]

Entertainments continued to be restricted to special occasions during the period of change that followed the Greek Revolution of 1821. Indeed, the chaotic spirit of undisciplined crowds in a country deeply scarred by a brutal war, with land being generally ruined, with unstable borders, and with internal political strife, resulted in instances of stringent control. Formal entertainments, in particular theater and opera, stepped into the breach. The infusion into Greece of more sophisticated and Westernized Greeks of the diaspora resulted in a split between native Greeks and those who, with the new Bavarian King Otho (invested in 1836), preferred the performances of imported Italian and French troupes. Only to a limited extent did the latter support the development of a national Greek theater.[61] The issue for the native Greek was freedom from foreign influence; the issue for the Greek of the diaspora, that new times required new, preferably Western, expressions. Neither side was willing to concede the ultimate similarity of both forms of theater. The Greek troupes were themselves formed by Greeks of the diaspora whose training was either Italian or French and whose repertoires included largely historical and sentimental French,

Italian, and classical Greek plays, sprinkled with modern Greek works modeled on Italian and French construction and themes.

Greek troupes had begun by mounting historical and patriotic productions of texts from as early as 1817 and 1818 in performances sponsored by the revolutionary secret society, Filiki Eteria, in Bucharest and Odessa. In the earliest years of establishing the state, they turned to plays on classical subjects that provided models of ancient heroism from which contemporary Greeks could draw courage and to plays on modern Greek historical subjects that could apply to the recent struggle against the Turks.

Neither the foreign nor Greek troupes could be said to have developed a revolutionary repertoire; rather, the former catered to an aristocratic taste for diversion (Italian comedy, opera, and melodrama), and the latter, to the common crowd's enthusiasm for patriotic sentiment. The "theater war" that ensued was exacerbated by government subsidies that favored Italian troupes and government regulations and censorship that inhibited the development of Greek theater until the third quarter of the century.[62] The live Greek theater was caught between the antitheses of Italian theater, on the one hand, and Karagiozis, on the other. Although essentially Western in its themes and construction, live Greek theater catered as well to Romaic support in its reliance on a common Greek audience to counter the effects of Italian theater. With these mixed attributes, live Greek theater became an amenable influence on the Karagiozis performance, which, in its attempts to mitigate the hostility of church and state, would develop a new form influenced by the patriotic texts of live Greek theater—the heroic text—to widen its own base of support and insure its survival. During periods of crisis, as Petropoulos demonstrates,[63] such socially divisive characteristics as sectionalism, class warfare, and church-state antipathies tended to be suspended or at least temporarily resolved. It was during such a period (the late nineteenth-century border wars) that Karagiozis capitalized on the minimalization of social frictions to solidify itself in its own naturalization.

The dramatic activity and the competition that developed in Greece during the last quarter of the nineteenth century was, in one respect, most fortunate. It provided a spattering of newspaper and journal commentary about Karagiozis that indicates, for the first time on record, not only the evolution of a Greek form from the Turkish performance but the robust state of health of that Greek form. From this point on, it can be said that Karagiozis was firmly established in Greece. It had developed in the context of a social and economic system whose rapid growth and political conflicts had eclipsed notice of the performance's gradual popular acceptance, just as they had exacerbated the debate that led to the theater wars. It is, in fact, likely that the interest aroused by the theater wars provided the impetus necessary for the success of the Karagiozis performance. Nevertheless, several notices have survived from which a short history of the evolution of the Greek performance can be gleaned. They allow us to reconstruct the faltering steps with which the performance separated itself from its Turkish progenitor and groped its way toward final acceptance.

The first notice of Karagoz in Greece is inconclusive, but nonetheless welcome. Foreign travelers—a prime source of entertainment notices throughout the Ottoman Empire from the sixteenth century on—who had freely noted Karagoz performances when visiting Constantinople, seem by the testimony of their memoirs not to have encountered them in Greece itself. The sparseness of references persists from the eighteenth throughout the nineteenth centuries. The first notice by a traveler of Karagoz in Greece was made by the Frenchman de Pouqueville during his 1799 trip to Tripolitza in the Morea, southern Greece. In a general catalogue of the servants provided and the services available in the pasha's palace there, de Pouqueville listed barbers, hairdressers, and bathers, as well as the following entertainers: "des musiciens, des jouers de marionnettes, des porteurs de lanterne magique, qui régalent le prince du spectacle de carageueus; des lutteurs, ou pehlevans, de joueurs de gobelets, des danseurs, un imam. . . ."[64] The "carageueus" referred to in the quotation is defined in a footnote on the same page in the following terms: "ce sont les marionnettes, mais d'un gout très-obscène."

De Pouqueville's reference is just that, a reference. He does not specify having seen performances, but merely notes that they formed part of the general entertainment of the serai. Moreover, he describes "carageueus" as a marionette performance and not as "ombre Chinoise," the period term used in French to specify the shadow puppet form. The spectacle is further introduced as presented by players of the "lanterne magique," a highly popular optical illusion show using projections. The performance indicated could as easily have been a show of slides depicting a Karagoz performance or themes taken from Karagoz as Karagoz itself. De Pouqueville's failure to record his attendance at an actual performance, taken together with his specification of the term "carageueus" in what appears to be a later addition to the text—a footnote, rather than in the text itself—leads one to suspect that his testimony is indirect. In addition, de Pouqueville, residing in Tripolitza during Ramadan, does not mention that the performance formed part of that season's entertainment, although it was traditionally performed at that time. One is, of course, free to argue that the omission was a conscious one, lending strength to the contention that the performance was not as closely wed to the Ramadan holiday as many critics believe. Indeed, one could say that de Pouqueville's list suggests a separation of the performance from special occasions, at least in Greece, and that it was simply performed in the palace whenever desired. The ambiguity of the reference cannot, however, be attributed to indifferent observation, for when de Pouqueville attended performances in Constantinople later in his trip, in 1802, he not only mentions his attendance and describes the nature of Karagoz, but he offers the testimony of a friend, M. L. B. Sevin, who describes a performance for the reader.[65] One is forced to conclude that de Pouqueville may not have seen "carageueus" performances in Tripolitza or was not at that time aware of their nature. Rather, he is reporting on what he has been told and only as part of a general note on services and performances in the palace.

By contrast, de Pouqueville's later description of Karagoz performances in Constantinople is well defined. They are introduced in a discussion of Ramadan, a season when the "grave et serieux" Turkish people, who were thought to have neither spectacle nor dances—"en un mot, aucune de ce réunions qui embellissent l'existence"—suspend their labors and find themselves "constamment occupés." The only entertainment discussed here is Karagoz, and that at length, as a possible exception to the general lack of spectacles. Nevertheless, he concludes: "On ne peut pas dire, à la rigueur, qu'ils aient un spectacle; car il n'est pas permis de donner ce nom à des scènes indécentes de marionnettes, que ces hommes, si jaloux de leurs femmes, font répresenter dans leur familles."[66] In support of his negative view of the performance, de Pouqueville invokes the testimony of Sevin, who first recalls the puppet hero's appearance with "tout l'équipage du fameux dieu de Lampsaque." Sevin describes the performance he saw as one in which Karagoz, in act 1, marries and consummates his marriage in full view of the audience; in act 2, his wife delivers a child who at once engages Karagoz in what the observer describes as a filthy dialogue; in act 3, Karagoz is disguised as a dervish and, together with the whole community, is eaten by a dragon who, unable to digest so terrible a dinner, vomits it up again. De Pouqueville himself recalls a performance in which the funeral procession for a dead Jew is followed by a merchant crying out his wares in Portuguese. The whole section then ends with de Pouqueville's reconfirmed judgment: "Ainsi, les Turcs n'ont ni spectacle, ni fêtes. . . ."[67]

De Pouqueville's Constantinople reference throws an interesting light on the performance of Karagoz in southeastern Europe by marionette or mime troupes rather than by a Karagoz player or shadow puppet entertainers. Although de Pouqueville clearly refers to a Karagoz shadow puppet theater performance, both he and Sevin identify the performance as "des scènes indécentes marionnettes." The term "marionettes" was, in fact, used both before and during this period as a general description of puppets of all types, a reflection again of the practice among individual artists since the Byzantine Empire of performing a variety of entertainments ranging from mimicry, juggling, and acrobatics to various forms of puppetry. Gerard de Nerval and Theophile Gautier, for example, reflect what was common practice among French travelers of the times, using the French terms "marionnette" and "ombre Chinoise" interchangeably to refer to Karagoz performances they viewed in Constantinople in the 1850s.[68] Even Sulzer in Romania in 1780 uses the term "marionette" to refer to a Turkish shadow theater spectacle. John Cam Hobhouse, who a full decade after de Pouqueville, in 1809, provides us with the first detailed, eyewitness account of an actual Karagoz performance in Greece, uses the term "Turkey puppet-shows" to refer to performances he heard about;[69] after having viewed such shows himself, however, he chooses the more carefully delimiting term, "ombre Chinoise."[70] The failure to make distinctions that clearly identify Karagoz as a shadow puppet theater performance is, at any rate, not an isolated event. As earlier indicated, confusion not only existed between Karagoz and other shadow puppet performances and mimes, but between shadow theater, religious shades, and dreams. A widely traveled student of life in the Turkish Empire, de Pouqueville inspires in his Constantinople description one final, new possibility that must be accounted for. By the manner in which he introduces his subject, he raises once more the possibility that the Karagoz performance was played outside of the Ramadan period, as a general entertainment. Considering his admission, "J'ai vu moi-même plusieurs de ces farces,"[71] one wonders if the numerous visits to which he refers could all have taken place during the short space of the Ramadan season. It appears that apart from public holiday performances at cafes, a precedent existed in Turkey from as early as the late sixteenth century for occasional performances of puppet plays in private houses, as indicated in Gazali's sixteenth-century *Dafi'al Gumum Rafi'al Humum,* which depicts just such an occasion.[72] Yet another account, in 1826, describes a foreign traveler's attendance at a Karagoz performance in a rich Turk's house in a men's room separated from the harem. This account offers further confirmation of private, nonholiday performances.[73]

Finally, one's curiosity is piqued by a question that has dogged historical accounts from as early as Chelebi's manuscript: What happens to itinerant performers between the month-long Ramadan holidays, royal circumcisions, and commercial fairs? If, as we have been told, popular Ottoman entertainments were played by professional troupes with the status of trade guilds, how was such a status achieved if not by year-round performing? Throughout the empire we find minstrels and story-tellers performing for travelers on the road and at local khans, or inns, over the course of the year. Is it not likely that these roving performers were masters of many trades, including Karagoz, just as Ottoman mimes were also shadow puppet players and manipulators of fireworks? One wonders, in particular, if occupied Christian lands, which were permitted a large decree of local rule, were very responsive to restrictions emanating from a distant, Moslem center of power. Certainly, the separation between court and countryside that existed in Byzantine times was even more highly exacerbated with the national and religious differences that existed between the two in Ottoman times. Thus, though Karagoz may have been traditionally restricted to special occasions in an Anatolian center of Ottoman culture, such as Constantinople, players may have had precedent, and perhaps some opportunity, for irregular performances of this particular specialty in the vast western reaches of the empire. We find just such a possibility suggested after the Greek revolution in two travelers' accounts, in which the seditious nature of the performance is said to have led to its censorship and exile from Constantinople. They report that the performance was forbidden in Turkish and had to be performed, if at all, in "la langue des esclaves ou des Hellènes."[74] In such circumstances, one can imagine the flight of Karagoz from its traditional home to new areas in the empire more amenable to its sedition and more immediate to its language. The largest barrier to its popular acceptance, of course, would continue to be the Orthodox church, which maintained strong influences in the provinces.

The church as a source of social, moral, and political leadership deserves note here for the role it played during the nineteenth century in inhibiting the assimilation of the Karagiozis performance in Greece. The church faced its own power struggle with the coming of the revolution, which led it to hold tenaciously onto its moral authority over the common class, its chief source of support. That power struggle centered primarily around the challenge to church authority and culminated in the establishment of an autocephalic Church and Caesaropapism in Greece under the terms of the Church Settlement of 1833–1834. Cut off by the war from two sources of its strength (the Patriarchate in Constantinople and Ottoman authority, which allowed it to rule in Greece under the millet system), the Orthodox church

found its institutional strength shattered. Its chief allies thus became
the Russians (themselves an Orthodox nation) and Greek peasants
(who still accepted the church's authority and led public outcries
against further dissolution by the new Greek state of church lands and
power).[75] Heterochthonous Greeks of the new government argued that
the revolution had been waged as much against the tyranny of the
church as against that of Ottoman rule, implying the collaboration of
the church with the old rulers to retain its privileges. These issues were
but part of the larger cultural conflict between secularism and spiritual-
ity, West and East, modernity and medievalism, in which the Karagiozis
performance became caught. In this confused picture of countermand-
ing forces, the church stood as both a bulwark and a tyranny to autochthonous Greeks. As long as the Karagiozis performance retained
its Ottoman ties, it was both associated with notions of collaboration
(from which the Church itself wished to escape) and with Islam (a pe-
rennial enemy of both church and state). At the same time, the Karagiozis performance retained its ties to autochthonous Greeks and their
essentially oriental attitudes and disassociated itself from anticlerical
heterochthonous attacks on the church, to which the common Greek
objected. The alliance forged between the Karagiozis performance and
its common audience rejected many of the Hellenic notions sponsored
by the new Greek state; in particular, it resisted placing a higher pre-
mium on the influence of western European forces than on that of native Greeks and resisted subsuming Christian values to values emanating from the pagan classical past. The church was, in sum, both an ally
of the Karagiozis performance as a Romaic force and an enemy in its
insistence on asserting its superior moral authority. The secular nationalism of the isolated and elite heterochthons, by contrast, was appealing (since it fostered a sense of pride and nationhood in the common Greek) and unappealing (since it did so with a clearly upper
middle-class and western European bias). It was, nevertheless, im-
pingent upon the Karagiozis performance ultimately to make its peace
with both the church and heterochthon forces if the performance was
to naturalize itself in the new Greek state. The meeting ground was to
be the newly developed heroic text (in particular, the history text), and
the moment was to occur in the late nineteenth century.

The next and most important step in recording Karagoz performances in Greece was taken by John Cam Hobhouse, an English
baron and travel companion to Lord Byron in Greece, who visited Epirus, northern Greece, in 1809. Referring to a performance put on during Ramadan in October, 1809, the author initially makes only a brief
comment: "In truth, although during this month the strictest absti-

nence, even from tobacco and coffee, is observed in the daytime, yet with the setting of the sun feasting commences, and a small repast is served; then is the time for paying and receiving visits, and for the amusements of Turkey puppet-shows. . . ."[76] Hobhouse saw one of these performances himself later in the month and referred to it specifically as a Karagoz performance:

An evening or two before our departure from Ioannina, we went to see the only advance which the Turks have made towards scenic representations. This was a puppet show, conducted by a Jew who visits this place during the Ramazan, with his card performers. The show, a sort of ombre Chinoise, was fitted up in a corner of a very dirty coffee-house, which was full of spectators, mostly young boys. The admittance, was two paras for a cup of coffee, and two or three more of those small pieces of money put into a plate handed round after the performance. The hero of the piece was a kind of punch, called Cara-keus, who had, as a traveller has well expressed it, the equipage of the God of Gardens, supported by a string from his neck. The next in dignity was a droll, called Codja-Haivat, the Sancho of Cara-keus; a man and a woman were the remaining figures except that the catastrophe of the drama was brought about by the appearance of the Devil himself in his proper person. The dialogue, which was all in Turkish, and supported in different tones by the Jew, I did not understand; it caused loud and frequent bursts of laughter from the audience; but the action which was perfectly intelligible was too horribly gross to be described. If you have ever seen the morrice-dancing in some counties of England, you may have a faint idea of it. If the character of a nation, as had been said, can be well appreciated by a view of the amusements in which they delight, this puppet-show would place the Turks very low in the estimation of any observer. They have none, we were informed, of a more decent type.[77]

The player described in Hobhouse's notice was an itinerant performer who played in a vulgar coffeehouse and used simple cardboard puppets. Admission required the purchase of a cup of coffee (presumably recompense for the cafeowner) and the price of a second cup (probably for the player himself) collected in a plate passed among the spectators. The audience was made up of male Turks, as Hobhouse suggests in expressing his low opinion of a nation that indulges in such entertainments and in referring to the audience as made up largely of young boys. The performance, as he describes it, must have relied to a great extent for its effect on Cara-keus's movable phallus (as Sevin indicated, a commonplace in Turkish Karagoz), manipulated by a string around the puppet's neck, for the performance appears to have been obscene and boisterous. Limited to five characters (Cara-keus, Codja-Haivat, a man, a woman, and a devil) and using a limited variety of dialects, the play must have been more primitive than the performances referred to by de Pouqueville and Sevin in Constantinople in

1802, apparently lacking the whole "community" of types available to the latter performances. It is worth noting here that de Pouqueville, who visited Epirus earlier (and whose book of travels served as a travel guide to Hobhouse), did not mention having seen Karagoz performances there.

Hobhouse's notice is interesting not only because it represents the earliest detailed reference to an actual performance of Turkish shadow theater in Greece, but also because it refers specifically to a Jewish performer who apparently visited Ioannina each Ramadan with his puppets. This Jew must be considered the first documented player in Greece, his appearance here providing a link with a popular Greek account of a Jewish player, Jacob, who was supposed to have played before the Greek revolution for the Albanian tyrant Ali Pasha (1800–1822) at his serai in Tepellene. Though Hobhouse's evidence disputes a second, and more prevalent, popular account in which the Greek player Barba Yiannis Vrahalis introduces Karagoz to Greece well after the revolution, c. 1860, it makes a third report more believable. This third account states that heroes of the Greek revolution attended Turkish performances of Karagoz, where they could meet without detection to plan revolutionary activities. This version is tenuously supported by secondhand, mid-twentieth-century testimony of Greeks who claim their grandfathers attended secret performances held before the war in caves and monasteries. These performances supposedly dealt with themes of Turkish-Greek conflict and were attended not only by villagers, both men and women, but by klephts fighting in the mountains.[78] This testimony, too distant from the event to bear much critical weight and too purposefully shaped to be entirely plausible, can at least be back-dated a full generation by a report in the periodical, *Estia* (1888), in which Babis Anninos describes the following:

About one of these, a distinguished Chief of the mainland, it is related that he came at times with a large retinue of armed lads to the humble theatre of a Karagiozis player. Completely indifferent to this common man, he haughtily ordered him to cut off the performance begun and to begin separately one of his pleasure. Crouched, the humble performer carried out the command; he set forth the ordered performance, an obscene one from his repertoire. The officer, having sat through the unbearable obscenity of this performance, afterwards addressed his followers with princely liberality, castigating the docile hunch-back for the performer's caprice. This was Karagiozis.[79]

This account does not, unfortunately, clearly place the event before the revolution. Its earlier reference to the performance as common Turkish theater does no more than indicate that Karagoz was still regarded a Turkish rather than a Greek form in the author's own times. The account does demonstrate, however, that a tradition linking "soldiers of the Greek revolution" with the Karagoz performance existed seventy years after the event was presumed to have taken place. Moreover, it views vulgarity as a common taste of the period described, among Greeks as well as Turks, and reveals the double standard maintained by performers who, sensitive to the presence of Christians, presented only their most insipid fare.

If Anninos's account can be taken as an accurate representation of the period described, it clarifies one troublesome issue: the supposed morality of the common Greek as the motive for rejecting "Karagiozis" (a term that will henceforth be used to designate performances in Greece following Greek liberation) through the early and mid-nineteenth century. Linked to that issue is the question about whether or not there was a taste among the Greeks for such a performance as Karagiozis early in the century. Both aspects of this problem hinge on some special morality within the Greek common class, an assumption that, given the development of oriental attitudes under 350 years of Turkish rule, cannot truly be made given the state of the common class's habits and manners, as distinguished from its politics and religion. The most important aspect of Anninos's account is the suspicion it raises that the perception of vulgarity and obscenity in the Karagiozis performance was not the same among those of the common class (those of the oral culture with which the performance made its home) as among those of the literate class, whose attitudes were created and fostered by what was written in newspapers and periodicals of the period.[80] The question one should be asking is not why Karagiozis took so long after the revolution to become popular, but rather—given its likely early acceptance among those of the common class, who found the performance's values familiar and accessible— why Karagiozis took so long to gain formal acceptance in Greece. The answer to that question, it appears, lies in the split of sensibilities between the common class and the upper-class, Westernized, diasporate Greeks and in government control of and resistance to popular entertainment rather than in moral objections among common Greeks to the performance's themes.

An 1852 notice of a Karagiozis performance to be played in Athens (*Tahypteros Fimi,* 9 February 1852) throws additional light on the performance's ability to inspire objections in mid-century Greece:

An oriental theater has been formed in the neighborhood of Plaka. By spending only ten lepta, that is five lepta for entrance and five lepta for a nargile, you can entertain yourself for three full hours of unending laughter the whole time. During the last performance a wedding was celebrated, that of Karagiozis, who, as he puts it, was eager to invite various people from the east, west, north, and south and all the Dodecanese. So, one could see there people from various nations in different attire such as ceremonial and ordinary turbans, Astrakhan fezes, towels, skullcaps, fezes, bonnets, and consequently full-skirted robes, ceremonial riding dress, Turkish trousers, bournouses, loose robes, tunics, greatcoats, fur cloaks, knee-breeches, baggy trousers, raincoats, shepherd capes, jackets, cloaks, cassocks, etc. Karagiozis himself wearing his official attire (in fustibus) and a lahuri shawl on his head received the guests repeating often, "Just because you're invited to a wedding don't be silly." Nasreddin Hotza riding on a camel standing between four minarets and surrounded by twelve dervishes was in charge of the religious ceremony. Hatzi Apturahmanis was the best man, wearing even more official dress than that of Karagiozis and in the best man's turban. In our next issue we will include the details of the wedding and the imaginary dinner given, where Karagiozis told those who asked for food, "Swallow it," and where Hatziavad subsequently developed the subject having proven on the basis of Stoic philosophy that everything can be achieved by means of ideas. During the ceremony Kutsutzuk Andrias, Karagiozis's nephew, played Kumuzulupe Maskaratzik with cymbals using the entire scale of the makam atzirem—or the initial grave tone, according to Kutuzelis—equivalent to the duet (duetto) of *Norma*.[81]

This performance is, apparently, heavily Turkish in its nature. In characteristically Moslem fashion, dervishes are presented in the play, a Haci (a Moslem who has made a pilgrimage to Mecca) acts as best man, and the well-known religious teacher and folk figure, Nasreddin Hotza, conducts the ceremony. The performance's costumes (fezes, pantaloons, and robes) and conveniences (nargiles were provided for its patrons), as well as the reference to "oriental theater" all support its Turkish nature. But the advertisement features a wedding parade as the performance's central event and stresses a debate on Stoic philosophy as one of its highlights, choices that indicate sensitivity to the immediate audience to which this performance must appeal. The advertisement has, first of all, avoided offending Greek tastes by eliminating any reference to the highly sexual nature of the wedding play as typically performed in Turkey. Moreover, several aspects of the advertisement acknowledge a responsiveness to local tastes and topical events that would ameliorate objections to the performance, including the following: its presentation of universalized customs through the suggested theatrical spectacle of a wedding parade that incorporates ethnic types and costumes from the Greek-populated (although Turkish-controlled) Dodecanese islands; its use of Stoic debate to prove "everything can be achieved by the means of ideas"; and its reference to a popular local event (the opera *Norma* was received with excitement in Athens when it was first performed by an Italian troupe in 1840).[82]

The wedding parade may have served here as a means of introducing Greek types and costumes into the performance. It certainly universalized the performance's appeal. Ironically, the parade belonged to a wedding play that was considered to be one of the Turkish form's most scandalously free performances (it permitted consummation of the marriage in full view of the audience).[83] The spectacle of the parade may here have completely obliterated the sexual scenes, since the advertisement indicates the parade was quite elaborate. On the other hand, it may simply have offset or diffused the importance of the sexual scenes by the attention it commanded (the performance did run two evenings). It is, in sum, quite possible that mid-century performances of Karagiozis were less morally objectionable than commentators of the period lead one to believe.

The history of official and upper-class objections to Karagiozis deserves its own chapter in any discussion of the performance. The evidence is, however, too sparse and incomplete to bear too extended a treatment. An impression is, nevertheless, generated (through government documents and commentary)[84] that from 1827 to 1894, Karagiozis was thought to need supervision and at times prohibition because of its ethics and vulgarity. The objections become more specific and more heated as the performance becomes more widely spread toward the end of the century. Indeed, as lines are drawn between oral and literary culture, the reception Karagiozis receives serves as a barometer of change. A useful starting point to trace the regulation of Karagiozis is the General Order of the King, No. 85, 31 December 1836, issued in Athens.[85] Article 5, No. 8, indicates a general category of "common games and moving theater," which was to be held under police supervision. That such supervision could have applied to Karagiozis is indicated by the word "kiniton" or "moving," apparently referring to puppets. The relevant section of the order includes a general proscription for all social events, which is followed by specific categories:

They intend to do away with these acts and prohibit whatever is corrupt for them. . . .

8. The all-night common players and the moving theater, inasmuch as their good character allows, is left to the discretion of the particular police on all-night duty.[86]

The General order included under its supervision such social events as games of chance, public bathing, and the presence of common women on public promenades. It took a firm position in its attempt to regulate social activity and to prohibit whatever deviated from its dictates. In that context, "moving theater" is treated with surprising tolerance. The standard established here, however, conforms more to the elevated tastes of the upper reaches of society than to those of the performance's natural audience.

Supervision was apparently irregular. *Athinas,* 4 January 1854, for example, depicts a police department whose laxity inspires public complaint: "We are sorry to see the governance of the police department tolerating and pardoning the Karagiozis performance in this cafe, when at other times it was strictly prohibited. The director seems ignorant of how many shameful and indecent acts were presented by the puppet theater in the lewd Asian theaters, and that this corruption spreads from them to our whole community since it touches numerous different children, and many of our high school and grade school students keep frequenting these theaters every evening, without letup." [87] The performance was closed, only to be reopened less than a month later under a new police chief, as we are informed in *Athinas,* 8 February 1854: "The Karagiozis performance resumed and this with the knowledge of the chief of police." [88]

By this time, the Karagiozis performance appears to have made the transition in Athens from a periodic performance mounted on special occasions to a general entertainment (where public performances had previously been limited to the month-long Ramadan holiday, we find Karagiozis performances in 1854 occurring in January, February, and December). The Karagiozis performance must have enhanced its ability to engender the loyalty and affection of its common audience. Thus, when officials undertook to control the performance, they did so in the face of a broadly based constituency, what a commentator in Kalamata was in 1896 to call a "new socialism, an entire democracy." [89] Indeed, when the police in Amarusi, a suburb of Athens, attempted to censor a performance in 1894 for having offered too bold a joke, the people reacted with an immediacy and force that soon reopened the theater: "This, then, was an immediate question for the Amarusians. They ran to the right, they ran to the left, they knocked on doors, they begged, they implored that the performance be permitted to return and after much doing it was finally allowed to do so." [90]

The popular response to police pressure was not merely a reaction to being denied a favored entertainment. The issue was much broader—less a question of resistance to government force than an undeveloped appreciation for government on a national level. The Karagiozis audience responded to a more highly generalized, informal source of authority, that of the traditional values of oral culture residing in the Greek people themselves. These popular values belonged to a broad folk group that included both the Greek and Turkish common classes. Such a view of authority, however unconsciously held, was anathema to literate, Westernized Greeks.

Complaints against Karagiozis can be traced to as early as 1872, in

Yeniki Efimerida, 17 December. Yerakaris, in this earliest known Greek reference to Karagiozis, explains why the term is used as a stigma by members of the Philanthropic Society: "Karagiozis in Turkey is the hypocrite of the Turkish theater performance at Ramadan, with shameless words presenting unstitched-together speech."[91]

In 1831 the performance still serves as a reference to oriental hypocrisy, as we see in Mavromihalis's work *Ellinika Simmikta* in which the author reviles those so blind they cannot recognize Hatziavatis (meaning here the Greek political figure Capodistria, leader of a pro-Russian faction) when he stands before them.[92] Perhaps the most revealing early comment appeared in the Athenian *Theatis,* 20 July 1837, in a review of the Fanariote Rizos Nerulos's comedy *Erotimatikin Ikoyenean.* Here, the Karagiozis performance is considered to be no more than an indicator of the Asiatic marketplace humor of the times. "And the fame and recognition of this loathsome concoction, called comedy, which claimed as its chef a Fanariote, given birth to and brought up in the bosom of Karagiozis and Hatziavatis, worn out at the humor of Asian loading docks and market places, those same ones who in youth were slavishly enthusiastic about the crooked dealing of the sodomites and all those deeply steeped in Arabic-Persian-Turkish aesthetics and life."[93] The author of the piece explains that his passion is inspired by that type of comedy born in and springing from the arms of Karagiozis and Hatziavatis. He describes Nerulos's comedy as a string of dialogue without moral purpose or dramatic plots, starved of imagination and either lacking a center or "vulgar-centered."[94] Embraced, in the author's words, by those whose feet sweat and others who smell, this kind of comedy exploits evil, defects, and peculiarities; this comedy does not contribute to the character of the nation as did such fathers of comic drama as Aristophanes. The author's interest here is not in Karagiozis itself, but in the deleterious effect he considers it to have had on the comedy of live theater. Nevertheless, he provides three important points of reference for this study: first, that Karagiozis, attractive to the laboring class and imitated by the literate class in its comedy, must by then have been widely known across class lines in Greece; second, that it was sufficiently influential to have infiltrated legitimate theater, demonstrating not only that Karagiozis was competitive with live theater at this early date, but that its own success was such that its rival mimicked its dialogues and themes; and finally, that the influence of Karagiozis, in the land of classical comedy, was considered to be so broad that Aristophanes himself must be brought in to reduce it to size.

The distinction between Karagiozis and Aristophanes drawn by this

Greek source is not shared by viewers of the Turkish performance such as Ampere in 1844[95] and Ubicini[96] in 1855, who found that Karagoz and Aristophanes had much in common. Ampere, in fact, argued that nothing gives a better idea of ancient comedy than the shameless words and licentious and motley satire of the scandalously jeering Karagoz. The contrast drawn both by Ampere and de Pouqueville is not between Karagoz and Aristophanes, but between the former and the progress in comedy represented by Aristotle. De Pouqueville expressed his position in his 1802 description of a Karagoz performance: "Je n'ai pas trouvé les règles d'Aristote plus respectées que les moeurs."[97] That the author of the *Theatis* review chose to ignore the more likely similarities and to stress what, to other viewers of the period, were less apparent differences between this modern performance and Aristophanes is a sign of the antipopulist and antioriental ideology of literate Greeks of the period. In these early days of the young Greek state, apparently a separation was being made by the upper classes between the Greek and the oriental. From the revolution until the end of the century, the upper classes associated Karagiozis with the Turkish oppressor, with lower-class morality, with illiteracy, and with oriental attitudes.[98] The view was an unforgiving one, for it implied that if Hellenization was to proceed, all traces of the Turkish occupation had to be eradicated. What could not be forgiven in Karagiozis was not its supposed immorality (the performance, in any case, was so much like Aristophanes in the freedoms it took that to deny the morality of one was to deny the morality of the other)[99] but the fact that it was a Turkish art.

Hellenization was viewed not only as a means of destroying vestiges of the Turkish occupation but of eliminating uncomfortable facts about the demoralization and debasement of the Greek people themselves during that period. Even the phallophoric Karagoz figure, which can be traced to classical Greek mime,[100] was attributed to Turkish influence. Thus not only Hellenization but bowdlerization was involved. Like the move to accept katharevusa, or elevated Greek, over the demotic or popular language, the de-vulgarization campaign preferred instructional art to what was responsive to and uncritically reflective of natural impulses in the population. We find in Hobhouse a kindred spirit, for he clearly takes the point of view of a European gentleman offended by the phallic "equipage of the God of the Gardens," the "very dirty coffeehouse," the boy-audience's "loud and frequent bursts of laughter," and the "too horribly gross actions" of a performance whose language he did not understand. Hobhouse juxtaposes the upper-class Westerner and the lower-class Easterner and finds the latter wanting in sensibility. Whether the performance presented its viewers with clever language play, earthy wisdom, or folk-rooted humor we are not told, for its virtues were locked behind culture and language barriers that this condescending visitor makes little effort to penetrate.

Literate Greeks mimicked the class bias and pro-Western sentiments evident in responses to Karagiozis among foreign travelers, accounting for much of the resistance experienced by the performance as it tried to find an audience and a form separate from its Turkish progenitor. An instance of police regulation of the performance in a suburb of Athens, Kifissia, in 1894 (reported in *Estia,* 1 August 1894)[101] further specifies the nature of that resistance. *Estia* reports that the Railroad Company of Attica had, by agreement with its council, established in Stathmon Square an outdoor theater for the performance of Karagiozis. Several items are of interest here. First, the sponsorship of a performance in a neighborhood setting suggests that, in spite of the performance's presumed vulgarity and the objections raised against that vulgarity, Karagiozis was considered sufficiently harmless to be endorsed by a public corporation as appropriate fare for neighborhood entertainment. The company's action, designed either to meet the tastes of its own workers or to serve as public relations, must have been perceived as an acceptable and popular course to take.

Played with the police in attendance, this performance was censored when its reportedly "customary vulgarity" surfaced. That a player would insist on asserting the natural state of his art, knowing the police to be in attendance, appears to have been a usual aspect of the performance. Such tests of official censorship undoubtedly contributed to the tension of performance situations. Objections, in this instance, were focused on the theme of the performance (described as the love of Fatme, or *The Urn,* the plot required various suitors to hide in an urn, ultimately to be discovered there and beaten) and the player's witticisms (among which the author points in particular to the line, "I'll break the chair on your face"). The performance was accused of offering *aplustata* (the most simple or artless) material. Presented out-of-doors rather than inside an enclosed cafe, as previously, and with the public endorsement of a respected company and its council, the performance, it was feared, would now be accepted as a family entertainment and thus affect those of tender years.

In Kalamata, the Peloponnesos, in 1896, a similar attack appears against the vulgarity of the performance. The author of an extended discussion in *Fare,* 14 July 1896,[102] calls the taste for Karagiozis a poisonous miasma and an infectious addiction. He wonders at the logic behind its attractiveness to a general audience. The grand terms of his attack are not, however, supported by the details he provides. Karagiozis, he claims, has merely to grab at Barba Yiorgos's (or Uncle George's) skirt or Dionisios's coattail for the crowd to dissolve into frantic laughter. The songs of Barba Yiorgos and Dionisios are heard on everyone's lips, while popular lines of Karagiozis and Barba Yiorgos are repeated throughout the city. Small children take up Karagiozis's cry, "Hey, you, little old man!" and the "immoral" phrase of Barba Yiorgos, "Go to the devil, you crumb, you!" [103] On such innocuous phrases rests this author's accusation of vulgarity and obscenity. The evidence presented against Karagiozis in Kifissia and Kalamata thus does not in itself, and in spite of the strong feelings of our sources, demonstrate a vile and corrupt performance. Indeed, when Karagiozis was prohibited to the troops of the Athens garrison in 1890, the prohibition was a response not to the nature of the performance but to the behavior of its audience. [104]

Descriptions offered by visitors to Turkey of the mid- to late nineteenth-century Karagoz performance provide us with a basis of comparison for our Greek sources. De Amicis in 1878, for example, calls Karagoz an "ultra Pulcinella, very much depraved; foolish, false, and cynical, foul-mouthed as a fish-wife and wanton as a satyr. . . ." [105] As a reflection of its culture, he claims, "Caragheus alone is enough to give an idea and a proof of the profound corruption hidden underneath the veil of Musselman austerity." Of the fool-hero's cynicism and self-indulgence, Thalasso's comments in 1887 should suffice:

Plus que ses confrères, Karagueuz est sensual, luxurieux, obscène. Avec son air de tout respecter, il ne respecte absolument rien: il ne croit pas plus à l'honnêteté qu'à la vertu, dont il prend souvent le masque pour atteindre plus facilement son but. Ce but consiste dans la satisfaction de ses passions. Il est d'ailleurs si blasé et tellement perverti qu'il les fait consister parfois, ses passions, à mal faire pour le plaisir unique de mal faire: c'est un raffinement de coquinerie qu'il se paie. Sans esprit, ou plutôt plein d'un esprit grossier et de bas étage, il souleve les rires de son auditoire par ses saillies d'un naturalisme dépravé et ses calembours tirés par les cheveux et renfermant toujours une obscénité. [106]

What, more than all else in the eyes of foreign travelers, contributed to the impression of Karagoz's grossness was the open wearing of a phallus, which bore the character of a second self. Gustave Flaubert, one of a few travelers capable of an ethnographic rather than a moralistic view of the performance, provides us in his *Voyage à Carthage*, 1858, with a description of the use of the phallus in the performance: "Quant au Carragheuss, son pénis ressemblant plutot à une poutre; ca finissait par n'être plus indecent. Il y en a plusieurs, Carragheuss, je

crois le type en décadence. Il s'agit seulement de montrer le plus possible de phallus. Le plus grand avait un grelot qui, à chaque mouve-
ment de riens, sonnait cela faisant beaucoup de rire."[107] Certainly numerous plots centered on Karagoz's sexual organ, most prominent
among them that reported by Gerard de Nerval in his *Voyage en Orient,* 1850. In the play he witnessed, entitled *Karagoz Victim of His
Chastity,* Karagoz goes to great pains to mask his sexual attractiveness
from a friend's amorous wife whose honor he has, ironically, been
asked to protect during her husband's absence. Karagoz finds himself
trapped in a number of compromising situations, the most comic occurring when he disguises himself as a bridge:

Caragueuz se couche sur le dos, et désire avoir l'air d'un pieu. La foule passe,
et tout le monde dit: Qui est-ce qui a planté là ce pieu? Il n'y en avait pas hier.
Est-ce du chene, est-ce du sapin? Arrivent des blanchisseuses, revenant de la
fontaine, qui étendent du ligne sur Caragueuz. Il voit avec plaisir que sa sup-
position a réussi. Un instant après, on voit entrer des esclaves menant des
chevaux à l'abreuvoir; un ami les rencontre et les invite à entrer dans une
galere (sorte de cabaret) pour se refraîchir; mais ou attacher les chevaux?
"Tiens, voilà un pieu," et on attache les chevaux à Caragueuz. . . . Les chevaux,
impatients, s'agitent: Caragueuz, tiré à quatre, appelle le passants à son secours,
et demontre douloureusement qu'il est victime d'une erreur.[108]

The Greek figure, unlike the Turkish, did not, however, wear the phallus; at least, there are no records indicating its use in Greece since that
country's liberation. One possible objection to the performance was
thus conveniently lost to Greek moralists who, nonetheless, chose to
apply the negativism of foreign travelers in Turkey to the Karagiozis
performance in Greece.

The second source of negativism among foreigners was the Turkish
performance's open attack upon authority. As minor entertainments in
Ottoman lands provided the sole legitimate outlet for the social and
political expression of the illiterate common class, foreign travelers
often found them to take intolerable freedoms. Karagoz in Constantinople is, in particular, described by the French travelers Michaud and
Poujoulet in 1830–1831 as a cynical exploiter of the naivete of its audience; they portray the nature and the end result of the performance's
close relationship with the common class in the following terms:
"Quant au pauvre Karagueuse, on l'accusait d'être l'idole et souvent
même l'interprète d'une multitude mecontente. Il est maintenant exilé
de Stamboul, l'usage de la langue turque lui a été interdit, et lorsqu'il
se montre sur quelque théâtre particulier, il ne lui est plus permis de
débiter ses lazzis que dans la langue des esclaves ou des Hellènes."[109]
Adolphus Slade goes further than his fellow travelers, complaining

during those same years in Constantinople of the seditious nature of Karagoz that spares neither sultans nor ministers. "Nearly all the popular commotions and revolutions," he offers, referring to the Karagoz performance, "have been planned in the nights of ramazan." [110] Karagiozis's most objectionable quality throughout the century was, indeed, its freedom to attack any and all with impunity. "Sa satire," Ubicini relates in 1855, "n'epargne personne"; "pachas, ulémas, derviches, banquiers, négociants; toutes les casies, toutes les professions sont passées en revue et marquées chacune du trait qui lui est propre. Les gouvernants eux-mêmes ne sont pas à l'abri de sa censure, et le vizir, qui assiste quelquefois *incognito* à ces représentations, s'expose à entendre plus d'une dure vérité." [111] The reaction of the audience of this performance required the placement before the booth of a man who "armé d'une longue gaule dont l'extrémité atteint jusqu'aux bancs les plus éloignés, frappe à grands coups sur les rieurs obstinés." [112]

Even the friendly voice of Richard Davey in 1894 refers to the performance as one in which "Karagheuz was constantly violating every law of Allah and his Koran." [113] Censorship, as we discovered in 1830, was not far behind each outbreak. Gautier, in 1856, another friendly voice, refers with distaste to censorship of the performance: "Cependant le Karagheuz du grand Champ-des-Morts a subi la censure, ou pour mieux dire la castration: il dit des obscénités, mais il n'en fait plus; la morale l'a désarmé; c'est un polichinelle sans bâton, un satyre sans cornes, un dieu de Lampsaque à l'état d'Abeilard, et, au lieu d'agir, il met en récits de Théramène ses lubriques exploits. C'est plus classique; mais, franchement, c'est plus ennuyeux, et l'originalité du type y perd beaucoup." [114] Like Gautier, Davey presents us with the strange and slightly sad picture of a Karagoz who, in 1894, is left posturing "with tongue slit, and wings clipped, by order of the Censor. . . ." [115]

In occupied Arab countries, the Karagoz performance, much in accord with its function in Turkey, was designated a role described by the Turkish theater historian, Metin And, as "agit prop in the Empire." [116] But in Greece, records do not indicate that the performance shared the discomforting political effect of the Turkish form. Though Karagoz is referred to as an "unfettered press" by one foreign visitor to Turkey, Joseph Mery in 1855,[117] and is seen as attacking not only British and French admirals but the Grand Vizir himself (in a mock trial in which the vizir is found guilty and imprisoned), we find no such references in nineteenth-century accounts about Greece. Thus, the true source of objections to the developing Greek performance must be sought elsewhere than in its sexuality or its power as a political statement—perhaps in the form's function as part of another yet larger problem.

A view into this larger problem is provided by our Kalamata author in *Fare*, 1896. In his discussion of the "miasma" born of the Karagiozis performance, he first makes the point that Karagiozis is responsible for the public's by-passing of live theater. An earlier issue, *Fare*, 9 July 1896, had placed Karagiozis's responsibility for capturing the audience in a kinder light, noting that since Kalamata had previously had no theater, the public passed its time with the "Karagioses and Punches." It questions continued attendance at the latter performances, however, now that the city had capable live theater.[118] A third issue, *Fare*, 23 June 1896, is more accusatory; though theater prices are cheap enough for the meanest pocketbook, it claims, friends of the theater sit "stuffed like sardines at the disgusting Karagiozis and the nonsense of Punch."[119] *Fare*'s complaint is not an isolated one. We find the same appeal made by Filaretos in Halkida in 1879 (*Evia*, 1 November 1879). In this instance, the issue is broadened beyond just a negative view of laic spectacles and an expression of preference for educating the provincial public through serious theater. Cultured opinion, here, contrasts the state of art in Greece with that abroad: "In Paris the very powerful Garnieros dispensed six to seven tens of millions for the Academy of Music; in Halkida, however, there exists a poor little cafe, a few meters walking distance into a very poor section, where Karagiozis became accepted with many jokes."[120]

But Karagiozis was not only performed in the poor section of the city; it played, as well, at the city theater of Halkida on Wednesday evenings, a scene our author describes with some degree of disbelief:

Coming to the Halkida theater, we found fellow workers drinking sensual coffee followed immediately afterward by an accompanying nargile. The audience of the show was eminently demotic. The orchestra and the gallery boxes were occupied by multitudes awaiting the beginning of the performance and composed of all kinds of common types and ages, of all kinds of religions but not sexes. This helter-skelter mixture of workers, those with independent means, employees or not, learned people, and industrialists was a spectacle which even this Blanke found amusing. Among the listeners were certain peasants, the first of such remarkable sights to be seen at the theater. And because of this, with fixed eyes and ears strained, the audience burst into loud laughter at every simple word from the stage.[121]

Though children attended with their fathers, women were not to be found either here or when live theater troupes appeared in the same hall. The provincial attitude toward women apparent in Halkida can best be understood by comparing it to a previously noted performance in Athens in 1890,[122] when women appeared with such abandon that the commander of the city garrison forbade his men to attend *thea-tridia* (a reference to puppet performances) to avoid "immodest indecencies" between his men and the women. Unmarried women of the working class came, dressed in simple evening dress and slippers and carrying infants in their arms, to stand throughout the performance. More significantly, however, ladies of breeding arrived to pass the evening as well. The scandalized author of the notice is particularly incensed at the poor Athenians who, in maintaining their own class of theater, corrupted public morals, military discipline, and more elevated classes.

The developing case against Karagiozis thus had much to do with the question of class taste in Greece, with the destructive effect the performance had on theater—which catered to more elevated tastes— and with the mixing of social classes to the detriment of the tastes of those in the middle and upper reaches of society. But it also had to do with the distinctions being made between urban and provincial life. Cultural leaders in the provinces, for example, resented paying a tax that went to subsidize live theater of a type not enjoyed in the provinces, for the French and Italian troupes visited only Athens.[123] At the same time, however, they secretly admired the wonders of European theater; moreover, they resented the fact that in Athens Greek theater performances were individually scrutinized before being licensed, while Karagiozis in Halkida was given "carte blanche."[124] Indeed, when competition with Karagiozis saw a Greek touring company in Kalamata—the Luludaki theater—eclipsed, the reaction was harsh: "Imagine that Karagiozis destroyed the Luludaki troupe. The Greek theater was buried at Kalamata by the Turkish screen."[125] Provincial leaders were impatient for a greater degree of local control and insistent on more conservative values in minor entertainments. But in their impatience, they failed to account for popular taste, which had developed its own momentum and, wherever possible, had taken into its own hands the satisfaction of its own needs.

Whereas the pre-eminence of the "Turkish screen" over "Greek theater" bothered those of culture, among the common class the presence of Eastern attitudes and influence in laic entertainments was not considered an issue of great moment. Filaretos in 1879, as a proponent of the cultured view, refers to the international mix of the Karagiozis audience (Christians, Jews, and Ottomans) as a means of countering public complaints by Turks of ill treatment under Greek rule.[126] Not only should the brotherly love expressed in its audience quell such complaints, he claims, but the events depicted on the screen (Greeks suffering under Turkish rule) should remind us of that which nullifies all complaint. But Filaretos is speaking here of a performance that was international in its scope from its inception. The use in the same performance of "barbaric tongues and Turkish, Italian, and Greek" is no more than what had characterized mime entertainments from the Byzantine period and Karagoz throughout the Ottoman period. The population mix was no more surprising to the common class, and carried no more real meaning, than the mixture of the performance's many languages.

Karagiozis's Eastern "vulgarity," too, lay in the eyes of the beholder. The common audience is described by Filaretos himself as being greatly interested in and unimaginably entertained at the Karagiozis performance. If fathers freely brought their children to Karagiozis as Filaretos reports, the conclusion must be drawn that they did so because they judged the performance to be within certain bounds of acceptability. That Karagiozis appeared at the city theater serves as a further indication of its public acceptance. That it was granted "carte blanche" by officials suggests that popular loyalty to the performance was so great and the danger to public morals so slight that public authorities did not feel irretrievably threatened.

The larger threat, thus far elusive, posed by the Karagiozis performance is taken up at length in Kalamata by the author of the *Fare* article of 14 July 1896. Having pictured modern Greece as the fatherland of dust, drunkenness and evil-doings, he contends that the new nation has lost its wartime sense of heroic struggle, its seriousness, and its sense of the tragic. The *agonistida* or "struggle" whose loss he bemoans is described as a time of committees, societies, guardianship, demonstrations, contribution, volunteerism, enthusiastic words, joy, and a sense of "centrality" from which to prick the outerlying parts of the political organism. In this nostalgic view, a heroic, past reality is contrasted with a contemporary degeneration of the sense of purpose, with desertion, and with a sense of loss that, coining a pseudo-medical term, the author calls "Karagiozitis." Ascribing to the term the meaning of phlegm, he calls it a disease like "meningitis, nephritis, arthritis, pleurisy." Highly infectious, it moves through the membranes, along the nerves, and into the cerebrum as it infiltrates the whole body. Extending his muddled medical metaphor, the author identifies the enemy as the infectious phlegm or spirit of the performance, which serves as an "icon" of the times "impressed within the center of particular people's minds." Just as the performance has spread far beyond Kalamata to other parts of the country, so the disease it carries is described as passing through the whole body of Greece. Thus, in a period of historical relapse and social slowdown, Karagiozis is represented as antistruggle, as an infiltrative virus exhausting the nation's sense of social purpose.[127]

Karagiozis had, nevertheless, been seen in 1879 in Halkida as a presentation of Greeks suffering under the Turks. Indeed, here in Kalamata in 1896 one of its highlights was still a scene in which Barba Yiorgos shoots at the Turks. One might, as a result, have expected the performance to have been credited with enhancing rather than depleting the Greek sense of struggle. Interestingly, the Karagiozis heroic history play was developed in Patras in the mid-1890s by the very same player, Mimaros, who was seen in Kalamata as the "king of buffoonery and marketplace punning" and who was credited with having exacerbated the progress of the disease with his visits to Kalamata of several summers running, having introduced Karagiozis to Kalamata in 1893.[128]

Thus, Karagiozis is seen in 1896 as a disease that, having spread quickly, has an explosive effect:

Here, indeed, in Kalamata, the enthusiasm for Karagiozis exceeded all limits; all received him with uncalled-for enthusiasm, during each new visit this enthusiasm is multiplied, spread-out, is enlarged as it goes over into rage. It is something, in the end, bordering on the mad, or more on the frantic towards hysteria. And you hear at night, whether it be evening, midnight, or dawn, day, morning, noon, sunset, wherever you go, to take a walk, to the countryside, to the market, to your house, to the cafe, to the square, when you go to sleep, when you awake, when you're dressing, when you're studying in your room, when you wander by the seashore, when you write in your solitude, it hunts you, and it deafens you, and it shatters your nerves, and drives you up a wall, when suddenly Barba Yiorgos's song is heard: "Oh Yio-mama mine, oh Yio, oh Yiorgos, he passed by. Hey, hey, hey, pssssssst, he passed by."[129]

The populace of the city took to imitating the behavior and habits of the puppets, mimicking their gestures, repeating their phrases, and singing their songs. The taste for Karagiozis was described as so strong that amateur performances by young boys began appearing. The announcement of one of these performances suggests the extent to which Karagiozis had penetrated into even the most intimate nooks of city neighborhoods: "At a house, near a military camp, opposite Aryiris's place, next to a paint store, a little farther down from a well, Karagiozis will be performed tonight."[130]

Estia, 7 August 1901,[131] reports that children were mounting Karagiozis performances in homes everywhere, and *Estia*, 26 April 1902, states that Karagiozis was being performed on every street corner.[132] All classes, all ages were involved, from teachers and students, to workers and managers: "An entire Democracy you see! There, near the cloth and oil Karagiozis scene, social barriers retreat, social fences collapse, different social strata, mixed-up texts, constituting a mass; a new populism would envy it, a new socialism."[133] The mixing of upper and lower-class patrons in the Karagiozis audience clearly disturbed those with cultural pretentions

Karagiozis's rival, the Fasulis and Periklitos performance (a puppet performance similar to Punch and Judy) did not, however, face the same degree of enmity with which the "Turkish screen" was greeted. Having appeared on the Greek scene sometime before 1870, Fasulis was introduced into Athens, Anninos reports, a few years before 1888 by an itinerant promoter from Kerkira. Fasulis was, unlike Karagiozis, more completely a lower-class entertainment. When, for example, a summer theater, expensively fitted to draw the public in 1870, was suddenly converted to a Fasulis performance and its audience became so mixed that the "kids couldn't be separated from the sheep," the common class simply drove out the upper classes, leaving an audience exclusively of "friends of laic theater." [134]

It is true that the Fasulis show was confused with Karagiozis when prohibitions were raised in 1890 against *theatridia*,[135] and that *Estia* refers in 1894 to officials forbidding a Fasulis performance to avoid complaints of favoritism when a Karagiozis performance was forced to close.[136] But, as Anninos makes clear, in the popular mind the two bore no relation to each other because of one point: in spite of having cleared the way for such an entertainment as Fasulis,[137] Karagiozis was clearly recognized as Ottoman in its origins while Fasulis was known as having been born of the Neopolitan Pulchinello. Having no Turkish blood in its wooden veins and having kept itself free of the upper classes,[138] Fasulis escaped the enmity of the Kalamata author, who bypasses that performance on his way to castigate Karagiozis. Indeed, as Hatzipandazis notes in a survey of historical sources of the late nineteenth century, the popularity of the Fasulis performance left Karagiozis, after 1890, open to attack. Even so, his review of police licenses in 1901 still show that of all the *theatridia*, Karagiozis was performed most frequently.[139]

The split between upper- and lower-class tastes in Greece thus constitutes an important element in the controversy over the Karagiozis performance. In reality, the combination of the performance's sexuality and its political statement only partially accounted for the resistance to the performance; more important was the inter-class mixture of the Karagiozis audience, the resulting competition between Karagiozis and serious theater for that audience, and the antioriental, pro-European bias of the Greek upper classes.

The common class as it moved into growing urban centers was undisciplined, un-self-conscious, and traditional in its attitudes and values, putting pressure on the new rulers of Greece and posing a problem in the growing nation that was not easily controlled. Themselves resistant to the western European ideas of their Bavarian King Otho and his circle of foreign advisers, members of the Karagiozis audience maintained their own ideas of what constituted Greekness, ideas tied, however unconsciously, to the continuity of the popular values that had been expressed by laic art over the course of the Turkish occupation.

The debate between the Purist (Hellenic) and Demotic (Romaic) perspectives in the study of Greek folklore should be raised here, for the struggle between these two concepts provides the context within which the Karagiozis performance grew up in the nineteenth century. Although the anthropologist Michael Herzfeld[140] refers to the Hellenic view as having developed during the nineteenth century and the Romaic view as having asserted itself at the end of the nineteenth century, it is probably more useful to think of the Hellenic as an eighteenth-century perspective and the Romaic as a nineteenth-century one, as Dimitris Tziovas does.[141] Indeed, the former, with its sense of unchangeable laws and timelessness, its homotropic or ethnically singular view of culture, its mechanistic and logical view of the universe, and its insistence on cultural continuity from ancient times, suggests a commonality of purpose similar to Neo-Classicism; the latter, with its sense of the organic nature and growth of culture, its total view of history as a continuous chain of events founded on general principles of repetition, its reliance on spontaneity and intuitive understanding, its heterotropic or ethnically mixed view of culture, and its differentiation of past and present (with a strong appreciation for the importance of the past in the present) suggests its comparability with Romanticism.

The Romaic view of history ultimately superseded the Hellenic view of order in the later nineteenth century, giving rise to cultural pluralism and appreciation of local and temporal conditions. Its sense of "nationism," based on the common will of the individuals who make up the national group,[142] replaces Hellenic nationalism and brings into play the autochthonous or native point of view to balance the heterochthonous influence that bowdlerized expressions of the peasantry, that denied popular attitudes acquired by illiterate, rural Greeks during Ottoman rule, and that identified with western Europeans whose antiquarian notions were tied to revolutionary ideals that had little to do with the social life of the Greek masses in the years of achieving statehood.

Nevertheless, at the time of the achievement of statehood, heterochthon Greeks asserted themselves in Greece, and the Hellenic perspective established itself as the theoretical framework by which the modern state was to begin to understand itself. We find, for example, that in the study of folklore, folksongs were selectively collected and studied by self-conscious ideologues among the Greek literati and that they were frequently edited and printed to conform to a pervading Hellenic perspective. Hellenists thus selectively retrieved folklore to engineer the selective survival of what supported their notion of a continuous and homotropic culture, a notion that they imposed as an ideological concept to institutionalize their own cultural image of the nation.[143] The relevant question, however, remains—To what extent did this foreign-influenced, literary, and upper-middle-class-bound description of culture have a determining effect on folklore itself? In particular, given the illiteracy, the oriental attitudes, and the autochthonous character of the Greek masses that resisted heterochthonous influence and that maintained its own distinct rural and lower-class values, it is difficult to maintain that Greek folklore was itself known or understood by the folk more completely by its Hellenic than by its Romaic face. This point is of particular interest considering the progress of the Karagiozis performance's development. Indeed, the performance remained stubbornly resistant to bowdlerization and to the nationalist perspective throughout the nineteenth century. Thus, *Avyi,* 20 November 1864, continued to describe the anti-Hellenic bias of the Karagiozis performance to the end of the century.[144] Referring to the closing of a performance because of its vulgarity, this source concludes, "This [performance] does not represent progress towards the cultural enlightenment of the nineteenth centry." Moreover, collection and printing of Karagiozis texts did not begin until 1918, just when the Hellenic view was loosening its hold and the Romaic view was coming into its own. Players had some control over the texts that were collected and the way they were printed, insuring that whole repertoires rather than selected examples were collected. Karagiozis's emergence as a significant entertainment thus coincided with the abatement of the debate between the Hellenic and Romaic perspectives and occurred at a time when the Romaic view was in the ascendency.

It is true, nevertheless, that the context of an already established, Hellenic national idea made it difficult for the Romaic notion to escape the influence of the theoretical framework the Hellenists constructed. We find this influence in two places. First, we find it in Karagiozis's borrowings of materials from patriotic plays of the live theater. Looking at the Karagiozis performance in the larger context of Greek theater, Karagiozis could have been swallowed up by the Hellenic theater sponsored by heterochthonous Greeks. Certainly, by the end of the nineteenth century, the appeal of national sentiments in live theater texts and Karagiozis players' desire to counter attacks on the Asiatic

morality of their performances led them to link with the Hellenic perspective by adopting themes, characters, and whole texts from live
Greek theater.[145] We find the second source of Hellenic influence in Karagiozis's ideological borrowings: the mythical quality of the performance's giant-sized heroes; its reluctance to acknowledge the ambigu-
ous attributes of the klephts both as a social institution and in their
relations with the Greek people; and the sense of national spirit sponsored by the performance's history texts. We clearly find this influence
in the folksongs used in the heroic performance texts, songs borrowed
from the same folklore tradition of which Herzfeld writes.

Where, however, erotic elements surface in the heroic texts,[146] and
where comic characters penetrate the heroic realm to confuse values,[147] there we find the Romaic face of the Karagiozis performance
putting itself forward. Also, insofar as the primitive nature of social
banditry is also expressed in the heroic texts (in which the klepht has
no coherent value system and no significant relationship to the context
of Greek society, and where the confusion of the roles of the klepht
and the brigand effectively erases distinctions that would lead to true
national consciousness),[148] we have no political consciousness or revolutionary ideology, but mere disruption, tension, and accommodation.
Indeed, the presence of a strong tradition of antiheroic *listi*, or brigand
texts, in the Karagiozis performance clearly demonstrates the presence
of an essentially Romaic attitude. These brigand texts (which take
place in the post-1821 period) express the mixed values of socially
marginal figures whose return home from the war of liberation was
less than glorious. Many took to the mountains to make their living,
escape their new rulers, or avoid imprisonment for acts that, if committed during the war years, would have earned them fame. Tales of
the brigands, taken up in popular *thrili* or adventure novels and
adopted by the Karagiozis performance, were warmly received, expressing the ambivalence of their laic audiences. The audience admired
the brigands' redistribution of wealth Robin Hood style, empathized
with their plight, and accepted them as one of its own, at the same time
recognizing their essential rapaciousness and their irredeemable hunger for the free life.

Karagiozis was not swallowed up by Hellenic theater nor coopted
by its ideological borrowings largely because it remained essentially an
independent tradition supported by autochthonous Greeks, expressing
the Romaic tradition of native views and oriental attitudes and reflecting a heterotrophic culture. Even as we freely acknowledge that, as a
part of Greek folk culture, Karagiozis remains tied to modern Greek
history and ideology,[149] it is clear, as Lukatos and Politis point out, that

Karagiozis remained an instinctive, native expression of the people.[150] Certainly, Karagiozis spontaneously and instinctively asserted itself in contradistinction to Hellenic attitudes, as we have seen in our review of the relevant, nineteenth-century historical documents. Extending this argument, we could say that, in the formative years of the Karagiozis performance, the common Greek made little sense of the Hellenic concept of nationalism. Among the merchants and artisans of early nineteenth-century Greece, there were few who played a significant role in the revolution. The peasants had little to fight for; in one description,[151] they were merely changing their Turkish masters for Greek ones under whom they were not necessarily better off. Horizontally divided into ruler and the ruled, Greece was a heterogeneous society of varied minorities (Armenians, Vlahs, Albanians, Turks, and Jews), characterized by a variety of centrifugal forces (including those of the church, the Greek primates, the klephts and armatoles, and the ruling Turks), sectionalism (between autochthonous and heterochthonous Greeks, but also between the various sections of Greece—Epirus, Rumeli, Morea, the islands, Attica, Thessaly, and Macedonia), and fear of centralized power (a result of Greek experience on a larger scale under Byzantine as well as Ottoman rule, and at the regional level under Orthodox ecclesiastics—bishops, archbishops, and metropolitans—Turkish voivodes, pashas, and beys, and Greek hodzabashis or primates). The Karagiozis heroic text thus grew to fill a vacuum by expressing and reflecting a demotic sense of "nationism."[152] The Romaic understanding of history has been effectively expressed[153] as a consciousness of the bond among people that exists in the collective memory, that is, consciousness of tradition that itself represents allegiance to values of the past. That past clearly represents, in terms of its social values, a bond with the immediate Ottoman period; in terms of its cultural values, it extends as far back as the Byzantine past. But, in spite of resurgences of the classical spirit, there is little evidence of a sense of bondedness with antiquity among either the Greek peasants or in the Karagiozis texts; rather, the texts share the same general lack of familiarity with the ancient past that foreign travelers found among Greek peasants of the eighteenth and nineteenth centuries.[154]

Thus, Karagiozis was to break away from its Turkish origins and accept a more national role as a Greek performance, but solely by developing heroic performances that accepted only some measure of Hellenic influence, almost entirely as an overlay on what was essentially a Romaic expression of the cultural values of the common Greek. Throughout the nineteenth century, the Karagiozis performance was thus national only in the sense that it expressed common Greek values.

It was certainly much closer to the Greek Vasiliadis's description in
1895 of the "authentic and only truly Turkish theater,"[155] than it was
to a performance capable of being supported by the Greek state. Referring to a performance he saw at Ramadan in Constantinople, Vasiliadis describes it as an expression of the practical life of the common
people, not of the nation as a whole. He specifies Karagiozis's drunkenness, his lying, his womanizing, his hunger, and his illiteracy as pre-
dominant themes. Nowhere does he indicate that a Greek form of the
performance existed separate from Turkish Karagoz. The Greek performance certainly does not appear in the catalogue of performances
to which Vasiliadis compares the Turkish form, a catalogue that includes the English Punch, the French Guignol, the Persian Ketse Pehli-
van, the Arab Hagias, and the Greek Fasulis and Periklitos.[156]

Vasiliadis goes on to note that the Turkish performance, infected by
live European theater, had begun to mellow, enriched by the latter's
romantic dramaturgy. Moreover, he credits the influence of European
theater with at least an attempt by some players to create substantial
plays of national drama. But it is difficult, he claims, for anyone to assert that these plays were "national" in the true meaning of the term.
Vasiliadis's commentary thus provides a picture of the Turkish performance that reinforces the likelihood that the two performances were,
at the end of the century, still very much alike in their characters,
themes, the influences to which they succumbed, and their effect on
their audience. This discovery should not lead us to minimize Greek
attempts to separate the Greek performance from that of the Turks,
but to acknowledge that nineteenth-century advances in that direction
were neither so great nor so original as was earlier suggested.[157] The
Karagiozis audience, in sum, was essentially the same as during the
Ottoman period. Karagiozis's effect on that audience and on the society of which it was a part was comparable to the effect created by
Turkish Karagoz. Its themes were neither as sexual nor as political as
those of its progenitor, but its subject matter and characters differed
insignificantly from its Turkish prototype. The addition of the Karagiozis heroic texts to the repertoire is commonly cited in modern
times as proof of the performance's nationalization and historical
consciousness.[158] If we believe the commentary of the Fare author,
14 July 1896, however, Greek history was not particularly well served
by the nineteenth-century Karagiozis performance. Indeed, his criticism points to just the opposite of a self-conscious, historical perspective. The sense of national destiny that latter-day critics attribute to the
Karagiozis performance of this period appears nowhere in the evidence. Karagiozis is, instead, accused of sapping the nation's sense of

struggle and diffusing its social and political focus, attitudes expressed most forcibly in the large body of *listi* texts the performance spawned. References to historical themes or characters in the performance do not appear in commentary of the period but only in players' recollections, which began surfacing in the 1930s.[159]

Yiannis Kiurtsakis[160] takes up the nature of the ideology and identity of these Karagiozis performances, examining its laic statement and the underlying question of the nature of its "Greekness." He finds in Karagiozis an expression of two paradoxes: first, that Karagiozis is referred to as a symbol of the modern Greek spirit and yet is "a wicked hunchback, a braggart blow-collector, a hungry speaker of obscenities";[161] and second, that Karagiozis, expressing the masses (a network of inferiors), is taken as a representative Greek expression.

Kiurtsakis poses the possibility that Greeks merely received the performance from the Turks and superficially Hellenized it, although he acknowledges that this prospect does not, however, explain the deep sympathy and recognition the Greek feels for Karagiozis. His position is that Karagiozis is neither a portrait, characterization, nor even a simple type, but something different, something rooted in the Carnival tradition that permits the coexistence of two conflicting streams in Greek life: slavery and anarchic freedom.

In the city setting of the comedies, Kiurtsakis describes the Greeks as strangers in their own land, slaves of their Turkish rulers. In the city, individualism prevails—the individualism of European society. In the mountain setting of the histories, by contrast, the Greeks are free. Here, the central value is that of the group, family, and kin, within which the individual must take his place. Whereas in the mountains Karagiozis's thievery (klephtism) is identified with heroism and honor, with personal, laic, and ethnic liberation, in the city it is identified with dishonor and serving one's own biological needs. Karagiozis's role is to assert the village within the city, the freedom of the mountains to counter the slavery of occupation. He represents, in Kiurtsakis's view, the coexistence of the continuity and discontinuity of the laic experience and ideology, the contradiction in which the *laos* lives.

In sum, Kiurtsakis argues that Karagiozis ties together the two worlds of the city and the mountains, the klepht and the city dweller. He combines in himself both hero and antihero, capturing both extremes of the human personality, linking the experience of the present tense, the specified past, and some exotic other time, and organically joining the group and the individual, the history of all and the situation of the individual in one self. Kiurtsakis's argument thus describes a primitive ideology that supports the Romaic view of the Karagiozis performance suggested by our period sources. It is this Carnival spirit, Kiurtsakis argues, that explains the immediate recognition the Greek audience feels for the Karagiozis performance.

In the end, three forces acted to change the perspective of the Karagiozis performance. The first was the criticism leveled against the performance by the upper classes, Westernizers, and moralizers who found Eastern aspects of the performance intolerable. Both church and state, the latter through regulation and the former through moral influence, played a role in minimizing the grossness of the performance's values and controlling its testing of authority. The church, however, was to play a second role, as discussed earlier, through ecclesiastical disapproval of Hellenism, thereby supporting the ascendency of the Romaic perspective in the late nineteenth century. The second force was a folk-life renaissance of the late nineteenth and early twentieth centuries, inspired by the interests of such foreign ethnologists as C. F. Abbott, Rennall Rodd, and John Cuthbert Lawson.[162] This developing interest insured a legitimacy for the performance that was to remain important to its survival in the face of the growing strength of live theater and the later success of early cinema. The final force was a regenerated historical sense that, appearing during the period of Greek border wars in 1899 and 1912, coincided with the crucial change-over period in the development of the performance. The patriotic fervor that accompanied those wars reinforced borrowings from live melodrama and hastily constructed, native patriotic dramas mounted to exploit the war atmosphere. Not only did tighter dramatic structure and more appealing themes in newly devised heroic texts attract an enthusiastic audience, but the spectacle of the plays began to reverse the performance's reputation as a force of antistruggle.[163]

The heroic text thus capitalized on the growing sense of nationalism in the country at the same time that it continued to reflect the common Greek's sense of "nationism" and to deflect attention from the Karagiozis performance's reputation for vulgarity and its identification with the lower class. The addition of heroic subject matter retained the audience being lost to the performance by the attack of moralists. At the same time, it served as a means of holding the interest of an increasingly literate adult audience. The reputation of the performance was ultimately such that several prominent voices, among them the writer Angelos Terzakis and the literary critic Leon Kukulas,[164] were to claim that Karagiozis was the only genuine form of popular theater in Greece when the nation got its independence from Turkey. Terzakis bases his argument not on Hermann Reich's position that Karagiozis is shaped on the ancient mimes, but on the premise that it truly embodies the popular aesthetic. Live Greek theater, Terzakis concludes—rightly or wrongly—should have taken its impetus from Karagiozis in the nineteenth century if it wished not only to represent itself as an authentically national theater but also to establish itself as a legitimate alternative to borrowed European forms and influences. Live theater, his argument implies, would itself have developed a more robust tradition had it followed, rather than resisted, the lead of its lesser brother. The irony of such a turnabout in thinking is not lost on students of the Karagiozis performance.

CHAPTER 2

THE HERO KATSANDONIS

THE KATSANDONIS TEXT

The klephts, the heroes of the Karagiozis history texts, were bandits who roamed Greece as early as the seventeenth century, when Ottoman governors recruited armed bands called *armatolikia* as law enforcers in the provinces. By the end of the eighteenth century, armatoli and klephts had become interchangeable roles in the popular mind because of the continuing pattern of collaboration and submission of klephts, who went on to themselves become armatoli as it suited their purposes. This collusion and merging of armatoli and klephts acted as a self-regulating system that was tolerated by weak central authorities. Thus, in the power vacuum created by the failure of the rebellion against the sultan by Ali Pasha of Epirus, which ended with the assassination of Ali Pasha in the 1820s, the klephts functioned as an instrument of social stability.[1]

As Koliopulos describes the klepht captains, they acted as entrepreneurs in the mountain districts, collecting levies and illegal fees, appropriating pay, and subcontracting services to the armatoli. Koliopulos makes a strong case that, in their self-serving banditry, klephts might have become proud freedom fighters in the minds of postliberationist, nationalist intellectuals and historians, but that notion did not translate into a pattern of support from the peasants who, rich and poor alike, they pillaged. In Hobsbawm's terms, by contrast, the klepht can best be described as a social bandit,[2] for through his reliance on the support of the peasants, whose champion he became, he remained part of his society and not a criminal. Characteristic of the rural pattern of poor societies, which are divided essentially into the ruler and the ruled and which are essentially pre-political, social banditry occurs during periods when the traditional equilibrium is upset. The nineteenth century was the classical age of the social bandit. As a social force, the adventurism of social banditry can be contrasted to the revolutionary organization of secret societies such as the Filiki Eteria, which can be identified as an isolated and elite ideological group of heterochthonous Greeks. The klephts, on the contrary, were primitive peasant rebels without a coherent ideology, a temporary auxiliary form and not a form of lasting revolutionary significance. The ideal of freedom pursued by the klepht was an index of his desire to bend to no authority, for even if he brought a new order, he would be as little a part of it as he was of the old world he struggled against. The klepht is a figure of the solitary rebel, a surrogate pursuing the freedom that evaded the helpless Greek peasant.[3]

The klepht as described here is distinguished in the Karagiozis texts from the *listi,* who is an unredeemable free spirit, one who does not pursue, as does the klepht, a religious or patriotic dream to liberate Greece. The *listi* is thus treated variously as an antihero and as a Robin Hood. Both this brigand and the audience's feelings about him are ambivalent. The figures are neither canonized nor Hellenized. They are accepted as they are and represent in its purist form the pluralistic and often negative Romaic view common to popular audiences of the Karagiozis performance.

These texts are not bowdlerized. Indeed, in one text a mother kills her own son to hide from him her illicit affair, while in another a son murders his father, who objected to the son's profligate ways.[4] The texts express a raw, naked energy that has not been retouched by elevated patriotic or moralizing sentiments. They reflect, instead, a natural and direct popular response to heroic events (see Chapter 1, note 148).

Michael Herzfeld[5] argues that intellectual ideologues took up the cultural aspirations and values of the klephts (as represented in selectively retrieved and edited folk songs), eschewed social reality, and used the songs for political purposes—to develop a sense of social and national consciousness. Jan Vansina's position[6] that traditions exist to serve the interests of their societies seems to support the notion that inherent in the songs was material that lent itself to such a use, even though, as A. Politis claims, there is neither social nor national consciousness expressed in the klephtic songs.[7] Beaton makes clear that it is the very distortions of history (the deviation from historical fact that is attributable to social interests or cultural values) that are the "real determinants of the nature and function of the tradition."[8]

Applying this perspective to the Karagiozis history text suggests we should find in it minimal historical veracity; moreover, the material of greatest interest should be that which deviates from historical fact, for it will speak to social, cultural, and personal values that express the function of the tradition. Indeed, the aim of a tradition is bound to interfere with its representation of the past, for it transmits a certain point of view about the past even if the degree of control exercised over that transmission is minimal. In general, the further a text is from its point of origin, the more likely it will forget historical facts and adapt to the cultural views of its tradition. The cultural values expressed will be those unquestioned assumptions of the group that give life its meaning, lay down ideals to strive for, and reveal unconscious dictates of behavior.[9] In sum, if a tradition survives, it is because it is highly valued. If it is highly valued, it is because it conforms to cultural ideals, meaning that it is likely, in historical terms, to be distorted.

Since its purpose is to satisfy the psychological needs of its audience, the Karagiozis history performance has no motive for transmitting historical information accurately. It is sufficient that it emphasize particular aspects of history, though that does not necessarily mean that major historical dislocations will occur. The performance chooses its own measure of time, a cultural rather than a historical perspective; it establishes its own view of truth, that which is worthy of belief; and it describes its own view of the nature of historical development, a pattern in which no progress and no causality exists between events and time remains unchanged from the distant past. Traditional history thus distorts perspective by choosing figures who are typical of some ideal or whose identification with certain regions or events is sufficiently well known or accepted to be typical of that ideal.[10] Traces of their presence in the landscape, through details of time, place, or person, provide all the guarantee of truth required by folk belief.

The history in the *Katsandonis* text exemplifies the player's treatment of traditional history. The specifics of the Karagiozis *Katsandonis* performance suggest the presence of the hero Katsandonis in a particular historical terrain. He is placed in Agrafa where he lived and fought. There, too, is the monastery Konithari, or Saint John of the Lice, at which Katsandonis is supposed, in the popular account adopted by the performance, to have sought refuge when ill. The performance has the captured hero sent to Ioannina, Ali Pasha's capital, and tortured at the historic site Platanon. His historical role in the liberation of the island Levkas, or Kerkira, and his likely participation thereafter in battles in Thessaly are tied ino the cycle through the hero's appeal to Capodistria, the famous patriot of Levkas, to provide refuge for his family and through the use of Tsara's Inn, the Thessalian headquarters of the Tsaras family of klephts, as a meeting place.

The events of the *Katsandonis* text do not, nevertheless, truly reflect history. Katsandonis was in real life the Greco-Vlah Kitsos Aidonis. He had in his youth apparently been jailed either by a local Turkish ruler or by Ali Pasha, an event omitted in the performance. Never married, he could not have rescued his wife and son as universally represented in the performances. Furthermore, unlike the giant pictured in popular tradition (a motif influenced by the depiction in myth of classical heroes as giants), Katsandonis was short and unattractive in real life. His legendary chivalry was equally fictitious, for he was known for his brutality to Turk and Christian alike.

Katsandonis, having fought beside his two brothers, Yiorgos Hasiotis and Kostas Lepeniotis, was not, moreover, the solitary martyr depicted in the performance, for he was martyred together with his brother Yiorgos. The hero was not betrayed by a lying monk, a folk tale influence, and his betrayal by a man (a farmer) who brought him his food (included in Mollas's play) is equally untenable. Indeed, according to eyewitnesses [11] a girl carried his meals. He was not given over to the famous General Yiusuf Arapis, as the performance claims, but to the less famous Aga Vassiaris. Finally, the cause of the hero's need for shelter was not a battle wound but smallpox, and his final refuge was a cave rather than a monastery.

The inclusion in the performance of period poems or songs maintained through memorization increases the sense of greater truth, when, in fact, these additions are themselves historical distortions with their own ideology. At the same time, some important events are not included in the performance; some are included but are not given any significance; while others are given a significance they do not deserve. Some events may continue in the performance as archaisms maintained without explanation; others are distorted by added explanations. Imaginary figures are introduced and historical figures are idealized.[12] Familiar events are mixed together, while complex aspects of history remain unrepresented and the larger events surrounding anonymous, historical forces are reduced or explained through easily comprehended, personalized exploits.[13] Lacking truly historical geneologies, demography, chronology, and geography, the form, as well as the perspective, of the performance's historical statement is best described as distorted by social interests, cultural values, or personal ideas.

Historical lapses in heroic texts based on historical events are largely dictated by popular cultural values. Both *Katsandonis* and *Athanasios Diakos,* for example, highlight Greek values that emphasize family life and moral struggle. *Diakos* ultimately speaks to the same larger questions as *Katsandonis*—apostasy, sacrilege, chivalry, and test of faith— although its initial events have broken off from the three-night cycle play to be represented in popular, pirated print editions as a separate play (*Athanasios Diakos and Karagiozis Churchwarden*)[14] that more pointedly describes this cycle's message. In the initial events of the *Diakos* cycle, a Turkish soldier seeks refuge from Andrutsos's troops at Saint John Prodromos, the monastery at which Diakos served in real life as a novice. Diakos admits him and, when Andrutsos's soldiers appear to claim their prize, hides him at the home of Diakos's mother and sister. Ali Pasha's officer Veli Gekas (in real life, Ferhat Aga performed this function) arrives at the monastery and appeals to Diakos's obligation to offer hospitality to travelers and strangers. When Veli's Albanian mercenaries abuse that hospitality by smashing icons and blaspheming, Diakos is driven to take up arms in the House of God and attack his guests. Having violated his vows as a monk, he flees into the mountains to join Andrutsos, stopping first to receive his mother's blessing.

The importance of sanctuary and the respect in which the custom of hospitality has been held in Greek culture since classical times have superseded, in the popular mind, the appeal of the other two major events of the play: the battle of Alamana Bridge and Diakos's refusal to convert (the latter resulted in his being roasted on a spit). Indeed, in Vango's version not only does the hospitality sequence constitute the most highly developed and well-detailed section of the play, but it continues to inform the second part of the play in Andrutsos's mountain camp. There, the soldiers who have pursued the Turk-in-refuge question Diakos's true loyalties. Andrutsos himself, admitting to his men that in war many strange things happen, advises Diakos not to treat war like an insult in one's house. The klephts embody the natural suspicion of common men for those of the cloth and doubt the appropriateness of such cultural values as hospitality and sanctuary. Although Diakos must prove himself in Vangos's version by being tested on a dangerous mission, he, nevertheless, vindicates those values and himself by both his earlier insistence on the values of traditional culture and his willingness to die for his faith and nation rather than submit to values outside his culture. *Diakos* thus becomes a play clarifying cultural values that encourage the continuity of traditional rules of behavior in modern times, at the same time marking a distinction between the dictates of patriotism and one's faith. Indeed, Vangos includes a debate on just these two latter, occasionally conflicting features in the third part of his performance.

A second advocate of popular cultural values, the heroic abduction plays (*Captain Gris, Kira Frosini, Astrapoyiannos, Captain Mavrodimos, The Abduction of Helen, The Orphan of Chios*),[15] offers the protection of female honor as a dominating motif. In individual texts, various minor events are celebrated as the major focus of the play (the reuniting of lost brothers, the symbolic raising of the flag of liberation, the call to arms, the rescue of hostages). Although these plays fail to explore single issues definitively, they present a picture of the values sponsored by the performance: justice to those who fight in the service of their nation; amnesty as a means of bringing marginal figures into the social center where their unique qualities can serve the people; resistance to conversion as a means of preserving traditional values; preservation of national values and customs in the face of pragmatic and efficacious pressures.

The depiction of the Greek warrior in the Karagiozis heroic text elucidates the cultural values sponsored by this performance. The hero[16] is described by his enemies as Satan, a genie, or a giant, a man who destroys his own weapons rather than surrender them and who prefers death at the hands of his lieutenant over capture by the enemy. He leads drastically outmanned troops that, nevertheless, outmaneuver the foe and take fewer losses. Enemy forces avoid battle at night, at close quarters, or in single combat, fearful of the Greek warrior's strength in a fair fight. They make hostages of old men, women, and children, and torture messengers who bear bad news. Many times stronger than the hero's forces, they lose battles through cowardice and lack of intelligence, they report greater losses than are actually incurred, list enemy forces several times their actual size, and exaggerate the heroism of their opponents.

The quality of action in the Karagiozis heroic texts is, as one might have anticipated, as brutal as the heroes are one-dimensional. The odor from the serai of burning Christians in the dark of night is said to silence the birds, and the Greek hero Katsandonis responds to the Albanian Ali Pasha's threat to scatter his body across the road with the claim that those parts will sprout forth into many more Katsandonians to shatter Ali's dry head. Ali, in the player Yiannis Mustakas's *Karagiozis, Ali Pasha, and Kira Frosini*,[17] is bounced so violently on his head that it flies off to drown in a nearby bay. Karagiozis, in Andonios Mollas's *Katsandonis, Ali Pasha, Kira Frosini, and Karagiozis*,[18] promises the ear and nose of Karderinis as a sign of that traitor's assassination; while in Mustakas's *Karagiozis and Captain Andrutsos*[19] the extermination of Turkish prisoners leaves the woods full of Turkish corpses and causes a thousand birds to fill the sky. Adding his voice to the fray in the latter play, Karagiozis calls out for heads to be lopped off like grape vines. Although it appears that Turks and Greeks are equally capable of brutality, the code espoused in the texts offers distinctions. Thus, the Greeks' enemies may be executed when captured, but, true to the warrior's code of honor, their bodies are saved from the ravages of wild animals, washed, and buried. Katsandonis may threaten desecration of the body of Sempsedin Aga as a ploy to exchange the body for a captured Greek, but he does not actually violate the corpse. The Turks, on the contrary, are shown hiring armies of Albanian mercenaries to fight their battles. These hirelings desecrate the dead, cutting off their heads and tossing their bodies into lime pits.

The songs[20] and poems borrowed from Greek folklore by the Karagiozis performance reinforce its themes by enhancing the audience's moral view of itself and by reconfirming the audience's commitment through appeals to God and country:

> Let us swear upon Holy Faith and upon the Cross,
> I fight for my country and my religion.
> Let us swear with our life's breath upon the Cross
> either our nation will be glorious again as once before
> or we will fall to earth filled with honor's bullets.
>
> (Kostas Manos, *Katsandonis*)[21]

Reiterating the primary message of the heroic texts, the songs contrast the faithful Greek with the faithless Turk, depicting the latter once again as perverse and unnatural. The distinction here is enriched, however, for the Turkish pasha is described in one verse as a snake that destroys itself in fires of its own setting and in another as an asocial animal that crawls off into a private mental world: "Death give me the key / to go dust off / my web-covered mind / where I will live" (Markos Ksanthos, *First of May of Karagiozis*).[22]

In the songs, the depictions of the klephts as children of nature and of the relationship between Greeks and Turks as analogous to that of the hunter and the hunted support the performance's dichotimization of values. The klephts drink and eat of the earth; the fruits of her trees and her vineyards and her flocks supply the warrior's banquets, which follow great victories, just as her wilds provide them sanctuary. The denial of basic needs—sleep, wine, bread—required of klephts is itself a testament to their dependence on the land and their loyalty to it. Indeed, they become nature's own in their ultimate tribute to the land:

"How long, warriors / shall we live in slavery / alone like lions / on the mountain's back" (Mollas, *Katsandonis*).[23] They are like the bird of dawn in a Panayiotis Mihopulos Karagiozis song, a bird that, its wings cut, longs to reach its high nest and its dependents there (*The Little Cafe of Karagiozis*).[24]

The hunters are depicted as being made up of varying predators, as in the *Katsandonis* text: the irredeemable infidel (Ali), the apostate Christian (Vagias), and the Christian ally of the Turk (the Vlah Veli Gekas). The function of the predator in the Karagiozis songs is to establish the limits of negative behavior. The Christian ally of the Turk, for example, serves as a barometer of change, for he stands at the pivot of the moral seesaw. A victim caught on the horns of a dilemma, described as laughed at by the stars and moon and plagued by nightmarish dreams, he is trapped between his religion and his national identity, the former antipathetic to Islamic rule of Christian land and the latter sympathetic to foreign occupation of the Greeks as a rival national group. He is thus both winner and loser. When, as inevitably happens in the histories, the tables are turned and the hunter becomes the hunted, we find Veli Gekas's synchronic, internal contradiction mirrored in a diachronic reversal. The suffering undergone by Veli Gekas is not, however, apparent in Vagias who, externalizing the former's conflict, has consciously chosen his role of turncoat and relishes having become even more threatening and devious than the master he serves. He is more to be blamed than Ali, for he has chosen to go against his own nature and thus consciously reverses the natural balance. The force of the opportunist apostate is intellectual (a suspect commodity in the moral realm) rather than physical (a force that is, at least, accepted as natural), as Vagias indicates: "Forty-five hunters / hunt my mind" (Mollas, *Katsandonis*).[25] Perverse mental force here, as in Ali Pasha, is the natural prey of the morality of the Greek warrior.

It is the Greek warrior, however, who is the true prey of the heroic Katsandonis songs; he is the one who establishes the positive balance on the moral continuum. It is his entrapment, his suffering and death, that preoccupies the singer of songs. Tied to nature's own imagery, the klepht is spoken to by birds and mourned by mountains; his fate is reflected in the red sun, the black moon, and the dawn that struggles to reign. The elements reflect and protect him: the pastures are green that he might eat; the heavy snows house him; and the mountains bend to reveal his struggle.[26]

The range of values exhibited in the songs of the Katsandonis performance not only provides an index of the moral continuum of the plays and the positions taken along that continuum by different characters, but points, more importantly, to the nature of the performance's ideology.[27] This ideology is expressed in appeals to the klephts to "fight gloriously . . . like Kolokotronis in Tripoli and Gravia / battle like lions . . . like worthy warriors / like Kanaris who burned the armada in Chios" (Mustakas, *Captain Andrutsos*).[28] It is also found in expressions of fear in the hero's camp: "How the shadow frightens us / of Markos Botsaris / or the skewering in Lamia / where they roasted Diakos. / How the shadow of Lambros Katsonis / frightens us or the voice of Agrafon / the hero Katsandonis / or the blessed sea-battling heroes / Kanaris and Miauli" (Manos, *Katsandonis*).[29]

Like the history texts, the Katsandonis text distorts events as a means of reinforcing conformity to tradition and consolidating national feeling in its audience. Such an expression and confirmation of cultural values appears most insistently in the text's treatment of characters and events in a manner similar to that found in folk morality plays. Katsandonis is portrayed with Christ-like virtues; his nemesis, Ali, is freely drawn and referred to as an anti-Christ, and his betrayer, Karderinis, has all the qualities of Judas. The gypsies who pound Katsandonis's flesh, called in the performance "torturers," are curiously similar to Christ's torturers in the medieval mysteries. In Mollas's treatment of the hero's life, Pontius Pilate and Herod are suggested, the first in the psychological portrait of the apostate Athanasios Vagias and the latter in Ali's out-Heroding of Herod in the hunting down of Katsandonis. Like a folk morality play, Mollas's version even provides us with the testimony of the common-man as jailer and with a ghost that warns of evil forces in the land. Indeed, in one performance of his *Katsandonis*,[30] Mollas shows Ali carried off in the end by devils. In a similar vein, Yitsaris's performance presents the devil and an angel fighting over Katsandonis's departed soul. In this instance, the angel prevails.

An essential contrast is thus drawn between two forces, that of good and evil. On the one hand, the audience is presented with the essential cowardice of both Ali and his henchman, Vagias, their bullying of the weak, their use of spies and torture, and Ali's revolt against heaven during which, like Lucifer, he defies the power of God. Set against this evil is the ideal hero Katsandonis, who refuses to be bound when captured and rejects conversion; he calls for single combat and insists on burial of the enemy dead; he lectures his son on the value of education and affirms in his behavior the importance of family life; he stands, above all, in the eyes of his men as a proponent of the democracy of men. The final ascension of Katsandonis, attended by angels and the allegorical figure of Greece, completes the series of parallels that suggests a Passion play in which the wedded forces of apostasy and Satanic evil battle the forces of faith in a great moral struggle.

Focusing on the distinctions it clarifies between East and West, Christianity and Islam, Greek and Turk, and the ruler and the ruled, the Karagiozis history text reinforces religious feeling and emphasizes epic feeling for one's race as part of a larger struggle for survival. The Karagiozis history text thus expresses an ideological view of history that has little to do with historical actuality; it is reducible to sentiments that express a primitive, national consciousness but that also essentially reflect the unquestioned assumptions of collective belief. These assumptions, which exaggerate virtues and repress failures, allow the audience to maintain within itself traditional habits, qualities, and conventions.

Because of his relatively minor role as a klepht captain in Greece prior to the Greek War of Independence, and in spite of the various antiheroic aspects of his character and person as noted in historical accounts, Katsantonis provided popular tradition with attractive material for expressing cultural values. The hero's terrible death at a young age and his call to the armatoli or mountain guards of northern Greece to take up arms against their masters were, of course, critical issues in his popular appeal. Nevertheless, the fact that his historical role was less well defined than that of more important figures in the Greek revolution provided greater freedom to embellish his life in ways that catered to audience interest and exploited cultural values. Certainly Katsandonis was sung of widely, receiving more attention than significantly more important klephtic captains such as Karaiskakis, Makriyiannis, or Kolokotronis. He was clearly taken up as an early model for the Karagiozis history performance when those same figures were being largely disregarded by players anxious to capture a large audience with their performances. Yet another reason for his appeal may have been that Katsandonis did not live long enough to encounter the jealousies of rival captains, which destroyed the reputations of other heroes, or to experience the fall in fortunes that afflicted yet others. His death, too, was far more romantic than merely dying of one's battle wounds or living out one's life.

The events of the *Katsandonis* cycle text can be outlined into four major lines of action: the murder of Katsandonis's father, Old Lepeniotis, at the hands of the Albanian tyrant Ali Pasha; the capture of Katsandonis's wife and child, their rescue from Ali's emissary Veli Gekas, and Veli Gekas's death at the hands of Katsandonis; the capture and exchange of Katsandonis's nephew Theodore; and the illness of Katsandonis, his betrayal by the monk Karderinis, and Katsandonis's death on the anvil.[31] The initiating action of the plot is the arrest by Veli Gekas of old Lepeniotis. The old man refuses to accede to

Ali's demand that he worship the pasha as a god and is boiled in oil. Turkish troops sent against Katsandonis are reported to have been shamefully defeated. As a result, Ali sends his trusted Veli Gekas to seize Katsandonis's wife and child. Manthos, the Greek secretary to Ali, sends a message through his associate Kentron to warn Katsandonis's wife, but she is seized. In retaliation, Katsandonis returns from the mountains to rescue his family and kills Veli Gekas. Infuriated by the death of his faithful officer, Ali sends additional troops against Katsandonis led by the powerful mercenary Yiusuf Arapis, a great black giant. Once again, Manthos sends a message to warn Katsandonis, and Arapis's troops are defeated. In the battle, however, Katsandonis's nephew Theodore is captured by the Turks. The corpse of Arapis's adopted son Sempsedin is retrieved by the Greeks and, to avoid threatened mutilation of the body, a great dishonor to a Moslem, Arapis agrees to exchange Theodore. Katsandonis, badly wounded in the battle, takes refuge in a nearby monastery where he is betrayed to Yiusuf Arapis by the monk Karderinis. Refusing to submit to Ali, Katsandonis is pounded to death on an anvil and his soul, attended by angels, rises to heaven.

Katsandonis is the most highly developed and most popular of the Karagiozis history performances. It survives, however, in only three print texts and one performance tape, largely because of its great length as a cycle play (it takes three nights to perform),[32] but also because this complex performance is arguably the most difficult for a player to perform and maintain in his repertoire. The earliest surviving version is an elaborate literary text published by Andonios Mollas in 1925. Published in six booklets of about thirty-two pages each, it totals 207 pages. A second print text was published c. 1940 by Yiannis Mustakas—an abbreviated, one part, thirty-two-page text. The most recent version is that of Savvas Yitsaris, collected on tape in 1969 by Mario Rinovolucri for the Center for the Study of Oral Literature.[33] An adumbrated, two-night performance, the Yitsaris *Katsandonis* runs two and a half hours; it adds to that length a prologue for each evening's performance and a one-act afterpiece for the second evening.

The fourth and most traditional of the surviving texts is a print text published by Kostas Manos c. 1930. A three-part text of 120 pages (this time in forty-page booklets), Manos's text was published as a separate text and not as part of a larger series of texts as was then common. It fell from sight almost immediately after it was published and, as a result, was not generally known to students of the form. It does not, for example, appear on any of the traditional Karagiozis bibliographies.[34] Fortunately, we rediscovered it in Athens in 1966 in an old bookseller's warehouse, and it is presented in this translation for the first time since its original publication. Not only was Manos particularly well known for his *Katsandonis* performance, but his few published texts (he published only eight compared to, for example, ninety-two texts by Yiannis Moustakas) have been described as those most carefully transferred from live performance to print.

Of the four extant *Katsandonis* texts, Andonios Mollas's version is both the earliest and the most elaborated. Mollas's version is four times as long as a conventional comedy, a length that permits the player epic scope in which to develop his legendary material. Mollas individualizes the familiar material of the Katsandonis legend, creating greater plot interest and more variety in his scenes than is commonly found in either the histories or comedies. The opening of act 1, for example, is not the traditional opening scene used in most Karagiozis texts, both comic and heroic (in which Hatziavatis engages in conversation with a pasha or bey). Instead, Mollas begins his action *in media res* as Vagias is caught by the klephts and brought to Katsandonis for questioning. The scene that follows is masterful in its suggestion of psychological nuances in the character of Vagias, who in this text takes on a complex meshwork of motives.[35]

Mollas, in his version of the *Katsandonis* text, elaborates on comic elements and elements of erotic love. The latter appears in Vagias's courting of the harem girl and in his claims that he was driven to his evil deeds by his passion for a woman. Even more significant is Mollas's depiction of Ali Pasha as a man desperately in love with the beautiful Vasiliki.[36]

Not only does Mollas individualize and develop the psychology of his characters, but he details events and provides a comic subscript to parallel the hero's exploits. Mollas includes, for example, minor details dealing with the political struggle in Greece, both adding an element of historicity and deepening the conflict within the two enemy camps. Here the internecine squabbles between the klephts and renegade brigands—presented as differences of opinion among Katsandonis's officers—are detailed, as are Ali's erratic favoritism among his officers, his solicitation of information about his enemy, and the debate between him and his counselors on military matters.

As for the comic subscript, Karagiozis's role is expanded in humorously treated scenes that act as a second line of development throughout the play: Karagiozis's donkey is eaten by a wolf; he is trapped in the midst of a battle on a runaway horse; he is captured by brigands, has a brush with death, and takes revenge against his captors; he deceives Vagias in their competition over a girl, is captured by the Turks, and kills both Vagias and Karderinis to avenge the death of Katsandonis. Karagiozis's comically treated mishaps and his final assertion of his value parallel, in fact parody, the serious heroic exploits of the hero Katsandonis, for the former's victory of physical valor occurs in the same scene as Katsandonis's spiritual victory over Ali and his ascension to heaven.

Comparison of the Mollas text with the Yiannis Mustakas *Katsandonis* and the *Katsandonis* of Savvas Yitsaris demonstrates the direction taken by the performance from its highly elaborated form in Mollas's early twentieth-century version to its mid-century state. Initially inspired by the spirit of nationalism that attended late nineteenth-century border wars with Turkey, the *Katsandonis* performance fell prey to a mid-twentieth-century disenchantment with history that overtook a nation distanced from its liberationist childhood of 1821 and the resurgent feelings of its late nineteenth-century adolescence. Performed less and less frequently in the mid-twentieth century, the long history cycles progressively lost their shape.

Mustakas's version is the most abbreviated of the four texts, the result of a movement to provide cheap chapbooks of Karagiozis performances for a popular audience. This undated print text was published during a period (1940–1950) of political unrest and economic deprivation in Greece, thereby making a developed version unlikely. Mustakas's version schematically presents three of the four traditional plot elements, excepting the capture and exchange of Katsandonis's nephew Theodore.

Mustakas's version suffers from the same audience disinterest that was to affect the Yitsaris performance. Separated from the Mollas and Manos texts by a forty-year period, Yitsaris announced his two-part performance as a seven-hour spectacle, but spent only two and a half hours with the actual events of the cycle history. The rest of his performance is devoted to the prologues and the afterpiece. The action is telescoped into a brief format characterized by shapeless scenes (Katsandonis's farewell to his wife and son, his farewell to his aid, Kostas, at the monastery, and his attempt to intervene in a dispute between Kostas and Yiusuf Arapis). Elsewhere, the player bypasses comic opportunities, using Hatziavatis, rather than Karagiozis, as messenger to the klephts, thus eliminating the possibility for humor at the klephts' hideout. In this role-switching, Yitsaris gives Karagiozis the role of Manthos, secretary to the pasha; here, in spite of the figure's illiteracy and characteristic incompetence, Yitsaris fails to exploit him comically.[37]

Not only his handling of the plot but his performance techniques reflect the deteriorated state of Yitsaris's version. Though his after-piece and prologues move smoothly and are well paced, the timing of the main performance has no edge. Scenes are poorly cut off and do not lay out well; moreover, distinctions between voices and individu-alization of character are not well developed. In sum, the inspiration of Yitsaris's *Katsandonis* is muted.[38]

As this discussion indicates, Yitsaris's text lies at one end of the spec-trum of *Katsandonis* performances, the spectrum running from Yit-saris's provincial folk performance to Mollas's urbane and theatrical version. Manos's *Katsandonis,* which stands at the middle point on the spectrum, exhibits the traditional and oral qualities of this Karagiozis performance. The Manos text preserves the direct characterization, the stereotyped scenes, and the repetitive and balanced plot most char-acteristic of products of oral culture. It displays the sentiments of tra-ditional values and exhibits the common understanding of folk culture and popular lore upon which Karagiozis is ultimately based. This is not to say that Manos's text is unaffected by the influence of live the-ater and melodrama. Indeed, it is characterized by a more suspenseful plot and greater psychological probing than is common for the comic performances in the repertoire. But while Manos reflects the trends that affected the Karagiozis performance, he remained essentially a traditional performer who resisted literary influences. His work re-mains an accurate reflection of the mainstream Karagiozis perfor-mance of the early decades of the century.

In Manos's *Katsandonis* text, repetition, balance, contrast, and cu-mulative effect represent the basic compositional techniques the player uses. The device of repeated messages is used, for example, to keep the audience aware of the progress of events: Karagiozis carries three sepa-rate messages, Barba Yiorgos, one, and Theodore, one. In each in-stance the events that necessitate sending the message are dramatized, then clarified by the author of the letter, and, finally, restated by the recipient of the message. The events themselves are more easily com-prehended by the listening audience through their repetition. Manos's balance is displayed in his organization of events as simple shifts back and forth from the Greek to the Turkish camps. The same process is used in his initiation of major actions. In each instance, the action is inspired by Ali Pasha who sends one of his officers against the Greeks: Veli Gekas is sent against Katsandonis's father, wife, and child; Atha-nasios Vagias, against a rich merchant; and Yiusuf Arapis, against Katsandonis—first through Arapis's capture of Theodore, then in his seduction of Karderinis, and, finally, in the capture of Katsandonis himself. Repetitious series are used to generate cumulative effects in establishing Ali's blasphemy. The basis of the repetition is established by Ali himself when he demands that Katsandonis's father worship him; Lepeniotis refuses, claiming Ali is neither his father, his ruler, nor his Christ. Ali next damns an Islamic priest who has come to provide his morning blessing; the priest withdraws as Ali damns his prophet to the devil. In the final scene of the play, Ali defies God himself, calling upon Katsandonis to forsake Christ and worship Ali as a new divinity. Contrasts are used throughout the play both for dramatic effect and emphasis, as when Ali's blasphemy is contrasted to Lepeniotis's faith, to the prayers of the klephts before battle, to Katsandonis's refusal to deny his God, and to Katsandonis's angelic ascension.

The straightforward simplicity of Manos's compositional techniques is expressed in a plot that rarely digresses. Although Karagiozis's anecdotes and the jokes he plays appear here as they do in all Karagiozis texts, only one major outburst of comedy—Karagiozis's capture by the Turks and the vestigial phallic humor that follows—can be said to function separately from the main action. Even that scene serves a dramatic function, for it delays the letter that would prevent the capture of Katsandonis's wife and child. Manos's dramatic effects are also economical, as in the text's last scenes. Here the author hesitates in the breakneck pace of his action to present a considered scene of almost ritual responses, or stichomythia, in which the torturers interject comments into a dialogue between Katsandonis and Ali Pasha. Similarly, and as is characteristic of all three *Katsandonis* texts, Manos's plot skeleton employs economical action and balanced scenes: the murder of Katsandonis's father; the capture of Katsandonis's wife and child; the capture of Katsandonis's nephew Theodore; and the martyrdom of Katsandonis.

Manos uses somewhat more developed techniques, though still relatively simple compared to Mollas, to contrast and balance his characters against one another. His Ali, for example, is a weak man who grieves at the loss of his trusted Veli Gekas, but who is easily assuaged by Vagias's plunder from a rich Greek merchant. A determined and convinced tyrant, Ali can neither understand nor tolerate the resistance of Christian faith to his iron rule. Though his evil counselor Vagias plays both on Ali's weakness and the weaknesses of others around him, Ali himself exploits Veli Gekas's loyalty, convincing the faithful officer to risk his life rendering a service that Vagias has refused to undertake. Unlike Veli Gekas, who feels himself humiliated by the unmanly circumstances of his capture of Katsandonis's wife and child, Vagias enjoys devising inhuman acts against the helpless. It is he who convinces Ali that the Greeks are capable of paying more taxes, and he

who recommends the kidnapping of Katsandonis's family. The human-
ity that Manos instills in Manthos Ikonomos—the Greek secretary to
Ali Pasha who acts secretly on behalf of the klephts (this role is played
here by Hatziavatis)—is used to balance the evil of the apostate Vagias. Manthos argues for leniency and acts as an intermediary, first to
moderate Ali's passion and finally to counter Ali's acts of vengeance,
thus countering the counsel of Vagias.

In the Manos text, sentiment plays a large part, being derived from
the patriotic espousals of Katsandonis and his men in the mountains
and of Manthos Ikonomos at the serai as well as from the spectacles of
Katsandonis's torment and his ascension, which Manos, alone of the
three players examined here, accompanies with a patriotic poem recited by the allegorical figure, Greece. The element of love also plays a
key role in the sentiment of the plays, but unlike Mollas and characteristic of the folk attitude Manos consistently observes, Manos keeps the
focus on family love, that of a husband for a wife and parents for a
child. The wife and son, for example, are depicted as waiting anx-
iously for Katsandonis's return and concerned for his safety, while
Katsandonis is shown to be brokenhearted when he receives the news
of their capture. The mother is seen fiercely defending her son's life
against their Turkish captors. The son is presented as being devoted to
his father when they must part. The father affectionately and at length
advises his son on the importance of preparing for the future. Of the
three extant texts, the Manos *Katsandonis* thus offers the most traditional statement of the cultural values, common psychology, and oral
compositional techniques characteristic of the Karagiozis history
performance.

THE PERFORMER KOSTAS MANOS

One of a handful of truly influential players who performed in the
golden age of the Karagiozis performance, Kostas Manos was born in
Argos, the Peloponnesos, in 1902. He was schooled through the first
grade, barely long enough to develop the ability to draw letters and
count change—basic knowledge for a player who must draw his own
posters and handle ticket sales. As was common with players of Manos's times, Manos adopted a pseudonym (his family name was Athanasios) to avoid embarrassing his family. Karagiozis players were, after
all, associated in the cities with the poorest working class, in the provinces, with vagrants, and in harbors and ports, with the criminal
underclass.

Manos began studying theater as a painter with the popular player

Markos Ksanthos in Athens in 1918, went on to work for the eminent player Manolopulos in the Peroki area of Athens, and became an independent puppeteer in Peristeri, Athens, in 1924. He fit into a tradition of players that traced itself back to Mimaros of Patras, the latter credited as the father of the Greek performance tradition. Mimaros's numerous reforms and his popularization of Karagiozis radically modified a tradition that had remained essentially Turkish from its introduction to Greece. The line of players that ultimately led to Manos passed from Mimaros to his most influential student, the founder of Athenian-style Karagiozis, Yiannis Rulias, then to Andonios Mollas, an acknowledged player's player in the Athenian style, and from there to Manos's first master, Ksanthos.

Despite his early start in Athens, Manos returned to his native Peloponnesos to perform, for the touring routes and the cities of the Peloponnesos were considered the true test of a Karagiozis player. The length of a player's stay in one spot varied greatly when he was on tour. A stay of only one or two days was not uncommon where the audience was difficult to please or quite small. If he was moderately well received, a player might stay thirty to sixty days, long enough to exhaust his basic repertoire. More often, however, a stay encompassed fifteen performances. If a player was well known in a particular area, he might be contracted by a cafe owner to perform and could thereby insure himself stable employment protected by the good offices of his employer. The proprietor arranged for the player's permit to perform, provided him with food, and paid for any damages incurred by boisterous or angry spectators. Together, they distributed handbills and placed advertisements in local newspapers.

Suffering the numerous inconveniences of the itinerant, players had to trudge from village to village searching for one in which they would be permitted to perform. They were subject to accusations of vagrancy by religious countryfolk, who believed puppeteering to be a sinful profession, and were forced to contend with moralizers who objected to the freedoms taken in their performances. Their performance inevitably attracted impressionable runaways and petty crooks. Indeed, some players were themselves thieves, pederasts, or vagabonds. Forced to contend with the jealousies of competing players[39] and proprietors of rival houses as well as the petty rivalries of their own apprentices, the Karagiozis player was often a helpless victim of his own art, a hungry and beleaguered figure who often bankrupted himself on tour and had to sell his equipment for fare home.

Responsive to the merest whims of their audience, Karagiozis players on tour developed a bond with spectators that determined, to some extent, the shape of the performance. In the north, players learned to perform heroic pieces, which, Kostas Manos explains, were preferred there. In the south, they had to demonstrate greater facility and provide more variety, particularly, says Avraam, in Salamina, Patras, and Kalamata where aficionados of the form would close out a player after only a few days if his performance did not meet their artistic standards. Audiences in villages around Tripolis and throughout Evoia were, according to Nikolas Lekkas and Dimitris Manos, particularly helpful to starting players. Those in Macedonia, on the contrary, were intolerant of players, regardless of their skill.

To engage an audience, Kostas Manos informs us, players had to know which of the different puppet types and texts appealed to it. Players salted Karagiozis's speech with examples of the dialect of the region in which they were playing, introduced local types, and judiciously selected those pieces most popular in the given area, even to the point of asking the audience which piece to perform. Careful to solicit the desires of those for whom they performed, players could thus avoid the risk of either losing their audience or their *kefi*, the high spirit needed to carry off a successful performance.[40]

Manos remained in the Peloponnesos to perform—using largely Kalamata and Argos as his home cities—returning only later in his career to play in Athens until his retirement in 1959. Although Manos was not among the players known for their singing ability, he was so well known for his designs that he was asked throughout his career to make puppets for other players. He was equally well known as a scenic innovator, sometimes performing without a screen and using numerous scenic properties. He prided himself most, however, on his ability to create new texts for his performances. He maintained some 250 performances, of which he claimed to have created 150.[41] Unfortunately, he published only eight texts. Just before his death in 1970, Manos was interviewed by Mario Rinovolucri for the Center for the Study of Oral Literature, thereupon leaving a record of his voice, if not of his live performances.

Manos is survived by a son, the Karagiozis player Dimitris or "Mimis" Manos, who himself became a Karagiozis player. Having studied and performed with his father over the course of fifteen years (not an uncommon term for an apprenticeship), Mimis ultimately developed a repertoire of 150 performances from the meager ten with which he began his career. In his own interview with Rinovolucri, Mimis Manos referred to his father's *Katsandonis* as the most serious Karagiozis performance of all, a work that, in his view, requires more skill and development from a player than any other text in the repertoire.

Heroic figures by the Karagiozis player Sotiris Spatharis.

Ο ΗΡΩΣ ΚΑΤΣΑΝΤΩΝΗΣ

ΔΡΑΜΑ ΕΙΣ ΤΡΙΑ ΜΕΡΗ

ὑπὸ τοῦ Καραγκιοζοπαίκτου ΚΩΝΣΤΑΝΤΙΝΟΥ ΜΑΝΟΥ

ΠΑΡΑΣΤΑΣΙΣ ΠΡΩΤΗ

ΠΡΟΣΩΠΑ

Κατσαντώνης
Ἀγγελικὴ (σύζυγός του)
Ἀλέξανδρος (υἱός των)
Γερω-Λεπενιώτης (πατὴρ τοῦ Κατσαντώνη)
Θεόδωρος (υἱός των)
Ζώστας (ὑπαρχηγός τοῦ Κατσαντώνη)
Γερω-Δῆμος (νονὸς τοῦ Κατσαντώνη)
Γούλας (Ἀνεψιὸς τοῦ Γερω-Δήμου)
Μπαρμπαγιῶργος
Πάνος Γκάκος Χανετζῆς
Ἀλῆ Πασσᾶς
Καρβερίνης (χοιροβοσκὸς Μοναστηρίου ἁγίου Ἰωάννου Κονίδρη)
Στρατιῶται—Ἀρματωλοὶ καὶ...

Χατζηαβάτης (ὢ: Μάνθος Οἰκονόμου Γραμματεὺς τοῦ Ἀλῆ Πασσᾶ)
Καραγκιούζης (ὢ: Κέντρον ψυχαγωγίας τοῦ Μάνθου Οἰκονόμου)
Ἀθανάσιος Βάγιας (συνεργὸς τοῦ Ἀλῆ Πασσᾶ)
Βελῆ Γκέκας
Γιουσοὺφ Ἀράπης
Σεϊφέδὶν Μπρεμὲτ (ψυχογυιὸς τοῦ Γιουσοὺφ Ἀράπη)
Χασὰν Ἀχμέτης (ἐξιωματικὸς τοῦ Ἀλῆ Πκσᾶ)
Ἡγούμενος Ἀμβρόσιος—Καλόγηροι

First page of the *Hero Katsandonis* text by Kostas Manos.

The cast of characters page from the *Hero Katsandonis* play.

Ο ΗΡΩΣ ΚΑΤΣΑΝΤΩΝΗΣ

ΠΑΡΑΣΤΑΣΙΣ ΠΡΩΤΗ ΕΙΣ ΠΡΑΞΕΙΣ ΤΡΕΙΣ

ὑπὸ τοῦ Καραγκιοζοπαίκτου ΚΩΝΣΤΑΝΤΙΝΟΥ ΜΑΝΟΥ

ΠΡΑΞΙΣ ΠΡΩΤΗ

Ἡ σκηνὴ παριστᾷ εἰς τὸ δεξιὸν τὴν Καλύβην τοῦ Καραγκιόζη καὶ εἰς τὸ ἀριστερὸν τὸ Σεράϊ τοῦ Ἀλῆ πασσᾶ).

ΣΚΗΝΗ Α΄.

Χασὰν Ἀμέτης. (μόλις ἐξερχόμενος τραγουδᾷ).

    Βαθειὰ ἀπὸ τὰ φύλλα σου
    καρδουλά μου τὰ βγάζης
    τὰ ὠμορφά σου δάκρυα
    τὴν ὑπαρξή μου σφάζης.

    Καταχαϋμένε ἄνθρωπε
    βαθειὰ ποὺ 'νε ἡ πληγή σου
    στὲν κάτω κόσμο ἀκούγονται
    οἱ ἀναστέναγμοί σου.

(Μονολογῶν) Ἕως τὰ Γιάννενα φθάσαμε καλά, ἀλλὰ τώρα νὰ ἴδουμε πῶς θὰ παρουσιασθοῦμε εἰς τὸν Ἀλῆ πασσά, αὐτὸ τὸ ἀνήμερο θηρίο, εὐτὸ τὸ τέρας τῆς Ἠπείρου, πῶς θὰ παρουσιασθῶ ἐμπρός του χωρὶς γρέσια; ὢ! ἀλλείμονό σου Χασὰν Ἀμέτη τί ἔχεις νὰ τραβήξης. Νὰ ἔλεγα τοῦ χὸρ Μάνθου νὰ ἐμεσολαβοῦσε εἰς τὸν Ἀλῆ; ἀλλὰ καὶ αὐτὸς ὁ δυστυχὴς μὲ ἔχει σώση δύο φορὲς ἀπὸ βέβαιο θάνατον, λοιπόν, δὲν πρέπει νὰ δυστάσω καθόλου, πρέπει νὰ φωνάξω τὸν χὸρ Μάνθο νὰ εἶνε μπροστὰ εἰς τὴν συζήτησιν ποὺ θὰ κάνω μὲ τὸν Ἀλῆ πασσᾶ (χτυπᾷ εἰς τὸ Σεράϊ),

ΣΚΗΝΗ Β΄.

ΜΑΝΘΟΣ—ΧΑΣΑΝ ΑΜΕΤΗΣ

Μάνθος. (ἐξερχόμενος) Μπᾶ καλῶς ὥρισες, κύριε Χασὰν Ἀμέτη.

An illustrated text of *Karagiozis, Alexander the Great, and The Cursed Snake* by Evyenios Spatharis.

Τήν Δευτέρα, 22 Μαρτίου, στό θέατρο «ΑΘΗΝΑ» τῆς όδοῦ Δε-
ριγνύ, ὁ παραδοσιακός καραγκιοζοπαίκτης ΘΑΝΑΣΗΣ ΣΠΥ-
ΡΟΠΟΥΛΟΣ, θά δώσει δύο παραστάσεις: α) 6 — 8 μ.μ. γιά
παιδιά, μέ τό ἔργο «Τό μαγικό μπαοῦλο καί ὁ Καραγκιόζης
νυχτοφύλακας». β) 8.30 μ.μ. γιά μεγάλους μέ τό ἔργο «Τό
διαζύγιο τοῦ Καραγκιόζη».

Newspaper advertise-
ment of a perfor-
mance by Thanasis
Spiropulos in Athens,
1974. A double bill
was performed: *The
Magic Trunk and
Karagiozis Night-
watchman* and *Ka-
ragiozis's Divorce.*

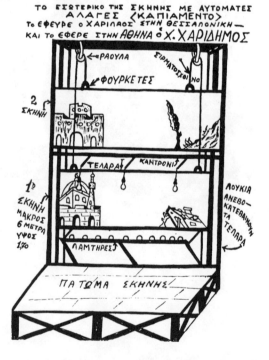

A sketch by Hristos
Haridimos of the
player's booth as viewed
from backstage.

A poster of a performance by Panayiotis Mihopulos at a
festival in Nancy, 1973.

Newspaper advertisement of a
performance by Manthos Athineos,
Alexander the Great and Karagiozis.

Newspaper advertisement of a
performance by Manthos Athineos,
Karagiozis at Galatsi.

THE HERO KATSANDONIS[1]
A DRAMA IN THREE PARTS[2]

BY KOSTAS MANOS

PERFORMANCE CAST

Katsandonis[3]
Angeliki, his wife[4]
Alexander, his son
Old Lepeniotis, his father[5]
Theodore, his nephew
Kostas, second-in-command to Katsandonis
Old Dimas, godfather to Katsandonis[6]
Goulas, nephew to Old Dimas
Panos Tsaros Hanitzis
Uncle George
Ali Pasha[7]
Hatziavatis, as Manthos Ikonomos, secretary to
    Ali Pasha[8]
Karagiozis, as Kentron, stepson to Manthos
    Ikonomos[9]
Athanasios Vagias, an accomplice of Ali Pasha,
    an apostate Christian Greek[10]
Veli Gekas[11]
Yiusuf Arapis, an Arab commander of Ali
    Pasha's army[12]
Sembsedin Bremetis, godson to Yioussouf Arapis
Hasan Ahmetis, an officer of Ali Pasha
Prior Amvrosios
Monks
Karderinis, swineherd at St. John of the Lice
    monastery[13]
Soldiers
Armatoli[14]
Klephts
Peasants, etc.

PART I in Three Acts

[*To the right of the screen, Karagiozis's hut; to the left, the palace of the pasha*]

HASAN AHMETIS: [*Sings a song as he comes out*]

> From deep within,
> my little heart, you grieve
> and shed your pretty tears
> to decimate my life.

> Wretched man,
> how deep your wounds must be,
> since even in the world below,
> your sighs resound.

[*Monologue*] We got as far as Yiannina, all right; but now let's see how we're going to face Ali Pasha, that wild animal, that Epirote monster.[16] How can I face him without money? Alas, Hasan Ahmetis, what lies in store for you? Should I ask Manthos for help?[17] Twice this poor man saved me from certain death. I better not waste any time; I've got to have Manthos there when I talk to Ali Pasha. [*He knocks at the serai.*]

ACT I, SCENE 2.

MANTHOS:[18] [*Coming out*] Welcome Hasan Ahmetis.

HASAN AHMETIS: Good to see you, Manthos.

MANTHOS: We've missed you at the serai, Hasan.[19]

HASAN AHMETIS: Didn't you know Ali had sent me to the villages for the poll tax, Manthos?[20]

MANTHOS: And what did you accomplish, Hasan?

HASAN AHMETIS: What could I do, Manthos? Since the villagers have nothing, I couldn't even collect a piastre. They're all poor. Whoever had anything, Ali took it, Manthos. He made the rich poor, like Old Lepeniotis. Remember what Old Lepeniotis had Manthos? All of Lepenos was his, and today he doesn't have shoes to put on his feet.

MANTHOS: Isn't that the truth. Imagine, even in his misery, poor old Lepeniotis is still loyal to Ali; he doesn't hold a grudge. He's never said a word against him.

HASAN AHMETIS: Yes, he hasn't complained at all. And yet, it's a Christian who ruined him, Manthos, this Thanasis Vagias. How do you bear this bastard, this assassin, this traitor?[21] How is it some Christian hand hasn't wiped this traitor off the earth? He's the cause, Manthos; whatever the Christians suffer, it's on his account; he singles them out to Ali who finishes them off. You see, Manthos, Ali is always after money; he's always poor; thousands of piastres arrive at the serai, but he's always complaining.

MANTHOS: You're right, Hasan, it's true. Ali has plenty of money, millions, but it's his nature to cry poverty.

HASAN AHMETIS: And what about Thanasis, Manthos?

MANTHOS: What do you want me to say? We all know what he is. He's hated by the Christians and the Ottomans. Whom has Thanasis left untouched? He's at the bottom of everything that happens in Epirus. If Vagias hadn't been spying around, Ali wouldn't have done anything. But don't worry, Hasan; you can be sure the Christians won't let him get away with it. He'll get just what he deserves. But we've talked too long and Ali might call me to bring him some proclamations to sign.

HASAN AHMETIS: Manthos, I'd like to ask if it's possible for you to announce me to Ali so I can report on my mission? I beg you, stay nearby if you can when I speak to Ali; you know how he is.

MANTHOS: Don't worry. Wait here. [*He exits toward the serai.*]

ACT I, SCENE 3.

[*Manthos enters and knocks at Ali's quarters.*]

ALI PASHA: [*Angrily*] Who is it, damn it?[22]

MANTHOS: It's me venerable vizir, Manthos.

ALI PASHA: Damn it, Manthos, what you want boy?

MANTHOS: Hasan Ahmetis is here, vizir; he asks to see you.

ALI PASHA: Tell him, damn it, he can wait till hell freezes over.[23]

MANTHOS: With your permission, sir. [*He comes out to Hasan.*] Did you hear him, Hasan?

HASAN AHMETIS: I heard him, Manthos. He's in a foul mood today.

MANTHOS: Yes, he's angry, because he can't find a way to get money.

[*Ali Pasha comes out, and Manthos stands behind him.*]

ALI PASHA: Welcome Hasan. You look said, damn it, Hasan, boy. What troubles you, damn it? You bring me money?

HASAN AHMETIS: I didn't bring any, Pasha.

ALI PASHA: Why, damn it, why?

HASAN AHMETIS: I went to all the villages as far as Arta, but wherever I went, not a single villager could pay the tax, vizir. They sowed their fields, but none harvested, vizir. You know this has been a bad year in the villages. The little they reaped lies on the threshing floors; no merchants came to buy it, so the villagers have no money to pay their tax.

ALI PASHA: Ah! And how we do it, damn it, boys, since I want lot of money; damn it, I need money damn it, to supply the army against klephts,[24] and I not have any. I poor, damn it. I poor. None of you do job right; only Thanasis Vagias do my bidding.

MANTHOS: Everyone serves you faithfully, vizir; all my officials love and respect you. If Hasan went and didn't bring money back, it's not his fault. If they didn't give him any, how could he bring any back? Should he mistreat the peasants? Should he force them? It wouldn't work, because in the end it would all fall on your head, Ali. The villagers who didn't give him money didn't have any to give; you heard what Hasan said. They've had bad luck farming, and the little that was grown is still on the threshing floors.

ALI PASHA: Yes, damn it, they right, Manthos.

MANTHOS: They have a good excuse, and you have to face that, vizir. When the villagers get money, they'll come by themselves to pay you first, as they do every year.

ALI PASHA: Damn it, go inside and you, Manthos, tell Thanasis Vagias to get here. I need him a bit.

MANTHOS: Certainly, vizir. [*He leaves with Hasan.*]

ACT I, SCENE 4.

[*Manthos comes out with Vagias.*]

ATHANASIOS VAGIAS: [*Falls at Ali's feet*] At your command, Ali.

ALI PASHA: Welcome, Thanasis.

ATHANASIOS VAGIAS: You called me, vizir?

ALI PASHA: Yes, damn it, Thanasis. I'm much depressed, damn it, boy. I don't have money, damn it, and I want much, damn it, for the troops, lot of money, damn it.

ATHANASIOS VAGIAS: Is this what bothers you, vizir? We have so many rich men here with so much money; why shouldn't they give some to Ali in his time of need?

ALI PASHA: Damn it, Thanasis, boy, which has money?

ATHANASIOS VAGIAS: Old Lepeniotis.

ALI PASHA: Damn it, he don't have it. I sent Hasan, damn it, and he told him he don't have it.

ATHANASIOS VAGIAS: It's a lie, he has money, vizir.

MANTHOS: Listen here, Thanasis, you and the vizir both know Old Lepeniotis well; he doesn't have any money. If he did, the vizir wouldn't have to send someone to ask for it. If he had any, he'd bring it himself.

ALI PASHA: Damn it, Thanasis, boy, you right. He don't have it, damn it. We must find another one with money.

ATHANASIOS VAGIAS: He has money, he has it, Ali; don't let Old Lepeniotis fool you; don't listen to what Manthos says. I know Old Lepeniotis very well; you'd even find money under his skin if you were to split him open. He has wells full of pounds-sterling; he's got plenty of gold. He hides it so he doesn't have to give you any.

MANTHOS: You're out of your mind saying Lepeniotis has wells full of pounds-sterling, Thanasis.

ALI PASHA: Shssh, damn it, Manthos. If Thanasis say he got it, he got it, damn it, and if he don't want to give it . . . damn it, go call Veli for me, and I'll send him to Old Lepeniotis to bring me money.

MANTHOS: Right away, vizir.

[*He goes and comes back with Veli Gekas.*]

ACT I, SCENE 5.

VELI GEKAS: [*Falls at Ali's feet*]²⁵ Phew!²⁶ At your command, sir.

ALI PASHA: Damn it, Veli, get up. Damn it, I want you to go to Old Lepeniotis, greet him, and, damn it, Veli, tell him to give you lot of money to bring me.

VELI GEKAS: Phew! What to say, sir: crumbs! Phew, that poor fellow, Old Lepeniotis, phew, not have money.

MANTHOS: Do you hear that, even Veli Gekas says he doesn't have any, vizir.

ATHANASIOS VAGIAS: He does, he does, don't listen to what they say.

ALI PASHA: Damn it, listen Veli. Thanasis know he has money, and he don't bring me any, damn it. Damn it go fix it like I told you.

VELI GEKAS: Phew! Yes sir.

ALI PASHA: Damn it, Manthos, boy, take off; fix me a pipe, damn it.²⁷

[*All go in except Veli Gekas.*]

VELI GEKAS: [*Alone*] Poor Old Lepeniotis, phew, not have money, phew; that Vagias behind it all. Come off it, now, Vagias, come off it, now.

[He approaches the rear of Karagiozis's hut and knocks.]

ACT I, SCENE 6.

[Enter Old Lepeniotis]

OLD LEPENIOTIS: Well, welcome, Veli, welcome, my boy. What are you doing down this way, Veli Gekas, my boy?

VELI GEKAS: Phew, how to put it, phew, how to put it?

OLD LEPENIOTIS: I can see you're stuck, Veli. Whatever it is, say it, spit it out, good or bad. You know, Veli, that by now the mountain is used to the snow; it doesn't matter how much falls on it. So speak, Veli.

VELI GEKAS: Phew, Old Lepeniotis, Thanasis Vagias say to Ali you have lot of money, and he be sending me now, phew, so give me to be taking it to Ali.

OLD LEPENIOTIS: Hang it, Veli, where will I find this money? You know the state I'm in.

VELI GEKAS: Phew, I tell Ali you don't have it, and Manthos say so. Phew! Vagias say you have it; that one fix everything.

OLD LEPENIOTIS: Bless Manthos. What did I ever do to Vagias? Why is he after me so?

VELI GEKAS: Phew! Me no know.

OLD LEPENIOTIS: Ah, listen Veli. Ali sucked enough from me. There's nothing left. Hang it, boy, you won't believe I've had nothing but a little sour milk since morning. I, Old Lepeniotis, the rich man of Lepenos, don't have bread to eat, Veli. Think of the thousands of goats I had. Ali took everything I owned. Ah, he ruined me.[28] Hang it, Veli, I'd go dry even if I was a well. Hang it, that's it. Tell Ali I don't have it. If I did I'd be glad to send it to him. I've got three blasted sheep; if he wants them, let him send for them. Hang it, Veli, put in a good word for me with Ali.

VELI GEKAS: Phew, O.K., Old Lepeniotis, phew. I tell the master. Bye.

[He leaves. Old Lepeniotis goes into his hut. Veli Gekas approaches, knocks at the serai.]

ACT I, SCENE 7.

MANTHOS: Welcome, Veli. How did you do? Did you bring money?

VELI GEKAS: Phew, what to say, Manthos, Old Lepeniotis not have money.

MANTHOS: We know that, but what can we do, Veli? You see, the master believes Vagias and not us. Wait here, I'll bring the master; you can tell him what Old Lepeniotis said.

[*He goes into the serai and comes out with Ali and Vagias.*]

ALI PASHA: [*To Veli*] Damn it, what'd you fix up, Veli? Damn it, you bring me money?

VELI GEKAS: Phew! What to say, master, poor Old Lepeniotis not have money. Phew, not have bread to eat, poor fellow. Phew, I know myself he not have money.

ATHANASIOS VAGIAS: Shut up, Veli. If Lepeniotis has money or not is for us to know and not for you. You do as you're told.

MANTHOS: Listen here, Thanasis, the vizir is here to listen to Veli. You're no expert. Veli tells the truth about Old Lepeniotis having no money.

ALI PASHA: Shut up, damn it. If Thanasis say he has money, he has it.

VELI GEKAS: Phew, Sir, Old Lepeniotis tell me, phew, he have three shabby old sheep, phew; if you want, he say, send, take them, too.

ATHANASIOS VAGIAS: What gall, vizir, how brazen.

ALI PASHA: Why, damn it?

ATHANASIOS VAGIAS: Because he takes you for a shepherd and sends you sheep.

ALI PASHA: Damn it, is that bandit make fun of me?

MANTHOS: No, sir, he's not making fun of you. With these three sheep the old man wants to submit to your power. He only has three sheep, he says, his last means of support; even these are yours if you want them.

ATHANASIOS VAGIAS: Send for him, vizir; bring him here and demand money. If he refuses to give you any, boil him in oil. Torture him until he confesses.

ALI PASHA: Yes, damn it, Thanasis. [*To Veli*] Go on, damn it, Veli, grab him by the hair and drag him here.

[*Ali and Vagias go into the serai.*]

MANTHOS: Listen, Veli, you're an old fighter; it's a disgrace for an old fighter to quarrel with old men. Go to Lepeniotis and persuade him to come here; tell him for me that if he has money to give it to you.

VELI GEKAS: O.K., Manthos. I bring Old Lepeniotis here without force. Phew, treat him like my old aunt.

MANTHOS: Very good, go, and remember what I said. [*He leaves.*]

ACT I, SCENE 8.

[Veli Gekas arrives at Old Lepeniotis's hut and knocks.]

OLD LEPENIOTIS: *[Coming out]* Welcome, Veli Gekas, welcome, my boy. Well, Veli, how about some raki?[29]

VELI GEKAS: No, Old Lepeniotis, I not want any, phew. Ali tell me to take you and lead you to the serai; phew, and Manthos tell me, phew, if you have money to give it to Ali so he not do you harm.

OLD LEPENIOTIS: Hang it, my boy, where can I find money? Where can I find it?

VELI GEKAS: Let's go, we go to the serai.

OLD LEPENIOTIS: Well, Veli, let me lock up my house and I'll come. Ah, Andonis, my boy, I'll never see you again. May my blessing's blessing be on you, my boy.

[He locks up the house and follows Veli, singing.]

A sea-bird and a mountain-bird,
two birds quarrel, two birds still quarreling today.
The sea-bird turning to the mountain-bird speaks,
"Don't scold me, fellow bird, don't even blame me,
for I, my feathered friend, cannot remain in your land.
Even if I remained all of May and through the thresher month July,
and even if I stayed five, six or ten days in August,
eventually I'd leave you to your health and to your good fortune.
—Remember my words and then turn back."

VELI GEKAS: Hang it, let's go old man, phew. It about time to be near the serai to call my master to come. *[He leaves.]*

OLD LEPENIOTIS: Ah, Andonis, my boy, don't forget your wretched father; if Ali destroys me, revenge my blood.

[Ali comes out, followed by Veli and Manthos.]

ALI PASHA: Welcome, old man, damn it, why don't you bow down?

OLD LEPENIOTIS: Hang it, Ali, why should I bow down to you? Hang it, for years I did nothing but bow down to you; that's enough, hang it. What are you, hang it, that I should bow down; are you my priest? My bishop? My Christ? What are you?

ALI PASHA: How you babble so? Damn it, I'll cut your tongue out.

OLD LEPENIOTIS: You might cut out my tongue, but it will turn into a ten-headed viper to strangle you, hang it, Ali.

ALI PASHA: Damn it, what's this, a teacher? Come on, damn it, Old Lepeniotis, give me money, damn it, money.

OLD LEPENIOTIS: Hang it, Ali, what money can I give you? Where would I find it? You've even taken my spit. Did you leave me anything? What can I give you if I don't have anything?

ALI PASHA: You have, damn it, and you give it or I boil oil and burn you, and I hang you on the plane-tree and skin you.

OLD LEPENIOTIS: Whatever you're going to do, do it fast. Why tell me, to scare me? Hang it, Ali, I don't have any money, but if I did, I wouldn't give it to you because you've taken enough already.

MANTHOS: He doesn't have any money, vizir; the wretch has nothing. If he had, you can be sure Old Lepeniotis would give it to you.

ALI PASHA: Damn it, Manthos, shut up. [To Old Lepeniotis] Damn it, you give me money, yes or no?

OLD LEPENIOTIS: Hang it, Ali, I don't have any money; didn't I tell you that?

ALI PASHA: I'll bleed you, damn it.

OLD LEPENIOTIS: Bleed me, hang it, and with this blood I'll be the first to water the tree of freedom.

ALI PASHA: What tree that, damn it?

OLD LEPENIOTIS: The tree that will spread its branches one day to cover Turkey from one end to the other.

ALI PASHA: Damn it, now you see how I fix you, damn it. [To Veli] Take him in, damn it, oil damn it, boiling oil to scald him in!

OLD LEPENIOTIS: Ah, Andonis, my boy, farewell; if you learn of my death, this hideous death Ali has prepared for me, don't leave things this way. Avenge me, Andonis, my boy, and receive my blessing's blessing.

[Manthos comes out after ten minutes.]

ACT I, SCENE 9.

MANTHOS: Oh, poor Old Lepeniotis, they boiled him in oil, ah. Wait till his son Andonis finds out!

KENTRON: [Exiting his hut, he meets Manthos.] What's up, boss? Manthos, what's the matter?

MANTHOS: Didn't you hear the news, Kentron?

KENTRON: Hear what? Are they cooking someplace so we can go eat?

MANTHOS: Why? Didn't you eat today?

KENTRON: Did I eat today? Why not ask me if I ate this month? Why the devil do I have such an appetite; strange isn't it?

MANTHOS: Ah, Kentron you wretch, poor Old Lepeniotis is gone; they boiled him in oil.

KENTRON: Boiled him in oil? What the devil did they take him for, French fries?

MANTHOS: Wait till his son Andonis finds out!

[*They leave.*]

ACT II, SCENE I.

[*To the right and left of the screen, the mountains in which Katsandonis's hideout is located.*[30] *Kostas and Uncle George come out.*]

KOSTAS: Hey, George, this way.

UNCLE GEORGE:[31] Here I'm, Kotsio, m'boy.

KOSTAS: Hey, George, do you see how nervous the boys are that the chief didn't show up yet?[32]

UNCLE GEORGE: Com'on, Kotsio, pipe down, the chif'll show. What you take him for, a crybaby who doesn't know what's up? If the cap'n ain't showed up yet, it means he's got work; that's why he ain't showed.

KOSTAS: I'm really afraid he fell into some trap. Ever since he left his father the other day, the Turks have been hunting all over for him.[33]

UNCLE GEORGE: Don't be scared, Kotsio, m'boy, the cap'n knows what he's up to; he's not a tyke to fall in a trap.

KOSTAS: Let's go dance a bit to cheer the other men till the captain comes.

UNCLE GEORGE: G'on.

[*They go in, greet all the men, and begin a song.*]

> If bravery you seek and klephts you want to be,
> I'm the one to ask how klephts pass their days.
> Twelve years I served
> as captain to the klephts (all exit).
> Warm bread, I've never eaten.
> On a mattress, I've never slept.
> Never did I my arms dishonor.
> Let a season like the present one
> never again arrive
> in which faithless friends
> betrayed me.

[*Continuous whistling is heard.*]

KOSTAS: Hey, guys, cut the singing, the sentry whistled from the foot of the mountain; I wonder what's up.

UNCLE GEORGE: Cap'n Kotsio, take a look-see down th'main road in th'plain, d'y'see som'n com'n runnin?

KOSTAS: Hey, George, you're right; you've got a good eye. The sentry must have seen him and whistled. Let's find out what he wants.

[*He whistles twice. Four whistles are heard.*]

UNCLE GEORGE: Hey, Kotsio, th'sentry says it's th'cap'n.

KOSTAS: Hey, you're right, George, its the chief coming on the main road. Let's wait for him here.

ACT II, SCENE 2.

KATSANDONIS: [*Comes with the flag in his hands*]

Greetings Souliotes, you bearded vultures and fearless men [34]
who live like proud lions on mountain tops
and undertake the cause of liberty in glory.

Lads, I came today so we can swear our allegiance to our country:
as long as there's one drop of blood in us, we will not stop
fighting the tyrant.
Tyrannical feet impiously trample our divine soil,
and from barbarian breath comes the air we breathe;
can we, then lads, accept this fate?

WARRIORS: [*All together.*] No!
KATSANDONIS:

> Let us all swear upon Holy Faith and upon the Cross,
> I fight for my country and for my religion.
> Let us swear with our life's breath upon the Cross
> either our nation will be glorious again as once before
> or we will fall to earth filled with honor's bullets.

WARRIORS: [*All together.*] Let us fall!
KATSANDONIS:

> Well, then, shoulder your arms for the attack,
> launch out against the foe, burn down their ramparts
> and retrieve our deeply troubled nation from slavery.

> Lads, shoulder your arms
> spread terror all about;

and may Christ be with us
to grant us victory.[35]

Have you heard lads, what this tyrant, this clever cat of Epirus, did to me?

KOSTAS: We haven't heard a thing, captain.[36]

KATSANDONIS: He took my father and boiled him in oil, thinking the burning flesh would satisfy him, the beast; the tyrant's made such things a daily event. Sometimes he takes a father and boils him in oil; sometimes he takes a sister[37] and a mother and throws them into his disgusting harem; sometimes he takes someone's property. Lads, we must show the tyrant that there is a handful of klephts who will punish Ali for his evil deeds. We must give courage to our suffering brothers, protect them from the tyrant, become defenders of the weak and the scourge of tyrants. From here on, brothers, we begin a dreadful war with Ali. Whoever of you wants to leave, let him leave. Leave now. I don't want anyone deserting in battle; the punishment then will be death. What do you say?

WARRIORS: [*All together.*] We'll all stay!

KOSTAS: Yes, we'll stay, captain, to die for our beloved country.

KATSANDONIS: Then, forward, brave ones. Let's begin the attack on Ali today. Ali keeps his chicken coops and haystacks below on the plain. Forward, brave lads, set fire to the chicken coops, set fire to the haystacks, and you, Kostas, keep your eye on my nephew Theodore; he's young and doesn't know anything about fighting. Don't let the boy get tricked. [*To Theodore*] Theodore, my boy, keep your eyes open. Stay close to Kostas and don't run ahead, you're still green in battle.

THEODORE: O.K., Uncle. Don't worry, I'll stay close to Captain Kostas.

KATSANDONIS: Then, forward, lads, set fire to the chicken coops, set fire to the haystacks, forward brave ones, and may God be with us.

[*They leave, set fire to the chicken coops and haystacks, wipe out the eighty-man guard, and leave two soldiers, one with a severed hand and the other with one foot, whom they send as envoys to Ali at Yiannina.*]

ACT II, SCENE 3.

[*The two wounded soldiers*]

HASAN: Ouch, m'foot.

MEHMET: Oh, m'hand.

HASAN: Say, what was that, Mehmet, m'lad?

MEHMET: Phew, what was it? I didn't even see it. Phew, phew, phew, m'hand!

HASAN: [*Calling loudly*] M'poor foot.

MEHMET: Phew, now how will we say to Ali? Phew, who'll be upset and destroy poor us.

HASAN: Ouch, ouch, ouch, m'foot.

MEHMET: Ouch, ouch, m'hand.

ACT III, SCENE I.

[*On the screen, Karagiozis's hut and Ali's serai.*]

ALI PASHA: Hey, damn it, come here, Manthos, lad.

MANTHOS: At your command, sir. [*He comes out.*]

ALI PASHA: Damn it, Manthos, lad, you notice clouds and bad weather today?

MANTHOS: Yes, Ali. [*He looks at the sky.*] It looks like rain, and that's good for the farmers; they will be able to work the soil now.

ALI PASHA: Yes, damn it, Manthos, lad, that's it! Look, look, how it booms and lights!

MANTHOS: The power of God is to be seen everywhere, Ali.

ALI PASHA: What God? There no God, damn it. Only me for Epirus.[38]

MANTHOS: [*Aside*] Curse you, taking on even God!

ALI PASHA: Damn it, Manthos, look at that, how thunderbolt pass through clouds; why that, damn it?

MANTHOS: I don't understand it, sir; I didn't study physics.

ALI PASHA: Damn it, Manthos, that Psalidas[39] tell me once that air pass through clouds to become thunder and light.

MANTHOS: Sir, Psalidas knows; he's well read and a wise man.

ALI PASHA: Damn it lad, let this Mukevelis[40] tell me how this work.

MANTHOS: Sir, he too knows a great deal; he's a world traveler and has seen much.

[*Thunder and lightning*]

ALI PASHA: [*Looking at the heavens*] Damn it, lad, look, look, how it do it.

MANTHOS: We'd better leave; the rain will start pouring any moment now.

ALI PASHA: Why, damn it, it frighten you?

MANTHOS: All fear God's anger.

ALI PASHA: What God, damn it, what God? That hidden up there, damn it, doing it's work like sneak? That which threw it's thunderbolt into gutter and burned donkey? Damn it, if it as strong as they say, why not it do it's work like me, damn it?

MANTHOS: But you believed in him and worshipped him.

ALI PASHA: I, Ali, believe him to fight him.

MANTHOS: [*To himself, frightened*] My, oh my, heaven help us! What is the beast saying? God forgive me.

[*Vigorous thunder and lightning*]

ALI PASHA: Damn it, Manthos, look. [*To God*] Look how it fight me, hidden in clouds, and little by little it take my life away every day.

> Give me your youth,
> and in its place take my own.
> Here I will wait
> for you to come and fight me.

[*He enters the serai hurriedly.*]

MANTHOS: Ah! You bum, nothing's sacred to you. You insult even the God you say you believe in and worship. Won't some hand snatch you off the earth so the world can rest easy? [*He leaves.*]

ACT III, SCENE 2.

[*The two wounded soldiers come out together on the hut side of the screen, behind Kentron.*]

MEHMET: Ach, Hasan, I really hurt.

HASAN: Hey, lad, I hurt too. Look here, they chop off m'foot at the root.

MEHMET: They do the same to m'hand. Oh, m'hand!

HASAN: [*Calling loudly*] Oh, m'foot!

KENTRON: Oh for crying out loud! What the devil's up? I'm hungry too, but I don't scream like that, damn their hide.[41]

HASAN: [*Calling out*] Oh, oh, oh, m'foot.

MEHMET: [*Calling loudly*] M'hand!

KENTRON: Damn! I'm going to spank them; I can't stand it; I'll give them such a wallop, it'll rearrange their brains.

MEHMET: Phew, listen, Hasan, phew, let we tell the master now; he destroy us. Damn it, boy, we going to take the blame; what say we cut out?

KENTRON: [*Comes near*] Hey, welcome, boys. What happened to you two?

MEHMET: Phew! Here, here what happen; phew! That Katsandonis fall on chicken coops, and haystacks. Phew! He burn, kill all Albanians, phew! And leave us two cripple.

KENTRON: Why, that ungrateful Katsandonis! What's that you say? He set fire to the chicken coops and the haystacks?

HASAN AHMETIS: Phew! He burn all.

KENTRON: So what can one do, boys; patience and by next year may God grant both of you a good memorial service.[42] [*He leaves.*]

HASAN AHMETIS: Phew! Mehmet we get going.

[*They approach, knock at the serai. Manthos comes out; the soldiers bow to him.*]

MANTHOS: [*Coming out*] So, what's the problem boys, what's wrong?

MEHMET: Phew! Not our fault, Mr. Manthos.

HASAN AHMETIS: Not our fault, Mr. Manthos.

MANTHOS: All right, boys, let's have it. What's the problem?

HASAN AHMETIS: What use to tell, Mr. Manthos; we be at chicken coops and haystacks, that Katsandonis come, set fire to chicken coops, fire to haystacks, kill all Albanians, leave us two cripple, cut m'foot and Mehmet's hand.

MANTHOS: Did you say Katsandonis?

MEHMET: Phew! Katsandonis, Mr. Manthos.

HASAN AHMETIS: Phew! Now, Mr. Manthos, you tell master so we not tell and he destroy us.

MANTHOS: Don't be afraid, boys, you go tell him yourselves; you can be sure, I won't let him hurt you. [*He goes to the serai and knocks.*]

ALI PASHA: Who is it, damn it?

MANTHOS: It's me, Manthos, Ali.

ALI PASHA: Damn it, Manthos, lad, what you want?

MANTHOS: Two Albanians arrived and ask an audience with your lordship.

ALI PASHA: What they want, damn it?

MANTHOS: I don't know, vizir.

[*Ali Pasha comes out, Manthos behind him. The soldiers bow down and kiss his feet.*]

MANTHOS: These are the soldiers, vizir.

ALI PASHA: [*To the soldiers*] Get up, damn it.

HASAN AHMETIS: [*On his knees*] At your command, master.

ALI PASHA: What you want here, damn it?

HASAN AHMETIS: Phew! Not my fault, master.

MEHMET: Not my fault, master.

HASAN AHMETIS: Not my fault, master.

ALI PASHA: Damn it, what you saying, talk straight.

MEHMET: Phew! How to tell, master.

MANTHOS: Speak, boys, don't be afraid.

HASAN AHMETIS: Phew! Master, how to say, us poor fellows at chicken coops and haystacks.

ALI PASHA: And what you do, damn it?

HASAN AHMETIS: Phew! Us guard and that Katsandonis come with men, phew! Set fire to chicken coups, set fire to haystacks. Us many Albanians, he destroy all, leave us two cripple.

ALI PASHA: Phew! phew! Damn it, how can this happen to me! Chicken coops burned, haystacks burned. Phew! phew! What a loss and you, damn it, why you here? [*Enraged*] Damn it, why you come? Damn it, I show you, damn it.

[*He reaches into his waistband to get a pistol to frighten the soldiers, but Manthos intercedes and restrains him.*]

MANTHOS: Vizir, what are you doing? Kill an Albanian by your own hand? It's disgraceful. [*He signals the soldiers to leave.*]

HASAN AHMETIS: [*Dragging himself, he leaves quickly.*] Phew! Phew! What a mess we got.

MEHMET: [*Leaving*] My, my, my.

ALI PASHA: What a loss, damn it, Manthos, the chicken coops and the haystacks. The chicken coops and haystacks, burned. Phew! What cost! Forty million piastres[43] loss, damn it, Manthos.

MANTHOS: As long as you've got your health, vizir, everything will be O.K. As long as you're well.

ALI PASHA: Kaskantonis, damn it, who this Kaskantonis?

MANTHOS: Who can he be, sir? Probably some goat-thief.[44]

ALI PASHA: You an idiot, damn it, to say it a goat-thief. It a genie, damn it, it a lion.

MANTHOS: Don't worry, vizir, your hand is long and reaches across the whole world.

ALI PASHA: Phew! Phew! Damn it, my heart, my heart.

[*Manthos kneels and restrains him.*]

MANTHOS: Take it easy, sir.

ALI PASHA: What misfortune, damn it, Manthos, a loss of forty million piastres, damn it.

KENTRON: [*Approaching Ali*] Say, what's up with the bear?

ALI PASHA: Why, damn it, Kaskantonis, if I catch you, I suck out all your blood. Kaskantonis, Kaskantonis!

KENTRON: [*Mockingly*] Kaskantonis! Well, what do you know, he's caught in the trap Katsandonis set, he's delirious; and he'll be seeing Katsandonis sleeping and waking.

MANTHOS: [*Softly to Kentron*] Go, Kentron, so he won't see you, he's furious; watch he doesn't catch you here.

KENTRON: So, if he's furious, let him take a bean-bath to calm his nerves.

MANTHOS: [*Softly*] Get going, you.

KENTRON: Hey, watch it, before I smack you.

ALI PASHA: [*To Kentron*] Who you, damn it?

KENTRON: Oupsy, daisy! Now what do I tell him?

ALI PASHA: Speak, damn it!

KENTRON: What should I say? You speak to me.

ALI PASHA: Talk, damn it, who you? You infidel?

KENTRON: You're the imbecile, not me.[45]

ALI PASHA: Greek, damn it, Greek.

KENTRON: Yeh, yeh, I'm a leek, and a carrot, and a bean, too.

ALI PASHA: Hey, damn it, you in for it; I hang you from your feet, set fire beneath you and squeeze your soul out little by little, infidel.

MANTHOS: [*Softly, to Kentron*] Now, look what your blindness has done. He'll kill you, he's so furious.

KENTRON: [*Crying*] Boss, may the living decrease and the dead multiply, but poor me, I'm not to blame. It's that other one. You know what he'll do to you when he catches you, he told me.

ALI PASHA: What he do to me, damn it?

KENTRON: He says, he'll set you running like the rabbits in my village.

ALI PASHA: And how rabbits in your village run, damn it?

KENTRON: Just watch how they go! [*He runs off hopping and calling out.*] Like this, hop, hop, hop. [*He goes into his hut.*]

ALI PASHA: Ah, damn it, clever fellow, he become rabbit to escape my trap.

KENTRON: [*From the hut*] No, I should be a dummy and stay so you can skin me.

ALI PASHA: Damn it, if I lay my hands on you I show you what I do.

MANTHOS: [*Aside*] How that ornery one got away, I'll never know.

ALI PASHA: [*To Manthos*] Damn it, Manthos, lad, tell me how to deal with this Kaskantonis, damn it.

MANTHOS: I don't know, sir, but don't worry. Your hand is long, and reaches across the whole world. Katsandonis will be caught just like the others.

ALI PASHA: How to catch him, damn it, Manthos, since he not like others. He genie, demon.

MANTHOS: [*Aside*] Here's a chance to get Thanasis Vagias out of the game. I'll tell Ali to send him after Katsandonis. If Vagias goes, I'll let Katsandonis know; he'll kill him, and the beast will be out of the game.

ALI PASHA: What you saying, damn it, Manthos?

MANTHOS: Do you want to catch Katsandonis?

ALI PASHA: Damn it, Manthos, you ask?

MANTHOS: If that's what you want, there's one way to catch him.

ALI PASHA: And how I do it, damn it, Manthos?

MANTHOS: Send Thanasis Vagias.

ALI PASHA: Damn it, you big rump, what you saying, that I send that scaredy-cat? How Vagias going catch him when Veli can't?

MANTHOS: There's no comparison, Ali; Veli went after him with troops; Vagias goes with his wits. It's Vagias whose wits encircled three hundred Gardikiotes and slaughtered them like lambs. He became a godfather, and Grimpovos Inn, where the Gardikiotes were slaughtered, was named Bleating Inn.[46]

ALI PASHA: You right, damn it, Manthos. Damn it, call Thanasis here for a bit; I need him.

MANTHOS: As you wish, Ali. [*He goes into the serai.*]

ACT III, SCENE 3.

[*Athanasios Vagias comes out from the serai; Manthos follows behind.*]

MANTHOS: Here's Vagias, sir.

ALI PASHA: Hey, damn it, Thanasis, come closer.

ATHANASIOS VAGIAS: Here I am, vizir.

ALI PASHA: Damn it, Thanasis, you know what I want from you?

ATHANASIOS VAGIAS: I'm at your command. Only command me and the impossible will be done.

ALI PASHA: Listen, damn it. This Kaskantonis sets fire to the chicken coops and the haystacks, costs me forty million piastres damage. Damn it, Thanasis, I want you to go and get him.

ATHANASIOS VAGIAS: What's that you say, pasha, me?

ALI PASHA: Of course, you, damn it.

ATHANASIOS VAGIAS: I, Thanasis Vagias, should catch Katsandonis?

ALI PASHA: Yes, damn it, why not? That seem strange to you, damn it, lad?

ATHANASIOS VAGIAS: Of course it seems strange. Even Veli

Gekas can't catch Katsandonis, and you're sending me, a coward, to get him?

MANTHOS: You know how, Thanasis, you . . .

ATHANASIOS VAGIAS: You pipe down, Manthos; if you want Katsandonis so much, you go.

MANTHOS: I didn't think you'd get angry; next time I won't say a thing.

ALI PASHA: Quiet, damn it! Cut the shouting. [To Vagias] So, what you say, damn it, Thanasis, you go?

ATHANASIOS VAGIAS: How can I go, pasha? Katsandonis will slaughter me if he catches me.

ALI PASHA: Damn it, you; don't go like a clown, go with your wits, your cunning, damn it.

ATHANASIOS VAGIAS: So I go with my wits; this Katsandonis is still cleverer than me; that's why he's a captain. Even if he takes me for a villager, he'll keep me around for two or three days to make sure I'm not a spy. A lot can happen in two, three days. Some warrior, some villager, someone could recognize me, and I've had it.

ALI PASHA: Damn it, Thanasis, your brains and cunning pen up three hundred Gardikiotas and slaughter them like lambs; damn it, Thanasis you become godfather.

ATHANASIOS VAGIAS: The Gardikiotas, vizir, were birds in a cage; but Katsandonis is a bird on the wing, and I don't intend to fly without a net.

MANTHOS: But if you really wanted to, Thanasis.

ATHANASIOS VAGIAS: I told you to keep quiet. If you want to go, you go for Katsandonis.

ALI PASHA: Damn it, Manthos, keep quiet.

MANTHOS: Very well, pasha.

ATHANASIOS VAGIAS: Do you want to catch Katsandonis, vizir?

ALI PASHA: Yes, damn it!

ATHANASIOS VAGIAS: Can we be alone?

ALI PASHA: Sure, Thanasis. [To Manthos] Damn it, Manthos, fix me a pipe.

MANTHOS: Right away. [He pretends to leave, but hides behind them.] [47]

ALI PASHA: Damn it, Thanasis, now it just the two of us.

MANTHOS: [To himself] He's up to something again. I better listen carefully.

ATHANASIOS VAGIAS: So, listen to me, sir.

ALI PASHA: I hear you, damn it.

ATHANASIOS VAGIAS: If you want to catch Katsandonis, or if you want him to come surrender to you, send someone to the village of Korthios. Katsandonis's wife and child live there. Send Veli to get the woman and boy and bring them here. As soon as Katsandonis learns you've got his wife and boy in Yiannina, he can't do anything but come here and surrender.

ALI PASHA: Bravo, damn it, Thanasis. Damn it, boy, I see you serve me well.

ATHANASIOS VAGIAS: I value the bread I eat, sir. I'm not like the others around here who kiss you to your face and knife you in the back.

ALI PASHA: Bravo, damn it, Thanasis, bravo. Now, tell Veli to take army and bring woman here to me.

MANTHOS: [*Under his breath*] Damn your hide, Thanasis. The bastard did it again, the traitor. I've got to head him off. That poor woman, if Veli brings her here.

ALI PASHA: [*Calling loudly*] Damn it, Manthos, where are you?

MANTHOS: [*Pretending to come out of the serai*] At your command, sir.

ALI PASHA: Damn it, call Veli to come.

MANTHOS: At once, sir. [*He exits into the serai.*]

ACT III, SCENE 4.

[*Veli Gekas comes out; Manthos is behind him.*]

MANTHOS: Here's Veli, whom you asked for.

ALI PASHA: Welcome, Veli, my fine warrior.

VELI GEKAS: Phew! Health to you, sir.

ALI PASHA: Damn it, Veli, you know what I want you?

VELI GEKAS: No, sir.

ALI PASHA: Damn it, Veli, listen. I want you take army to village of Korthios where Katsandonis's wife and child live. Damn it, Veli I want you catch them and bring them here. Damn it, Veli, this way I make that animal Katsandonis worship me.

VELI GEKAS: Phew! To catch the Katsandonis woman and boy and bring to Yiannina?

ALI PASHA: Yes, damn it!

VELI GEKAS: Phew! Shame, sir, shame. I be warrior and warriors not fight with woman. You want me take army and go after Katsandonis, I go. For woman, I not go.

ALI PASHA: [*Angrily*] Damn it, curse you, curse the bread you eat.

[*Veli bows his head and goes into the serai.*]

MANTHOS: It's disgraceful, sir, disgraceful to make Veli Gekas suffer so. He's the finest warrior you have. Veli is an honorable warrior; you saw what he told you about Katsandonis. He'll go after warriors, if you want, but not after a woman. Warriors have a code of honor that does not make war with women. You shouldn't make Veli suffer so, vizir.

ATHANASIOS VAGIAS: Yes, sir, it won't do.

ALI PASHA: Damn it, Manthos, you right; call him here to forgive me.

[*Manthos enters the serai and comes out with Veli.*]

ALI PASHA: [*To Veli Gekas*] Forgive me, damn it, Veli, forgive me; I make you sad, damn it, boy; I make you sad. Damn it, Veli, mistake, damn it; I make mistake.

VELI GEKAS: Phew! No matter, sir.

ALI PASHA: Damn it, Manthos, cure my heart, cure my heart.

ATHANASIOS VAGIAS: Veli, how can you refuse when your master begs you?

VELI GEKAS: Since you wish, sir, I go.

ALI PASHA: Bravo, damn it, Veli, bravo. That genie[48] Kaskantonis will submit to me, damn that rebel.

VELI GEKAS: Phew! I go.

ALI PASHA: Bravo, damn it, Veli. [*To Manthos*] Where are you, damn it, Manthos?

MANTHOS: Here, sir.

ALI PASHA: Damn it, give Veli money and choose Albanians for his work.

MANTHOS: Yes, Ali.

[*All enter the serai, except Ali.*]

ACT III, SCENE 5.

ALI PASHA: [*Alone*] Come on, damn it, Kaskantonis; if I get my hands on you, just once, I suck you dry, damn it. I beat you to pulp. Come on, damn it, Kaskantonis; come on, where can you hide?

KENTRON: [*Coming out of the hut bent over and without noticing Ali*] Damn it to hell, damn it, would you believe it, I can't sleep? I have this belly that acts like a broken alarm clock from hunger; can you believe it, I'm hungry! I'm hungry! How can I put it? Now, you'll say I should go eat. You'll tell me to eat, but since I have nothing to eat and since everyone knows me, and I mean everyone—the bakers, the greengrocers, the grocers—wherever I go, I have a reception waiting.

You'd think I was running for mayor, damn them all; what the hell can I do? Forget my hunger? I can tolerate sleep; I sleep for fifty-seven hours straight and get my fill because sleep is free, you see; but hunger, there's the rub. [*Approaching close enough to Ali to notice his feet.*] Boy, oh boy, clogs,[49] that spells a beating. I wonder what devil it is this time. [*He raises his head.*] Oh boy! The bear! How will I get out of this one? The first time he caught me, I escaped, but what am I going to do now?

ALI PASHA: Ah! Damn infidel!

KENTRON: Sir imbecile!

ALI PASHA: I got you.

KENTRON: As if I had you; why tell me?

ALI PASHA: Now damn it, I make ground meat of you.

KENTRON: Ground meat? Fix me hamburgers with ketchup, and I'll eat them myself, since I'm so hungry; mama mia, what a meal I'll make of myself.

ALI PASHA: Damn it, now I show you who you fool, making like rabbit to take off. Now, damn it, Greek.

KENTRON: Oh boy, he remembers I got away the first time; this time I won't make it. Get some wheat[50] ready so the world will forgive you. Boil it yourself, so you can eat some and be forgiven a little.

ALI PASHA: Now then, damn it, how you want to die?

KENTRON: Throw me in a pot full of beans so I can go from bean-death.

ALI PASHA: No, damn it, that no good death. I fix another death for you. I skin you.

KENTRON: So, I'm to be skinned? Skin me and take my skin to the tanner to treat it and make some fur or rug for some woman to walk on or wear so I'll be tickled; or put me in some shop window so people will say, "Hey, what a lovely skin," and so all the world will admire me.

ALI PASHA: Now, damn it, I call tanners to skin you; now you see.

KENTRON: Oh, mother! [*He cries out.*] Master, what have I ever done to you, poor me? I'm just a poor man.

ALI PASHA: Quiet, damn it.

KENTRON: O.K. since you want to kill me, kill me, but I've got a request.

ALI PASHA: What, damn it?

KENTRON: I'll tell you a story.

ALI PASHA: A story?

KENTRON: Yes.

ALI PASHA: What story you tell me, damn it?

KENTRON: I'll tell you, but you have to swear that you won't kill me until I finish the story.

ALI PASHA: Why, damn it?

KENTRON: So you'll hear it all, that's why.

ALI PASHA: By the prophet, I swear it. If story not done, I not destroy you.

KENTRON: Then listen, since you've sworn. Do you know I'm a barber?

ALI PASHA: A barber? So what!

KENTRON: So, take it easy; don't be in such a rush. So, once I was a barber to the sultan.

ALI PASHA: To the sultan, damn it?

KENTRON: Yes, to the sultan. I shaved him myself. And so, to continue, sir; one day, I went to shave the sultan and his vizir came while I was shaving him and brought a decree.

ALI PASHA: And what happen, damn it?

KENTRON: You'll find out, now; don't be in a rush. So, as the sultan read the decree, I shaved him; the vizir looked at me from head to toe because I shaved so well. So, as I was shaving, the vizir turns to me and says, "I beg you, sir, when you've shaved the sultan, I'll wait to get shaved, too, for I see you shave very well." I tell him wait and it won't be long. Having shaved the sultan, then we go to some other room to shave the vizir as well; what can I tell you, he had a long beard like your own. [*He indicates Ali's beard.*] [51] But while his was as long and white as yours, it had a special quality.

ALI PASHA: So, damn it, what quality it have? Speak quickly, so I hang you.

KENTRON: Will you look how impatient he is. I'm not in a hurry, but he is. So, it had the special quality of being gold.

ALI PASHA: Gold, damn it?

KENTRON: Yes, gold.

ALI PASHA: What you do, then, damn it?

KENTRON: Then, I begin to shampoo him. I rub it well, and I wait while the beard softened.

ALI PASHA: It soften, damn it?

KENTRON: Not yet. So, sir, you too must sit; don't kill me; and wait for the vizir's beard to soften so I can shave him first; then, you can kill me.

ALI PASHA: Damn it, what you say?

KENTRON: Didn't you swear by your propshit that you wouldn't kill me until I finished the story?

ALI PASHA: Yes.

KENTRON: Then, wait for me to finish the story; the beard will soften, I'll shave it, and afterwards you can kill me.

ALI PASHA: When the beard be soft enough, damn it?

KENTRON: It'll be soft when you take a piece of gold, throw it into soapy water, and you see it dissolve; then the vizir's beard will be soft. Come find me then to kill me. Farewell. [*He bows down to Ali and leaves.*]

ALI PASHA: Why, damn it, the thief tricked me with his story.

KENTRON: What am I? A fool for you to kill? The vizir's beard will stay that way for two thousand years so Kentron can save himself. See you. [*He goes into his hut.*]

ALI PASHA: Go on, damn it, next time I not spare you. [*He leaves.*]

PART II in Four Acts

ACT I, SCENE I.

[*The scene shows Karagiozis's hut to the right of the screen, Ali Pasha's, to the left.*]

HOTZAS:[52] [*Enters singing*]

> Even with all its suffering
> life is sweet.
> Whoever seeks to end it
> should plead insanity.
> We complain how unjust
> Allah can be.
> For some he feels compassion.
> For others he brings misery.

What blessing can I bring Ali? He demanded I come every day to bless him. Oh, Allah! The beast thinks a blessing brings Allah's forgiveness. Blessings won't help, Ali. No, no, one needs good deeds to be forgiven. But what good have you done, son of darkness; what good? God in heaven, stretch out your hand and save the people from the claws of this wild beast; Ali is a tiger, a hyena, and worse who drinks human blood to quench his thirst. Damned Ali! Curse the hour you were born; born to tyranny and merciless slaughter, unfeeling beast! I better knock so Manthos can tell Ali that Hotzas has come to bless him.

[*He knocks and Manthos comes out.*]

MANTHOS: Well, welcome, Hotzas.

HOTZAS: Good to see you, Manthos.

MANTHOS: Of course you've come to bless the master, Ali.

HOTZAS: Yes, yes, Manthos, I'm here for the blessing.

MANTHOS: I don't know if he'll let you bless him; he's very upset today.

HOTZAS: About what?

MANTHOS: About Katsandonis, Hotzas; he torched Ali's haystacks and destroyed more than forty million piastres worth of goods.

HOTZAS: Who's this Katsandonis?

MANTHOS: You haven't heard of him?

HOTZAS: No.

MANTHOS: He's someone who gathered some twenty-five ruffians and took to the mountains to play captain.

HOTZAS: And he torched the haystacks?

MANTHOS: Yes.

HOTZAS: But, why?

MANTHOS: To avenge his father whom Ali boiled in oil.

HOTZAS: The beast! He boiled him in oil? Every day he commits crimes and has the gall to ask a blessing for forgiveness. Savage beast, how can Allah forgive you for your crime?

MANTHOS: What do you care Hotzas, what Ali does? It would be better if he had a human, compassionate, calm soul, but what can we do if he has the soul of a wild beast?

HOTZAS: Will you tell him I'm here, Manthos, so I can bless him?

MANTHOS: Glad to; please wait; I'll be right back. [*He goes to the serai and knocks for Ali.*]

ACT I, SCENE 2.

ALI PASHA: Who damn it?

MANTHOS: Me, vizir, Manthos.

ALI PASHA: What you want, damn it, Manthos?

MANTHOS: Hotzas is here, vizir, if you'll receive him, for your daily blessing.

ALI PASHA: Damn it, tell him go before I catch him and cut him in ribbons and toss him to dogs. Devil take him and blessings and prophet.

MANTHOS: [*Coming toward Hotzas*] Did you hear, Hotzas?

HOTZAS: I heard, Manthos; no one can figure out what Ali is and what he wants. I'd better leave while I still have my head on my shoulders, I have no intention of losing it. Good-bye, Manthos. [*He leaves.*]

MANTHOS: Poor Hotzas.

ALI PASHA: [*Comes out.*] Damn it, Manthos, where Hotzas?

MANTHOS: He left on your orders, Ali.

ALI PASHA: Let him go to devil! Tell me, damn it Manthos, lad, what Veli doing, damn it?

MANTHOS: What can he be doing, sir; he's doing what you ordered. He's getting everything ready; in two hours at the most, he'll leave for Korthios.

ALI PASHA: Yes, damn it, Manthos, he should get going; bring me Kaskantonis's wife and son so I make this wolf who eat my sheep obey me, damn it, obey me, the dog.

MANTHOS: Don't worry, pasha, he'll bring Katsandonis's wife; then Katsandonis will obey you, so you can pardon him and satisfy yourself, once and for all.

ALI PASHA: Yes, damn it, he fine warrior and if he obey me, I forgive him. Damn it, Manthos, listen, when Veli leave tell him come here first. I got something to tell him. [*Ali enters the serai.*]

MANTHOS: Whatever you wish, sir. [*Alone*] Good! I have the letter ready for our trusted contact. I must send it before Veli Gekas leaves so I can head off trouble before he gets there and takes the woman and something horrible happens. Now, where the hell will I find that Kentron to get him to deliver the letter. He's not the sort of man to come around the serai and ask for work; all he thinks of is sleep. I've seen sleepers, but never like this one. He sleeps from morning to night. Nothing interests him, not food, not bread, nothing. What a jerk! Let's see if he's at home. [*He approaches the hut and knocks.*]

KENTRON: [*From within*] Who's there, please?

MANTHOS: It's me.

KENTRON: Who is you?

MANTHOS: Me.

KENTRON: So! I'm me too. Why tell me about it?

MANTHOS: Listen you, it's me Manthos.

KENTRON: Sorry, boss, I didn't catch your drift.

MANTHOS: Hurry out here, it's important.

KENTRON: I'm there, already.

MANTHOS: Come on, now.

KENTRON: Right away, damn your hide.[53]

MANTHOS: What's your problem, you?

KENTRON: What do you think's my problem? I got drowsy and went to sleep; and I got into the sack upside down and got so twisted up, I can't get out now.

MANTHOS: Still?

KENTRON: Hold your horses, boy, I'll break a foot tangled up like I am; how the devil did I get into this thing?

MANTHOS: Hey, Kentron, come on now; I'm late, and Ali's likely to ask for me. I've got to be at the serai.

KENTRON: Hold on and I'm out, Manthos; hold on.

MANTHOS: Hurry out here.

KENTRON: [*Coming out*] There, here I am. What's up?

MANTHOS: Did you hear the news?

KENTRON: You're going to ask me out to dinner?

MANTHOS: No. Your mind is always on food.

KENTRON: What else can I do, since I'm hungry? Can't you hear the chorus singing in my belly?

MANTHOS: Forget that now and pay attention to what I'm going to tell you.

KENTRON: Go ahead, speak.

MANTHOS: Since Ali can't catch Katsandonis by standing up to him, he's decided to do it backhandedly; he's sending Veli Gekas to Korthios to grab his wife and son and take them to Yiannina. In that way, he'll force Katsandonis to give himself up.

KENTRON: No kidding?

MANTHOS: Mind what I tell you. Do you know who thought of the woman?

KENTRON: Who?

MANTHOS: Thanasis Vagias.

KENTRON: Why that good-for-nothing! Let me tell you, boss, he's not a Christian; he's a Christian-hater; whatever hard times the Christians come on, it's Vagias's doing. He sets the traps that Ali Pasha springs on the Christians. Now, Manthos, what's going to happen to Katsandonis's wife?

MANTHOS: That's where you come in, Kentron; we can't let Veli grab Katsandonis's wife and son and take them to Yiannina.

KENTRON: How?

MANTHOS: How? We'll have to get there before Veli does and warn them to hide, to leave the village; then, when Veli arrives, he won't find them there; he'll return empty-handed, and Vagias won't get his way.

KENTRON: But how are we going to warn them?

MANTHOS: We'll warn them; I've figured it out, but you'll have to help me.

KENTRON: Help you?

MANTHOS: Yes.

KENTRON: Why, are you crippled?

MANTHOS: What crippled, you? You've got to help me save the woman.

KENTRON: How?

MANTHOS: Here's a letter. I give it to you, and you deliver it right away to our contact. You know where?

KENTRON: I know, at Old Man Dimas's.

MANTHOS: Good. Tell him to read it immediately, carry out what I wrote right away, and then to burn the letter.

KENTRON: O.K. I know. Where's the letter?

MANTHOS: [*He takes out the letter and gives it to Kentron.*] Here, take it, but watch yourself so the Albanians don't catch you and find the letter; then, we've all had it. It'll be curtains. You'll have to cut open your heart and hide it there. Let's rehearse to see how you'd handle things. If some soldiers on the road were to ask you where you're going, what would you tell them?

KENTRON: I'm taking the letter to Old Man Dimas.

MANTHOS: What are you saying? Is that what you'll do?

KENTRON: I'll tell the truth, my boy.

MANTHOS: No, dummy. You have to lie. Pretend you're sick, that your belly hurts, and you're going to a village nearby to get pills.[54]

KENTRON: I got it.

MANTHOS: Let's try again. Now then, I'm a soldier and I stop you on the road. "Halt! Where are you going? Who are you?"

KENTRON: What do I say to you?

MANTHOS: Damn your hide![55]

KENTRON: Thanks, same to you!

MANTHOS: Didn't I tell you what to say? That your belly hurts, and you're going to a village nearby for pills?

KENTRON: I got it, I got it. Let's do it again.

MANTHOS: Again! "Halt! What's your name?"

KENTRON: [*Holding his belly, he cries out*] Oh! oh! My belly hurts, my belly hurts.

MANTHOS: [*Playing the soldier*] "Your belly hurts? From what?"

KENTRON: From hunger.

MANTHOS: Not from hunger, dummy.

KENTRON: My belly aches only from raving hunger; there's nothing else wrong with it.

MANTHOS: Just say it's from some other illness, and that you're going to a village nearby to get pills.

KENTRON: O.K. Oh, my belly.

MANTHOS: "Where are you headed to? What's the problem?"

KENTRON: My belly hurts, and I'm going to a nearby village to get some thrills.[56]

MANTHOS: Listen, dummy, not thrills, pills.

KENTRON: Same thing, my boy, thrills, pills; they sound alike.

MANTHOS: All right. Be careful, keep your eyes open so they don't find the letter on you.

KENTRON: Not to worry, Manthos, not only won't they find the letter, they won't even find Kentron.

MANTHOS: Good! How are you going to get there? On foot? Don't you have an animal you can ride to get there faster?

KENTRON: I have an ocean liner; I'll go with that.

MANTHOS: There's no ocean here to use an ocean liner.

KENTRON: This is an ocean liner for dry land; it's a good, fine one, too; it takes me half way and I take it the other half. This way, neither owes the other.

MANTHOS: What's this ocean liner, you?

KENTRON: What else but Mr. Lucidity, my donkey!

MANTHOS: Good, mount up and go as fast as you can, so you'll get there in time. Godspeed. [*He leaves.*]

KENTRON: God damn it![57] Even the donkey is blind from hunger. I wonder who's taking whom? Will he take me or I him? [*He enters the hut, mounts his donkey, and departs.*]

ACT I, SCENE 3.

ALI PASHA: Damn it, Manthos, lad, where you? [*He comes out.*]

MANTHOS: At your command, vizir. [*He comes out.*]

ALI PASHA: Damn it, where Veli?

MANTHOS: Here below in the garden, preparing the men he'll take with him.

ALI PASHA: Call him to come speak to him, damn it, lad.

MANTHOS: Yes, right away.

[*He goes in and comes out with Veli Gekas.*]

MANTHOS: Here's Veli, sir.

VELI GEKAS: [*Bows*] Phew! At your command, sir.

ALI PASHA: Welcome, Veli, welcome, my fine warrior. Damn it, Veli, I want you don't embarrass me, damn it; I want the wife and the boy, damn it, be brought to me. I know it not worthy of warrior to fight the women, but, damn it, Veli, you know I not have another faithful warrior to send; that why I send you, damn it, Veli. You will do this favor for me.

VELI GEKAS: Phew! I pull it off, sir.

ALI PASHA: Good! You not break my heart. You take money?

VELI GEKAS: Phew! I get it.

ALI PASHA: Damn it, Veli, then go and good luck.

[*All go in. Veli Gekas lines up his men, inspects them, and departs for Korthios, leading his troops.*]

ACT II, SCENE I.

[*To the right, Angelikis's house and to the left, the Turkish jail, behind which is Old Man Dimas's hut.*]

ANGELIKI: [*Coming out*] Almighty God, it's been several days since we've seen Andonis; could something have happened? May God help him and guard him from enemy bullets.

ALEXANDER: [*Coming out*] Mother.

ANGELIKI: Here I am, Alexander, my boy.

ALEXANDER: Where's father; why hasn't he come yet?

ANGELIKI: Don't be so impatient to see your father, child; you know he has work. He roams the mountains for the love of our country; he's trying to free our enslaved land.

ALEXANDER: Oh, Mother, how much I wanted to be with Father to fight too.

ANGELIKI: It's not time for you yet, child; you're still young.

ALEXANDER: But I can shoot a rifle.

ANGELIKI: You can shoot a rifle, but you have to run at the same time, because in war, Alexander, my boy, you must be able to do everything.

[*Distant shots are heard.*]

ALEXANDER: Listen, Mother, listen, they're fighting.

ANGELIKI: Yes, child, they're fighting, but who is it?

ALEXANDER: It must be Father.

ANGELIKI: May God protect him and keep him strong.

ALEXANDER: Oh! Let me go fight, too, Mother.

ANGELIKI: You must keep your mind on getting an education now that you're young, because an education is very important; when you grow up, then you, too, will take up a rifle and go into the mountains for the liberation of our beloved country.

ALEXANDER: When am I going to grow up?

ANGELIKI: Have patience, child, and you'll grow up. Come inside, now, my boy. Old Man Dimas is late in bringing news of Andonis. I wonder why he's so late. Come, Alexander, my boy, come inside.

[*They go in.*]

ACT II, SCENE 2.

OLD MAN DIMAS: [*Coming out of his hut*] Damn, I've put off seeing Angeliki, and she'll be worried. I haven't gone since yesterday; I wonder what she's saying. Let me go over for a minute and see what's

going on. [*He approaches and knocks at Angeliki's house.*] Angelikula,[58] where are you, Angelikula?

ANGELIKI: [*Coming out*] Welcome, Old Man Dimas; you've delayed your coming somewhat, Godfather.

OLD MAN DIMAS: Yes, Angeliki, my child; I was late coming, because I was alone with the flock.

ANGELIKI: Have you any news to tell me of Andonis, Godfather?

OLD MAN DIMAS: What can I tell you, Angeliki, my child. Here's
all I know: yesterday Gulas went high into the rocks to tend the sheep
and saw some ragged men there chasing some who were well equipped.
It seems, Angelikula, the ragged ones were Katsandonis's men and the
well equipped were Ali Pasha's.

ANGELIKI: Then, there was a battle?

OLD MAN DIMAS: It seems that way, because Gulas heard a lot of
gunfire.

ANGELIKI: Oh, my God! Do you think anything happened to
Andonis?

OLD MAN DIMAS: Don't be afraid, my child; nothing will happen
to Andonis. When I baptized him, I used an extra handful of oil and
prayed he be fortified in steel. You mustn't fear. Where's Alexander?

ANGELIKI: He's inside, Godfather, reading his lesson.

OLD MAN DIMAS: Call him so I can take a look at him. I miss the
boy; he's just like his father.

ANGELIKI: Yes, Godfather, he always asks for his father. He says
he wants to fight beside him too.

OLD MAN DIMAS: Wouldn't you know it, a morsel of a boy asking
for a gun; but, then again, he's Katsandonis's blood, isn't he? What do
you expect? The apple doesn't fall far from the apple tree.

ANGELIKI: Do you want to see Alexander?

OLD MAN DIMAS: Call him over so I can see him a bit.

ANGELIKI: [*Calling*] Alexander, come here, my boy; your godfather wants to see you.

ALEXANDER: [*Coming out*] Welcome, Godfather, let me kiss your
hand. [*He kisses his hand.*]

OLD MAN DIMAS: My blessing, Alexander, my child. Good, I see
you're a well-behaved child. Let me kiss you, too. [*He kisses him.*] To
your health, Alexander!

ALEXANDER: Where's my father, Godfather; why doesn't he come,
so we can see him? He hasn't been by for so many days.

OLD MAN DIMAS: He's busy, Alexander, that's why he doesn't
come. He can't just come whenever he wants to; he has his soldiers
with him. Be patient, and you'll see your dad; you'll grow up, you'll go
off into the mountains, and whatever else you want will happen.

ALEXANDER: May God make it all happen, Godfather.

OLD MAN DIMAS: It will all happen. [*To Angeliki*] Eh! Now, Angelikula, I'm off.

ANGELIKI: Good luck, Godfather, remember us.

OLD MAN DIMAS: Of course, I always remember you; if I get any information, I'll come immediately. [*He leaves.*]

ANGELIKI: May God protect you. Come inside, Alexander, my child.

[*They enter their house. Shortly, Kentron's voice is heard, as he comes riding on his donkey to deliver Old Man Dimas's letter.*]

ACT II, SCENE 3.

KENTRON: [*Coming out riding*] Git up, you, git up, damn your hide. You're gonna conk out now at the end? What the devil's the matter with you? Now that we're here, you'll eat. I'm hungry, too, but I'm not carrying on like that, my boy. [*He hits the donkey.*] Git up, git up, you, git up. [*The donkey stops.*] Well, that's just dandy, now he stopped. Well I'll be, he just made up his mind not to go any farther. Now what do I do? Get going, damn it, boy; I'll get you some candy later to pass the time and forget your hunger. Come on, now, damn it! What's this! Welcome, boys![59]

FIRST SOLDIER: Phew, hey, you steal pistol?

SECOND SOLDIER: Phew, it the one. Hey, you, what do with pistol?

KENTRON: What do I do with my pistol?

FIRST SOLDIER: Ah! What do it?

KENTRON: I use it for a saddle.

FIRST SOLDIER: Phew, you steal it.

KENTRON: Steal what?

FIRST SOLDIER: Pistol.

KENTRON: The pistol.

SECOND SOLDIER: Yah, you steal it.

KENTRON: [*Showing his pistol*] Hey, you mean this pistol? What are you talking about? I have this pistol from my ancestors; what pistol did I steal from you?

FIRST SOLDIER: Phew, hey, you, you steal pistol.

KENTRON: [*Shouting loudly*] Listen you, my pistol is my inheritance, since my father had it, and my grandfather, and my grandfather's grandfather's grandfather's grandfather, and you tell me I stole it? A plague on you! What did you take my gun for? Laundry, a wallet that I'd steal it? Get out of the way, so I can pass; I have work to do before I'm late and my boss has a fit.

FIRST SOLDIER: Phew! You not go nowhere.

KENTRON: Why?

FIRST SOLDIER: Other now come from Yiannina. We ask if you him, then we let you go.

KENTRON: And if this guy doesn't come from Yiannina?

FIRST SOLDIER: We hold you inside.

KENTRON: Oh, my God,[60] now I've had it for good; they'll hold me inside, and what about the letter I have to deliver? How the devil I'm going to work it out, I don't know. [*To the soldiers.*] Hey, boys, I'm not the one you're looking for; I've never been this way before. What pistol did I steal? This good-for-something[61] doesn't have the slightest idea what you mean. Let me go about my business; my boss will have a fit.

FIRST SOLDIER: Phew, they give us description of thief, and he look much like you. Now that you caught, he who know thief will look you, and if you not him, then you go. Go, now, inside, go on, now.

KENTRON: More problems. You know what it is to be put in prison hungry? Just as I was about to say thank God, I made it and I'll eat. Blessed Mother help me again. How long will they keep me in here? Not long enough to die from raving hunger, I hope. I guess we'll see.

[*The soldiers take him and lock him in their jail.*]

ACT II, SCENE 4.

[*Veli Gekas comes out and approaches Angeliki's house; he addresses himself to the soldiers.*]

VELI GEKAS: Phew, hey, you all surround the house so she not escape; all together, put the house in middle.

[*The soldiers encircle Angeliki's house.*]

VELI GEKAS: Phew, now bang on door. [*He knocks.*] Phew, Mrs. Angeliki, Mrs. Angeliki.

ANGELIKI: [*From inside*] Who is it?

VELI GEKAS: Phew, come out; I see you a bit.

ANGELIKI: But who is it?

VELI GEKAS: Veli Gekas.

ANGELIKI: [*Coming out*] Welcome, Veli Gekas. What brings you by my house, Veli?

VELI GEKAS: Phew, what say, Mrs. Angeliki. My master give orders to catch you and take you Yiannina.

ANGELIKI: [*Startled*] To catch me and take me to Yiannina?

VELI GEKAS: Phew! Yes, Mrs. Angeliki.

ANGELIKI: Why?

VELI GEKAS: Phew, I not know why; they order me catch you.

ANGELIKI: Aren't you ashamed, Veli Gekas, an honorable soldier like you, kidnapping a woman? Do brave men fight with women? Cowards fight with women, and you are a brave man; how can you fight a woman? I respected you as a brave, worthy man, Veli, even though you fought my husband.[62] I see now I was mistaken; you're not a brave man but a fraud and a fool.

VELI GEKAS: Phew, Mrs. Angeliki, not my fault, poor me, phew. Me not want to come, but not be able to fix it otherwise.

ANGELIKI: Officers take their soldiers and go fight man to man in the mountains, Veli; find Katsandonis to fight; don't come to me.

VELI GEKAS: Not be able to fix it otherwise; come now, go Yiannina.

ANGELIKI: Then you insist on taking me to Yiannina?

VELI GEKAS: I take you.

ANGELIKI: Very well, then, wait till I close the house and leave the child with someone, and I'll come.

VELI GEKAS: Phew, kid come with us.

ANGELIKI: Must I take the child with us?

VELI GEKAS: Phew, take him.

ANGELIKI: Very well, wait.

[*She goes in, takes Alexander, locks the house, and comes out.*]

ANGELIKI: Here we are, Veli.

ALEXANDER: Who's this Turk, Mother?

ANGELIKI: No one, my child; it's nothing.

ALEXANDER: What does a Turk want at our house?

ANGELIKI: He came, my child, to take us to Yiannina to Ali Pasha.

ALEXANDER: [*To Veli Gekas*] Is that right, you came to take us to Yiannina? I'm not going anywhere. I'm staying right here.

VELI GEKAS: [*Shoving Alexander*] Phew, get going, kid.

ANGELIKI: Take it easy, Veli Gekas; why shove the boy like that? He's just a child; he doesn't understand. [*To Alexander*] Come with me, Alexander, my boy, stick close to me.

VELI GEKAS: Phew, come along, lads, all together now.

[*The soldiers put Angeliki and Alexander between them and leave.*]

ACT II, SCENE 5.

[*The soldiers come out with Kentron.*]

KENTRON: Didn't I tell you? I told you my pistol's inherited. It's in the family. Now, what am I to do?

FIRST SOLDIER: Phew, hey, boy, mistake made.

KENTRON: Beef steak, ground steak, what do I care? [63] What'll I tell my boss, hey? You've had me inside here for twenty hours.

SECOND SOLDIER: Who your boss, you?

KENTRON: Manthos.

SECOND SOLDIER: Phew! Manthos?

FIRST SOLDIER: The Manthos?

KENTRON: Yes, the Manthos; what am I to say to my boss, now? He'll fire me.

FIRST SOLDIER: Phew, say to the Manthos to forgive us, boy, mistake made. We not to blame to take you for pistol thief.

KENTRON: Beef steak, fine. All I can say is you Turks are made of fish eggs.

FIRST SOLDIER: Phew, go, now, not be late.

KENTRON: They kept me locked up all these hours, and now they want me to leave, so I won't be late.

FIRST SOLDIER: Phew, take off!

KENTRON: Tell me.

FIRST SOLDIER: Phew, what, you?

KENTRON: Is detention over for the other one?

FIRST SOLDIER: Who, you?

KENTRON: The other one.

FIRST SOLDIER: What other one, you?

KENTRON: My party.

FIRST SOLDIER: What party, you?

KENTRON: My donkey, you. He got a stiff sentence.

FIRST SOLDIER: Phew, we bring him now.

KENTRON: [*To himself*] Detention's over for him too.

[*The soldiers leave; Kentron whistles, and his donkey comes out.*]

KENTRON: Come over here, you, Mr. Donkey, detention's over. Now, where's Old Man Dimas's house. Ah! It should be over this way. [*He approaches behind the jail and knocks at the hut of Old Man Dimas, shouting.*] Hey, owners of this house!

ACT II, SCENE 6.

KENTRON: Hey there! You in this dwelling!

OLD MAN DIMAS: [*Coming out*] Well, welcome, son. What's up?

KENTRON: Say, tell me, is this Old Man Dimas's place?

OLD MAN DIMAS: I'm Old Man Dimas.

KENTRON: I know it's you; they told me so, and they told me the moment you saw me you'd ask me to eat. You know they told me that you're good, and right away you'd ask me to eat.

OLD MAN DIMAS: Hey, are you hungry?

KENTRON: Are you kidding? I'm not hungry, just curious.

OLD MAN DIMAS: Listen son, if you're hungry, you'll eat; but, first, why did you come here? Tell me what's up, then we'll eat.

KENTRON: Let's eat first and talk later.

OLD MAN DIMAS: No, first tell me, then you'll eat.

KENTRON: Here, you, I've got a letter for you.[64]

OLD MAN DIMAS: Let me see it.

[Kentron takes out the letter and gives it to Old Man Dimas.]

KENTRON: Here, take it. Now, let's eat.

OLD MAN DIMAS: It's not time yet.

KENTRON: That's the last straw. I'm gonna go mad from hunger.

OLD MAN DIMAS: Hey, can you read?

KENTRON: Sure I can.

OLD MAN DIMAS: Read what it says here.

KENTRON: [Takes the letter and examines it] Now, let's see which ones are the letters, the black or the white? Hey which ones are the letters?

OLD MAN DIMAS: You're asking me, you? If I knew, I'd have read it myself; I wouldn't have given it to you. Well, go on, read it.

KENTRON: [Preparing to read] Old Man Dimas, as soon as you receive this letter feed Kentron, because he's hungry; feed Kentron, because he's hungry; feed him, because he's hungry; feed him . . .

OLD MAN DIMAS: Hey, wait a minute.

KENTRON: What's the matter?

OLD MAN DIMAS: This letter is all about food?

KENTRON: Since I'm hungry, it's all about food.

OLD MAN DIMAS: Hey, you, give me that letter; you're not worth a damn.

KENTRON: Here, take it. [He gives him the letter.]

OLD MAN DIMAS: Come on in and bring the animal.

[All go inside the hut.]

OLD MAN DIMAS: Gulas? Hey Gulas, where are you?

GOULAS: Here I am, Uncle.

OLD MAN DIMAS: Listen you, go to the village and bring Father George here at once. It's an emergency.

GOULAS: Right away, Uncle. [He leaves.]

KENTRON: Good, am I going to eat?

OLD MAN DIMAS: All right, you, you'll eat. Your mind is always on food.

KENTRON: Where else do you want it to be?

OLD MAN DIMAS: Don't carry on; I'll give you something to eat now.

KENTRON: O.K. feed me, and I won't carry on.

[*Gulas returns, followed by Father George.*]

GOULAS: Just wait here, your reverence; my uncle wants to see you. [*He goes into the hut.*] Uncle, Uncle, Uncle!

OLD MAN DIMAS: What is it, Gulas?

GOULAS: Come out, it's the priest.

KENTRON: It seems I don't eat again.

OLD MAN DIMAS: May a wolf swallow you! Wait a bit; you'll eat. [*He goes out and kisses Father George's hand.*] Welcome, my dear Father.

FATHER GEORGE: Bless you my child,[65] I'm glad to see you; you sent for me?

OLD MAN DIMAS: Yes, dear Father; I called you for a great emergency.

FATHER GEORGE: Bless you my child, but couldn't you wait for day to dawn?

OLD MAN DIMAS: Forgive me, dear Father, but it's a great emergency; you must read this letter to me so I can see what it says. [*He gives him the letter.*]

FATHER GEORGE: [*Coughing two to three times, he reads it.*] Old Man Dimas, as soon as you receive this letter, rush at once to Korthios, take Katsandonis's wife and young son and hide them, even if you have to split open the earth to do it. Veli Gekas is coming with his army to take them to Yiannina. Greetings from He-Who-Is-Known-To-You. [*Father George to Old Man Dimas*] Who is this He-Who-Is-Known-To-You who writes you, my child?

OLD MAN DIMAS: [*Taking the letter*] This isn't the time to ask, dear Father; some other time I'll tell you, some other time. Go, now, and I'll send Gulas to you with a sack of cheese. Go, now, dear Father, and may the Virgin Mary bless you.

FATHER GEORGE: Good-bye, Old Man Dimas. [*He leaves.*]

OLD MAN DIMAS: [*Going into the hut*] Oh, how could this happen? Can I make it in time? How could this happen?

KENTRON: What's the matter? I bet you're out of food.

OLD MAN DIMAS: Hey, stop whining about food. Here we're being ruined, and you've got food on the brain.

KENTRON: Hey, what's the matter?

OLD MAN DIMAS: Gulas, get a goatskin of cheese and take it to Father George. [*To Kentron*] You come with me; we have a job to do. Kentron, let's get going.

KENTRON: Let's eat first and then go.

OLD MAN DIMAS: Come on you, let's get going.

[*They exit running and approach the village from which screams are heard. "She's lost; Katsandonis's wife is lost." Old Man Dimas approaches Father George.*]

OLD MAN DIMAS: What's going on, dear Father?

FATHER GEORGE: Veli Gekas took Katsandonis's wife and son and is taking them to Yiannina.

OLD MAN DIMAS: I didn't make it in time. What a mess. Good-for-nothing, what am I to do now? What is to become of me? Angelikula is lost.

KENTRON: Hey, Old Man Dimas, what's wrong?

OLD MAN DIMAS: Didn't you hear what happened?

KENTRON: What's to see and what's to hear? Everybody's shouting, and nobody can make sense of anything.

OLD MAN DIMAS: Listen, you, Veli Gekas came and took Katsandonis's wife and child and is taking them to Yiannina. Kentron, we must get to Katsandonis and inform him before Veli Gekas makes it to Yiannina with them.

KENTRON: Let's see if we can make it, then.

OLD MAN DIMAS: Get going, we've got to move fast.

KENTRON: How far is it?

OLD MAN DIMAS: Not far, hereabouts.

KENTRON: How many hours?

OLD MAN DIMAS: Six.

KENTRON: Just like you said, around the corner.

OLD MAN DIMAS: Come on, keep up.

[*They leave running.*]

ACT III, SCENE I.

KOSTAS: It's been some time since Veli's come around, captain.

KATSANDONIS: You're right, Kostas, quite a long while and I don't know why.

KOSTAS: Ali must be up to some mischief again.

KATSANDONIS: And are we the type who fall into traps, Kostas? Whatever Ali's up to won't do him any good.

UNCLE GEORGE: I'm tellin ya, Veli ain't comin, ev'n though we've turn'd monks up 'ere on th' mount'n.

KATSANDONIS: Patience, George, patience.

UNCLE GEORGE: What pati'nce, cap'n, what pati'nce! We ain't

com 'ere to sits and looks at e'ch other and shoots th' bre'ze. We com's 'ere, ya know, to fights.

KOSTAS: Say, George, what can we do if an army won't come?

UNCLE GEORGE: If th'y ain'ts comin, let's go finds 'em.

KOSTAS: It doesn't work that way, George. It's one thing for us to go find them, but think, there are many of them and very few of us; hey, we can't just expose ourselves like that. The job requires a plan. Just imagine, twenty-five, thirty men against a hundred, two hundred, and, often against three hundred Albanians. It's not a simple thing. Listen, George, it's better we wait. In that way, the boys will be rested; and if the enemy should appear, they'll fall on them in force and put an end to them.

UNCLE GEORGE: Calls it lik's ya sees it, cap'n.

KATSANDONIS: Hey, Kostas, where are you?

KOSTAS: I'm here, captain.

KATSANDONIS: Say, put a sentry here on this path; this place shouldn't be unguarded.

KOSTAS: As you order, captain.

KATSANDONIS: And you, George, butcher the goat and let the boys eat.

UNCLE GEORGE: O.K. cap'n.

[*They all go in, except Kostas.*]

KOSTAS: [*Alone*] I should leave a sentry here, the captain is right.

[*He whistles, and a warrior comes out.*]

ACT III, SCENE 2.

WARRIOR: At your orders, Captain Kostas.

KOSTAS: Come here, lad.

WARRIOR: Yes sir.

KOSTAS: You'll have to stand guard here and keep your eyes peeled. Don't let anyone pass; don't speak to anyone who comes from below the ravine; if anyone comes your way, grab him and whistle for the captain.

WARRIOR: Yes sir, Captain Kostas.

KOSTAS: Good lad; keep your eyes peeled.

WARRIOR: Not to worry, Captain Kostas.

KOSTAS: Good. [*He leaves.*]

WARRIOR: [*Alone*] Ah, this is the life. Long live the life of the klephts. May it go on forever. [*He watches the road.*] Hey, it seems something's moving down below; what the devil is it? It must be some kind of animal. Hey, would you look at that, look at that, it moves like a salamander; if it's a man, he must be a spy. I'd better hide and see what's up. [*He hides himself behind a rock.*]

OLD MAN DIMAS: [*Coming out, bent over alone*] Ah! May Christ and the Virgin Mary help me find Andonis here; I've gotten as far as the hideout, but I don't see a sentry or anything. Just my luck there's no sentry here.

WARRIOR: [*Comes out angrily, the rifle stretched out in front of him*] Halt!

OLD MAN DIMAS: [*Sitting on his haunches*] Halt, my son, halt!

WARRIOR: Hey, where are you going in such a hurry; where are you off to; where are you coming from; who are you?

OLD MAN DIMAS: I'm a good man, my son.

WARRIOR: Hey, how good can you be, coming here all bent over and hunched up? You say you're a good man, but that's how much you know, old man; to come here like this, you must be a spy. Say your prayers, you, before you die.

OLD MAN DIMAS: Don't hurt me, my son, I'm a good man.

WARRIOR: Hey, how can you be a good man? Say your prayers.

OLD MAN DIMAS: I'm your captain's Godfather.

WARRIOR: Quiet you, keep the captain's name off your lips.

OLD MAN DIMAS: Call him here, my son and see if I'm lying; then, you can kill me.

WARRIOR: You sit there and don't budge an inch; if you do, I'll take your head off in one clean sweep.

OLD MAN DIMAS: O.K., my son, I'm not moving.

WARRIOR: You'd better not move. [*He turns and whistles three times.*]

KATSANDONIS: [*Coming out*] What is it, lad?

WARRIOR: I caught some spy, captain.

KATSANDONIS: So, where is he?

WARRIOR: Right here. [*He points to Old Man Dimas.*]

KATSANDONIS: [*Catching sight of his godfather*] This is the spy?

WARRIOR: Yes.

KATSANDONIS: What have you done, you? You caught my godfather.

WARRIOR: He's your godfather, captain?

KATSANDONIS: Yes.

WARRIOR: I'm sorry, I didn't know.

KATSANDONIS: You did what you had to, lad; go on, now, go inside and eat.

OLD MAN DIMAS: Andonis!

KATSANDONIS: Let me kiss your hand. [*He kisses his hand.*]

OLD MAN DIMAS: Andonis, my son.

KATSANDONIS: You're flustered. What's the matter? The truth is, I didn't expect you.

OLD MAN DIMAS: Ah! Where do I start, my son?

KATSANDONIS: What's wrong, Godfather, tell me?

OLD MAN DIMAS: Andonis, my son, don't waste any time; rush while there's still time and try to head off disaster.

KATSANDONIS: But tell me, what's wrong?

OLD MAN DIMAS: Ali Pasha, my son.

KATSANDONIS: What did he do?

OLD MAN DIMAS: He sent Veli Gekas to Korthios, got Angeliki and Alexander, and took them to Yiannina.

KATSANDONIS: Are you sure, Godfather?

OLD MAN DIMAS: Yes, my son.

KATSANDONIS: Why that dirty bastard; he tests his manhood against women and children.

OLD MAN DIMAS: Rush, my boy, and head him off!

KATSANDONIS: Don't worry, Godfather, I know his plan. He grabbed my wife and child and takes them to Yiannina to force me to surrender. But the joke is on Ali. No, never! As long as I'm alive, I'll never surrender. Wives and children I can have, but another country, no. Me surrender? Ah, Ali, Ali, how wrong you are. Next to my country, my wife means nothing, my child means nothing.[66]

OLD MAN DIMAS: Andonis.

KATSANDONIS: Don't worry, Godfather. Are you hungry? If you're hungry, come and eat.

OLD MAN DIMAS: No, my son, I'll be going. I have work.

KATSANDONIS: Well, then, good luck, Godfather, and don't worry. Listen, did you ask which road they took?

OLD MAN DIMAS: They took the road to Simos's Inn.

KATSANDONIS: All right, Godfather, go in peace.

OLD MAN DIMAS: So long, Andonis, my son; may God fortify you with steel. [*He leaves.*]

KATSANDONIS: [*Alone*] So, he took my wife and son. You bastard Ali, if Almighty God ever puts you in my hands. Ah! Alexander, my son, I'll never see you again.

ACT III, SCENE 3.

KENTRON: [*Shouting*] Hey, Old Man Dimas, hey!

KATSANDONIS: Who's shouting like that?

KENTRON: Where the hell did he go, damn his hide; he's nowhere to be seen. Hey, Old Man Dimas. [*He comes out.*]

KATSANDONIS: Halt, you!

KENTRON: Halt!

KATSANDONIS: Say, who are you?

KENTRON: I'm me.

KATSANDONIS: Who, damn it?

KENTRON: Who are you?

KATSANDONIS: It's none of your business.[67]

KENTRON: What about me? None of your business, either.

KATSANDONIS: Speak up, you; either say who you are or it's your head.

KENTRON: Stop, I'll tell you. Kentron's my name.

KATSANDONIS: So, you're Kentron?

KENTRON: That's me, and who might you be?

KATSANDONIS: Don't you recognize me?

KENTRON: No!

KATSANDONIS: Shame on you, don't you recognize Katsandonis?

KENTRON: Captain, how are you? How are things going? Don't be afraid; I won't hurt you; I won't kill you, since you're a good man.

KATSANDONIS: Hey, you louse, what are you talking about? What's all this about not hurting me because I'm good?

KENTRON: Captain, I'm rabid from hunger; I haven't eaten since Easter. I'm dying from raving hunger; give me a little bread to eat.

KATSANDONIS: You're hungry, eh? Go inside; right now your uncle's dividing up the goat. Go, see if you can get yourself a piece, go on.

KENTRON: Like a shot! [*He enters the hideout.*]

UNCLE GEORGE: [*Seeing Kentron*] M'rciful God!

KENTRON: And God be merciful!

UNCLE GEORGE: Wh't ya 'ere, ya spitball?

KENTRON: Don't hit me, Uncle; I couldn't stand a beating; I haven't eaten for days.

UNCLE GEORGE: I'll giv's ya goat, but ke'p yar dist'nce.

KENTRON: O.K., Uncle, I won't come any closer.

UNCLE GEORGE: 'Ere, tak's some. [*He gives him goat.*]

KENTRON: Thanks, Uncle, may God oust you from your house. [*He eats.*]

KOSTAS: [*Coming out*] Captain, I see you serious and sad. What's wrong?

KATSANDONIS: Nothing's wrong with me, Kostas.

KOSTAS: But something's bothering you, captain; why don't you tell me? This is Kostas. Haven't we sworn to die together? Tell me what's troubling you, captain. Your problems are my problems, and your joy is my joy.

KATSANDONIS: I know, Kostas.

KOSTAS: Then, why don't you tell me what's wrong? If it's sad we'll be sad together; and if it's happy, we'll both be happy.

KATSANDONIS: But there's nothing wrong.

KOSTAS: Your face gives you away, captain.

KATSANDONIS: I'm all right. [*He draws a little farther off from Kostas and sits thoughtfully.*]

KOSTAS: [*Beginning to speak to him, singing*]

> Andonis, what are you thinking
> why are you so thoughtful?

KATSANDONIS: [*Singing*]

> Lads, try not to force it out of me,
> and I will confess my sorrow.
> Sad news arrived for me
> by way of Old Man Dimas.
> That dog and false friend Veli Gekas,
> laid hands on my wife
> and my little son, Alexander
> Now they go all the way to Yiannina
> into the hands of Ali
> Pasha.[68]

KOSTAS: Captain, what did I just hear? Did I hear right, or am I just hearing things?

KATSANDONIS: You heard right, Kostas. Veli Gekas got my wife and son and is taking them to Yiannina to his filthy serai. The night birds have been hushed and nature is putrid with the foul smell that comes from that dirty Ali Pasha's serai where he burns poor Christians alive in the dark of night; the beast boiled my father in oil, thinking the odor would snuff out his passion, that animal! He tests his strength against small children, old men, and women, Kostas!

KOSTAS: Order us, captain; your command will be our religion.

KATSANDONIS: The time, the moment, has come when we must uproot the Turkish tree from one end to the other.

KOSTAS: We'll uproot it, captain; but what about the captainess?

KATSANDONIS: What can we do, Kostas? It's too late, now; Veli left Korthios seven hours ago.

KOSTAS: Do you know the route he's taking to Yiannina?

KATSANDONIS: By way of Simos's Inn.

KOSTAS: He left seven hours ago; since he has a woman and a small child with him, he needs another three hours to get to the inn. He'll have taken the main road. From here, it'll take five to six more hours to overtake and get ahead of him, captain.

KATSANDONIS: Veli needs five to six hours to get there; but don't forget that from here, it's fourteen hours, Kostas. How can we overtake him?

KOSTAS: We'll put wings on our heels, captain, and we'll overtake him; all you need to do is give the word; we'll take all the troops with us, and whoever gets there, even if only you and I get there, it'll be enough to save Katsandonissa.[69]

KATSANDONIS: Then what are we waiting for? Call down the sentries, and let's get going.

[*They go in, gather the warriors, and leave quickly toward Simos's Inn.*]

ACT IV, SCENE 1.

[*The scene shows a tree on the left and mountains on the right.*]

KOSTAS: Captain, come this way. [*He comes out.*]

KATSANDONIS: Is everyone here, Kostas?

KOSTAS: Everyone, my captain, except that Kentron doesn't seem to be anywhere around.

KATSANDONIS: He probably stayed behind.

KOSTAS: So it seems, captain.

KATSANDONIS: What do you think, Kostas, did Veli Gekas pass by already?

KOSTAS: I don't know.

KATSANDONIS: Say, come take a look; are these tracks ahead fresh or old? Where do they come from? Who passed by here?

KOSTAS: [*Looking down*] Ah, ah! Not many footsteps appear.

KATSANDONIS: What is it, Kostas?

KOSTAS: They're not tracks, captain, some villagers must have passed by with some kind of animal; those are the only tracks.

KATSANDONIS: Thank God, if we're in time! Come inside.

[*They go in.*]

ACT IV, SCENE 2.

KENTRON: Thank God, I finally made it.

KATSANDONIS: Welcome, Kentron, you made it.

KENTRON: How do you know I made it? But since I'm here, it seems I made it.

KATSANDONIS: Enough, you; didn't you wear a kilt?[70]
KENTRON: How could I if they didn't give me any?
KATSANDONIS: Hey, George, where are you?
UNCLE GEORGE: 'Ere I'm cap'n.
KATSANDONIS: Give your nephew a kilt and clogs.
UNCLE GEORGE: 'E'll sell 'em b'fore 'e w'ars 'em, the wr'tch.
KATSANDONIS: Come on, cut out the nonsense and give him a kilt.
KENTRON: Yeh, you, cut out the nonsense and give me a kilt.
UNCLE GEORGE: Which kilt should I giv's 'em, cap'n?
KATSANDONIS: Give him Mitros's, may he rest in peace.
KENTRON: What? I'm going to put on "may-he-rest-in-peace's" clothes?
KATSANDONIS: Yes.
KENTRON: Damn it to hell, it's just my luck to always wear "may-he-rest-in-peace" leftovers.
UNCLE GEORGE: Tak's 'em, ya.

[*He gives him the kilt, and Kentron takes it and wears it; in his hand, he holds a pistol.*]

UNCLE GEORGE: God b' m'rciful!
KENTRON: And merciful bishop! What's wrong with you, uncle?
UNCLE GEORGE: Looks 'ow th'y fits th' wr'tch.
KATSANDONIS: Say, Kentron, the kilt does suit you.
KENTRON: What can I say, I've got the body.
KATSANDONIS: Come on, now, Kentron; I'm posting you sentry.
KENTRON: I haven't eaten, yet, and I'm to stand guard?
KATSANDONIS: Come here, you glutton.

[*They come out.*]

KENTRON: Here I am, captain.
KATSANDONIS: Do you know what you're going to do here?
KENTRON: I know.
KATSANDONIS: What are you going to do?
KENTRON: How do I know.
KATSANDONIS: Then why say you know?
KENTRON: I thought I knew, but I don't.
KATSANDONIS: You'll stand guard; do you know what your job is?
KENTRON: I know.
KATSANDONIS: What is it?
KENTRON: To eat.
KATSANDONIS: No.

KENTRON: No, No!

KATSANDONIS: Your job is to watch for the enemy on all sides. If you see the enemy, do you know what to do?

KENTRON: What'll I do?

KATSANDONIS: You'll whistle like this. [*He gives a sustained whistle.*] Go on, whistle.

KENTRON: [*Whistles*] I can whistle now, but let's see if I can whistle when the enemy comes; I'll be scared out of my mind.[71]

KATSANDONIS: All right, now, be careful. Keep one eye on the ravine and the other on the pine forest; keep one ear on the ravine and the other on the pine forest. Do you understand?

KENTRON: And my nose?

KATSANDONIS: You won't need your nose.

KENTRON: Ah! So, it's not needed. Hold on a second, captain; what do you take my eyes for—marbles to be rolled around? And what are my ears, codfish, that I should peel them off and throw them about?

KATSANDONIS: I don't think you read me right. I didn't tell you to peel or roll anything around; I said you should keep your mind on your work and keep your eyes open.

KENTRON: Say, I've only got two, but you'll think they're twenty-four, you'll see. Now, when do we eat?

KATSANDONIS: It's not time to eat, yet. Keep your mind on your work. [*He leaves.*]

KENTRON: [*Alone*] Damn it to hell! Do you call this life of mine worth living? Damn your hide, to be hungry and not be able to eat; can you believe it, friend? Hey, what the devil do I hear? A lot of marching feet. [*He observes.*] Oh, oh, Turks, and a lot of them. I wonder where I can hide. [*He whistles.*]

KATSANDONIS: [*Comes out, behind him, Kostas.*] What's up?

KENTRON: Turks.

KATSANDONIS: Where?

KENTRON: [*Indicating*] Over there.

KATSANDONIS: Hey, Kostas, take a look.

KOSTAS: [*Approaches bent over and observes*] Let's greet him with open arms, captain; it's Veli Gekas.

KATSANDONIS: [*Observing*] Good work, Kostas; you've got good eyes. Let's get going; we don't have a moment to lose. Take half the boys and go down into the ravine and get them in position. I'll give the signal myself. As for Veli Gekas, I don't want anyone to harm him; I want my own shot to take him out.[72]

KOSTAS: O.K., captain. [*He goes in.*]

ACT IV, SCENE 3.

[*Veli Gekas comes out, behind him, Angeliki with Alexander, and behind them, soldiers*]

VELI GEKAS: Phew! Come on, Mrs. Angeliki, walk a little.
ANGELIKI: I'm walking, Veli, but think of the little one; he can't walk.
VELI GEKAS: Phew! Hey, kid, walk!
ALEXANDER: I'm not budging. [*He sits down on the ground.*]
VELI GEKAS: Get up, so we get going, you; I'll hit you.
ANGELIKI: Veli, lay a hand on the child, and I'll tear your eyes out.
VELI GEKAS: Phew, you going to pay for that, now.

[*Katsandonis comes out in front of Veli with a pistol in his hand.*]

KATSANDONIS: Hey, Veli, halt!
SOLDIERS: Phew! Phew! Katsandonis. [*They flee.*]
KATSANDONIS: Well, Veli; I had you down in my book as a soldier.
ANGELIKI: Andonis, Andonis.

[*She faints while Alexander moves away.*]

VELI GEKAS: Phew, that was long ago, Captain Andonis!
KATSANDONIS: I took you for a good soldier. I didn't think you'd stoop so low you'd set upon a woman. Now, I'm crossing you off my list. Take this!

[*He shoots him with his pistol and leaves him dead.*][73]

KATSANDONIS: Fire, boys!

[*A fearsome battle begins in which the Katsandonians triumph and capture two soldiers at Katsandonis's orders.*][74]

UNCLE GEORGE: [*Approaching the fainted Angeliki, he lifts her up and carries her inside the hideout, crying out*] 'Ush, captain'ss, it's all right; m'nam's George, George.
KATSANDONIS: Kostas, where's Alexander?
KOSTAS: [*Leaves and comes out carrying Alexander in his arms*] Here he is, captain.
ALEXANDER: Father.
KATSANDONIS: Alexander, my boy. What's this blood on your hand?
ALEXANDER: It's nothing, Father. While I was watching the battle to see who would win, a bullet suddenly hit me. It's nothing Father.

KATSANDONIS: That's my boy, Alexander, my treasure. Hey, Kostas where are you?

KOSTAS: Here, captain.

KATSANDONIS: Find a mule right away so the soldiers can load Veli; we'll take him as a gift to Ali Pasha. Have my nephew Theodore get ready, right away. Have him wear these monk's clothes, and tell him to come here right away, so I can send him on a job.

KOSTAS: Right away, captain.

[*He leaves. Theodore comes out shortly, dressed as a monk.*][75]

KATSANDONIS: Greetings, Theodore; you're unrecognizable. Listen, now; here's what to do. Go to Levkada[76] and find my uncle, Kapodistrias.[77] Tell him I send him greetings and ask if I can leave the captainess in Levkada for two months. Go now Theodore and good luck to you; be careful they don't catch you on the road. Do you know what to say?

THEODORE: I know, captain. Till we meet again. [*He leaves.*]

KATSANDONIS: Come, Alexander, so you can rest.

[*They go in.*]

PART III in Five Acts

ACT I, SCENE I.

[*The scene shows a serai on the right and a hut on the left.*]

ALI PASHA: [*From within*] Damn it, Manthos, lad, where are you?

MANTHOS: [*Approaching Ali*] At your orders, sir.

[*Ali Pasha comes out with Manthos behind him.*]

ALI PASHA: Damn it, Manthos, seems like Veli late.

MANTHOS: Consider, sir, it's very far. He can move quickly going; but returning, he has a woman and a small child with him; he won't be able to move quickly, and so he'll take longer. That's why Veli's late.

ALI PASHA: Damn it, Manthos, I fear this Katsandonis learn about it and make more trouble again before Veli get here with the woman. I hope he not attack Veli on road.

MANTHOS: And how would Katsandonis learn of this thing? No one knows; you only told me.

ALI PASHA: I very afraid, damn it, because Katsandonis be clever, damn it, Manthos, very clever.

MANTHOS: Don't be afraid, vizir, don't be afraid; for sure, Veli will carry out your order without any problems.

ALI PASHA: Damn it, Manthos, fix me pipe.

MANTHOS: As you order. [*Goes into the serai*]

ACT I, SCENE 2.

KENTRON: Ah, good, Kentron! You got here before the soldiers. Now you've got the right to eat. But I've got to see my boss, Manthos. But how the hell can I get to him, since I can't go near the serai where that bear is? It's curtains if he finds me there. Still, I've got to talk to him. [*He approaches the serai and shouts.*] Manthos, Manthos.

MANTHOS: [*Coming out*] Well, what do you know. Welcome, Kentron. What took you so long? Where have you been?

KENTRON: What do you mean where have I been, boss? I wouldn't know where to start. Big problems. Ah, never mind.

MANTHOS: What? Did something happen?

KENTRON: Lots of things.

MANTHOS: Like what? Talk.

KENTRON: Can't we eat first?

MANTHOS: Talk first, and later we'll see about eating. Speak. You didn't come here to eat. You came to tell me what's going on, so tell me.

KENTRON: I'm going to go hungry again, damn your hide.

MANTHOS: Speak quickly, so I can learn what you did with the letter. Did you take it to Old Man Dimas? Did you give it to him? What did you do?

KENTRON: As soon as I left here, I went to Old Man Dimas's sheepfold; but on the road, some soldiers grabbed me and held me in jail for twenty hours; in the meantime, Veli Gekas came and got the woman.

MANTHOS: He got her?

KENTRON: Yes, but the minute they let me out of jail, I went to Old Man Dimas and gave him the letter; as soon as he read it, he went to the village, but Veli had gotten the woman. Then, Old Man Dimas and I leave for Katsandonis's hideout. We find him and tell him what's going on; he gets his soldiers together and goes to Simos's Inn along the road Veli Gekas took.

MANTHOS: Had Veli passed by already?

KENTRON: No.

MANTHOS: Then what happened?

KENTRON: We waited, and in about one to two hours Veli appears with the woman and child; Katsandonis loses no time. He jumps in

front of him and kills him with his own hands. The soldiers are bringing in Veli, now, dead.

MANTHOS: What are you saying, Kentron?

KENTRON: Just that.

MANTHOS: That Katsandonis killed Veli Gekas?

KENTRON: Did he kill him? He gave it to him right between the
eyes.

MANTHOS: Goodness! Now, what will Ali do? Pity the poor Christians, Kentron; they'll have to pay for it all. The beast will take his
anger out on the Christians; he loved Veli better than his own children.
Go hide, and don't come out of your house at all the next few days or
it's bad news for you, poor devil. I have a job for you, I'll come myself
to get you. Don't come out at all.

KENTRON: And what do I eat all those days in there?

MANTHOS: Here, two lira will last you. [*He gives him two lira.*]

KENTRON: Thanks, albatross.[78] [*He leaves.*]

MANTHOS: Remember what I said. [*He leaves.*]

[*Two soldiers come out with Veli dead on a mule.*]

FIRST SOLDIER: Phew! Say, how we tell master, now?

SECOND SOLDIER: How tell him; he be sad. Poor Dervenagas[79]
gone; Veli gone.

[*They approach and knock at the serai.*]

MANTHOS: [*Coming out*] Welcome, boys, what's the matter?

FIRST SOLDIER: What say, Manthos; that Katsandonis find Veli
Gekas on road, phew, and give him one on noggin and he go down.

MANTHOS: What are you soldiers saying?

SECOND SOLDIER: Phew, your health, Manthos.

MANTHOS: Oh, poor Veli Gekas. What is it you want, now?

FIRST SOLDIER: Phew, you tell master about Veli, Manthos.

MANTHOS: I should tell the master?

FIRST SOLDIER: Phew, yes, Manthos.

MANTHOS: No, better you tell him yourselves; it's better that way.
[*To himself*] I'm not in the mood for fireworks. [*To the soldiers*] Wait
here five minutes; I'll tell the master there's news so he'll come; you
can tell him yourselves.

[*He goes into the serai as the soldiers set Veli Gekas down and go back
to their places. Manthos, from within, knocks for Ali.*]

ALI PASHA: Who's it, damn it?

MANTHOS: Manthos, sir.

ALI PASHA: Damn it, Manthos, what you want? Veli come, damn it?

MANTHOS: Two soldiers are asking for your lordship.

ALI PASHA: What they want, damn it?

MANTHOS: I don't know, sir.

[*Ali and Manthos go out and the soldiers bow down.*]

ALI PASHA: What you want, damn it?

SOLDIER: Phew, what say, master?

ALI PASHA: Veli bring the Katsandonis wife and child?

SOLDIER: No, master, phew! Long life, lordship.

ALI PASHA: What long life to my lordship, damn it?

SOLDIER: Phew, Katsandonis kill Veli.

ALI PASHA: [*Startled*] Katsandonis kill Veli? What! What! Damn it, what calamity; great calamity for me. And you, what you do, damn it? You loaf? Now I show you, you pack animals.

[*He tries to take his pistol out of his sash, but Manthos holds him back. The soldiers leave quickly.*]

MANTHOS: Sir, you gain nothing by killing the soldiers.

ALI PASHA: Damn it, Manthos, Veli, damn it, they kill my Veli. I have no other soldiers like Veli. Oh, my heart!

MANTHOS: Don't go on so, sir; you have other fine soldiers like Veli. You'll make yourself sick; you also have Yiusuf Arapis, a fine soldier.

ALI PASHA: You dolt, damn it, Manthos, there no one like Veli, damn it, no one.

MANTHOS: Don't say that, Yiusuf is a fine soldier, too.

ALI PASHA: Ah, damn it, Veli you make my heart hurt, damn it, I not find another like you.

MANTHOS: Don't say that, sir; Yiusuf Arapis has proven himself over and over.

ALI PASHA: Damn it, Manthos, send soldier to call Yiusuf; I want him.

MANTHOS: I'll send for him right away, chief.

ALI PASHA: Send me Thanasis Vagias.

MANTHOS: Right away. [*He leaves.*]

ACT I, SCENE 3.

VAGIAS: [*Coming out*] At your service, pasha.

ALI PASHA: Damn it, Thanasis, listen what I want. Here at Pazagoris, damn it, come some Triantafyllos from Europe [80] and, damn it, Thanasis, brought lots of money; he have a boy, an only son. Damn it, go tell him many, many greetings from master, and I want his son to make him my own child, a godson. You understand me, damn it, Thanasis?

VAGIAS: Do I understand you, you ask, my Ali? We're birds of the same feather and I shouldn't understand you? How much should I ask for this job?

ALI PASHA: More than 10,000 piastres.

VAGIAS: Don't worry; the money will be here in a little while, sir. [*He leaves.*]

ALI PASHA: Farewell, damn it, Thanasis. [*Alone*] This will fix my heart.

ACT I, SCENE 4.

MANTHOS: Listen here, soldier, go find Yiusuf Arapis right away; tell him the master wants him. He must come to the serai right away.

SOLDIER: Phew, O.K., Manthos. [*He leaves and returns shortly.*]

MANTHOS: What did he say?

SOLDIER: Phew, he come with godson.

MANTHOS: Very well, come inside.

[*They leave together. Yiusuf Arapis comes out, behind him Sembsedin Bremetis.*]

YIUSUF ARAPIS: Hey, Sembsedin, master want us. Hey, boy; we go.

SEMBSEDIN BREMETIS: We go, agas.

[*They approach and Sembsedin knocks at the serai; Sembsedin's dog follows them.*]

MANTHOS: [*Comes out*] Well! Welcome, Yiusuf Arapis.

YIUSUF ARAPIS: Welcome, you too, Manthos.

MANTHOS: The vizir called you, Yiusuf, to make you a derve-nagas; he'll give you troops to capture Katsandonis who has killed Veli Gekas. [81]

YIUSUF ARAPIS: Phew, I Manthos, take whole army to catch this good-for-nothing Katsandonis; where can he go?

MANTHOS: Yes, but the vizir wants him alive. In battle, take care to order your soldiers not to shoot at Katsandonis; if he's brought in alive, Ali will be very happy.

YIUSUF ARAPIS: Good, Manthos, I catch him alive.

MANTHOS: Good, wait now, I'll call the vizir to see you.

[*He goes out and returns behind Ali.*]

ALI PASHA: Welcome Yiusuf Agas, welcome, my fine soldier. Damn it, Yiusuf, I called you . . . .

YIUSUF ARAPIS: [*Bowing*] Phew, I be to your command, sir.

SEMBSEDIN BREMETIS: Phew, I bow down, sir. [*He kisses Ali's feet.*]

ALI PASHA: Damn it, Yiusuf, listen! I make you the commander of all Epirus. I want this Katsandonis dead or alive; hey Yiusuf, bring him here alive, so I suck his blood, bite by bite, because he make my heart hurt.

YIUSUF ARAPIS: Phew, I go there, phew, grab him, sir; grab him by hair; bring him jail.

ALI PASHA: Damn it, good! Damn it, Yiusuf, I take you for a fine soldier. [*To Manthos*] Damn it, Manthos, where are you?

MANTHOS: At your command, vizir.

ALI PASHA: Give Yiusuf lot of money and soldiers;[82] let him choose whatever and whoever he want to go for Katsandonis.

YIUSUF ARAPIS: Phew, I choose soldiers and go now!

ALI PASHA: Damn it, Yiusuf, get going and not shame me also in front of Katsandonis.

[*All exit as Yiusuf selects soldiers, takes money, and departs. Sembsedin Bremetis is followed by his dog.*]

ACT I, SCENE 5.

[*Vagias comes out with a sack full of money in his hand.*]

VAGIAS: Very nice; the game ended well. Now, let me give the money to Ali, so he'll be pleased.

ALI PASHA: [*Comes out*] Welcome, Thanasis.

VAGIAS: Glad to see you, Ali.

ALI PASHA: What you fix up with Triantafyllos, damn it, Thanasis?

VAGIAS: What did I fix up, pasha? Here's the money you asked for.

ALI PASHA: The right amount, damn it?

VAGIAS: Not a penny missing, Ali!

ALI PASHA: Damn it, Thanasis, good! Come in.

[*They go in.*]

ACT I, SCENE 6.

MANTHOS: [*Coming out, he approaches Kentron's hut.*] I must notify Katsandonis that Ali sent Yiusuf Arapis to hunt him down. [*He knocks at the hut.*] Kentron, Kentron.

KENTRON: Well, welcome, albatross.

MANTHOS: Take this letter and run as fast as you can to Katsandonis's hideout. It's absolutely essential you give it to him. Run as quick as you can; don't waste any time.

KENTRON: [*Taking the letter*] I'm off like a plane.[83]

[*They leave.*]

ACT II, SCENE 1.

[*The scene is a dry coastal place.*]

KOSTAS: Theodore is awfully late coming back from Levkada, captain. I'm worried.

KATSANDONIS: Don't worry, Kostas; Theodore is clever; he isn't easily trapped.

KOSTAS: But he's young.

KATSANDONIS: Even so, I know why I sent Theodore; I know what I'm doing. At any rate, he's dressed as a monk; who's going to notice him?

KOSTAS: Still, our enemies suspect everything.

KATSANDONIS: There's no reason to worry, Kostas. Come on in, lad.

ACT II, SCENE 2.

THEODORE: [*Comes out cautiously*] So far, so good. Thank God, I got here without any trouble on the road.

YIUSUF ARAPIS: Hey, monk, halt!

THEODORE: Yes sir, my son.

YIUSUF ARAPIS: Where you going this way, you?

THEODORE: Where would I be going, agas? I'm going to my monastery.

YIUSUF ARAPIS: Phew! Hey, you see Katsandonis anywhere?

THEODORE: Where would I see Katsandonis? I, my son, mind my own business; what business would I have with the klephts?

YIUSUF ARAPIS: If you see him come, tell me.

THEODORE: Of course, when I see him, I'll come tell you. What else do I have to do?

YIUSUF ARAPIS: Hey monk, good, good, phew; now, get going, good. [*He leaves.*]

THEODORE: Can you believe that dim-sighted Arab? What a nitwit. If I see Katsandonis, I should go tell him? What an imbecile, not even a pea-size brain. [*He approaches cautiously and arrives at the hideout.*][84]

ACT II, SCENE 3.

UNCLE GEORGE: [*Seeing Theodore*] Praiz' th' Lord! Welcome Father Onufrio, welcome Saint Lavrentio,[85] Praiz' th' Lord!

KOSTAS: Welcome, Theodore!

THEODORE: I'm happy to be back, Captain Kostas; I'm happy to see you all.

KOSTAS: Say, Theodore, how are you? How did your trip go?

THEODORE: Fine, Captain Kostas, fine; how about yourselves?

KOSTAS: Fine, Theodore, fine.

THEODORE: Where's the captain?

KOSTAS: There he is, Theodore; he's coming this way. [*He whistles.*]

KATSANDONIS: Hey, Kostas, what is it?

KOSTAS: Your nephew Theodore, captain.

KATSANDONIS: Well, welcome.

THEODORE: And welcome to you, captain.

KATSANDONIS: Did you go to Levkada?

THEODORE: I went, Uncle.

KATSANDONIS: Did anybody question you on the road?

THEODORE: Both on the way and back.

KATSANDONIS: What did they say to you?

THEODORE: What business did I have in Levkada.

KATSANDONIS: And you, Theodore, what did you say?

THEODORE: I told them I'm going to Levkada to buy oil for the monastery. When I returned, and the customs-clerk saw me without oil, "What?" he says to me, "You're returning empty-handed?" So I told him the Europeans Europeanized the islanders, and they gave me neither oil nor vinegar.

KATSANDONIS: Good for you Theodore! You're a clever boy, and your luck will change soon. Now, come inside and change to your kilt and leather belt.

THEODORE: Right away, Uncle. [*He leaves.*]

KATSANDONIS: Kostas, send me Angeliki.

KOSTAS: Right away, captain.

[*He leaves, Angeliki comes.*]

ANGELIKI: Andonis.

KATSANDONIS: Angeliki.

ANGELIKI: Did you call me?

KATSANDONIS: Yes, Angeliki, I have a few things to tell you.

ANGELIKI: I'm listening, Andonis.

KATSANDONIS: This evening, you'll leave for Levkada; I must advise you about our son Alexander. Angeliki, you must educate him as much as you can, for education is man's best guide.

ANGELIKI: Don't worry, Andonis, Alexander is the best student at school; his teacher has often praised him.

KATSANDONIS: I can see the child's clever and lively; that's why you must guide him.

ANGELIKI: Don't worry; but why must I leave you so soon?

KATSANDONIS: You must go, Angeliki; this mountain is no home for you. We don't know ourselves where we'll be from one minute to the next, and you're a woman and can't run with us. So, you must go to Levkada to stay with our godfather Kapodistrias. This place here is dangerous for you; as long as you stay, it's dangerous for me, too. What will my mind be on if I get caught in battle? On you? On our child? Or to inspire my small band by being with them? You must leave, Angeliki, and if God grants His help and our land is liberated, you will see me very soon. You must realize, Angeliki, that before the individual, the family, and honor, is Country! First, we must do for our country and then for everything else.

ANGELIKI: Whatever you think, Andonis; may God grant we soon see our country free.

KATSANDONIS: Go rest now and send me Alexander.

ANGELIKI: Very well, Andonis.

[*She goes in and Alexander comes out.*]

ALEXANDER: Father!

KATSANDONIS: Alexander, my boy, come give me a kiss.[86] [*He kisses him.*]

ALEXANDER: And I kiss your hand, Father.

KATSANDONIS: Bless you, my son.

ALEXANDER: Well, Father, will you keep me with you, so we can fight the tyrants together?

KATSANDONIS: No, Alexander, my child; you're still young. You must go with your mother and get a good education. If I had a better education, I might have ruled all Epirus and Macedonia.

ALEXANDER: But how do you create such fear in the enemy with so little education?

KATSANDONIS: Because I have an inseparable companion.

ALEXANDER: Kostas.

KATSANDONIS: No, my boy.

ALEXANDER: Who Father?

KATSANDONIS: Hatred of tyranny and love of my country. The only legacy I leave you, Alexander, is this: to love your country and hate its enemies. I have nothing else; whatever we had, Ali, the tyrant of Epirus, took. Guard these words deep in your heart.

ALEXANDER: I swear I'll guard them, Father.

KATSANDONIS: Good, Alexander; now go to your mother.

[*Alexander leaves, while Katsandonis whistles for Theodore.*]

THEODORE: Here I am, Uncle.

KATSANDONIS: Say, Theodore, come here; now that it's just the two of us, tell me what my godfather said.

THEODORE: He told me to greet you warmly; when I told him you want to send the captainess, he told me she can stay for a year, not merely a month or two. They love and respect you, captain; everyone swears by your name.

KATSANDONIS: I'm grateful to him; how will he get Angeliki out of here?

THEODORE: He told me he'll send the dugout canoe that belongs to an old man named Sikelianos to this desolate place; he'll have a light in his canoe so we'll recognize him. Then, we'll light a second fire from here, so he'll know where to come.

KATSANDONIS: Is he going to take long?

THEODORE: According to what they told me, he'll be here tonight.

KATSANDONIS: Very good.

THEODORE: I haven't told you the rest, captain.

KATSANDONIS: What's that, Theodore?

THEODORE: On the road, I also met Yiusuf.

KATSANDONIS: Yiusuf Arapis?

THEODORE: Yes, captain, and he asked about you; but I played the fool and pretended not to know anything.

KATSANDONIS: Good, Theodore, good; now, go in and have Uncle George sit on a rock as a lookout over the sea. When he sees the canoe with the fire, let him light another fire, so old man Sikelianos will know to come here.

THEODORE: At your command. [*He goes in calling*] Hey, George, Uncle George, where are you?

UNCLE GEORGE: I'm all 'ere, what's up, Ted m'boy?

THEODORE: The captain says you should sit on a rock near the sea; if you see a fire in the sea, light a fire so old man Sikelianos will know to come here.

UNCLE GEORGE: O.K., I knows.

ACT II, SCENE 4.

KENTRON: [*Coming out*] God damn it to hell, which way should I go? I'm lost like a fish out of water; now, where's the hideout? I know it's around here someplace, but where? Let's see now, God damn it to hell.

KOSTAS: [*Coming out*] Freeze, you!

KENTRON: I froze, I'm not budging.

KOSTAS: Hey, who are you?

KENTRON: [*Recognizing Kostas*] Who am I?

KOSTAS: Yes, you, who are you?

KENTRON: Don't you recognize me?

KOSTAS: No.

KENTRON: Aren't I Katsandonis?

KOSTAS: Who did you say is Katsandonis?

KENTRON: I am.

KOSTAS: [*Laughing*] Ha, ha, ha.

KENTRON: The dummy's laughing.

KOSTAS: Hey, quiet you, you physical wreck. Who do you think you are, calling me a dummy?

KENTRON: Then why are you laughing?

KOSTAS: Because you say you're Katsandonis; now, say who you are, or I'll take your head off with this sword. Speak!

KENTRON: Hey, come on now, cut it out; don't joke around with swords; I'm ticklish. Do you want to know who I am? I'm Kentron, and I'm looking for Captain Andonis. I want to give him a letter from my boss Manthos.

KOSTAS: You're Kentron?

KENTRON: Of course; I'm the one.

KOSTAS: Hey, why didn't you say so, instead of saying you're Katsandonis?

KENTRON: I thought you'd take me for the captain and give me something to eat, that's why.

KOSTAS: You think you're clever, don't you, Kentron? Wait here, I'll send you the captain.

[*He leaves and Katsandonis comes out.*]

KATSANDONIS: Well, welcome, Kentron; what do you want?

KENTRON: Good to see you, captain. Here's a letter Manthos gave me to bring you. [*He gives him the letter.*]

KATSANDONIS: [*Reading*] "Captain Andonis, greetings from Manthos and from all those who love you. Know that Veli Gekas was brought in dead to Yiannina; Ali was furious. He put Yiusuf Arapis in Veli Gekas's place and he took his soldiers into the mountains. Keep your eyes peeled; when you read my letter, burn it. With great love and respect, Manthos."

KENTRON: That's my boss, captain.

KATSANDONIS: What a patriot! If we had a few more men like Manthos, the fate of our enslaved nation would be different. My hat is off to you,[37] brave Manthos; you might not be fighting in the mountains, but you do a job that no one else could do. Our nation is indebted to you.

KENTRON: And he told me that you should feed me.

KATSANDONIS: Quiet, you, you hardly got here and your mind's on food already. Don't you have any other work to do?

UNCLE GEORGE: [*From within*] Praiz' th' Lord, m'y th' Virg'n help us!

KENTRON: Uh, uh, it's Uncle George.

KATSANDONIS: Yes. Let's go; the canoe is coming.

[*They leave.*]

UNCLE GEORGE: Hey, would'ya looks at that; th' sea caughts fire.

KATSANDONIS: What is it, George?

UNCLE GEORGE: Hey, cap'n, m'boy, would'ya looks at that; fire in th' sea.

KATSANDONIS: You light one, too.

[*They light a fire, and the fire on the ocean comes nearer.*]

KATSANDONIS: It's the dugout canoe. Angeliki, come; take Alexander and go to Levkada.

ANGELIKI: Good-bye, boys.

ALL: Have a good trip, captainess.

ANGELIKI: Thank you, boys, may God keep you like iron.

ALL: Thank you, good luck.

KATSANDONIS: Go, with God's blessing, Angeliki; come on, Alexander.

ANGELIKI: Andonis, write so I'll know what's going on.

KATSANDONIS: I'll write regularly.

[*She enters the canoe with Alexander and goes off.*]

UNCLE GEORGE: Hey, looks, looks, 'ow th' sailboat mov's. It walks cross th' sea likes a donk'y.

KENTRON: He thinks the canoe's a donkey.

UNCLE GEORGE: Ya' 'ere? Ya wolf in she'ps clothin; takes that.

[*He hits him.*]

KENTRON: Hey, Uncle, watch it!

KATSANDONIS: Hey, George, leave him alone.

KENTRON: Yeah George, leave me alone.

KATSANDONIS: Leave the poor fool alone, why hit him?

KENTRON: Yeah, leave the poor fool alone, why hit me?

UNCLE GEORGE: Don't com' clos'r, or I'll cuts off yar navel.

KATSANDONIS: Kostas.

KOSTAS: Here I am.

KATSANDONIS: Gather the boys and take to the road.

KENTRON: [*Noticing the road*] Captain!

KATSANDONIS: What is it?

KENTRON: Look over there, where it's red; are they poppies?

KATSANDONIS: Where?

KENTRON: There, on the road.

KATSANDONIS: It's the soldiers; no doubt about it, it's Yiusuf Arapis. I'll teach him a lesson that will make him a proper Agas of Epirus.

KENTRON: There, he's going into the ravine.

KATSANDONIS: It seems he knows where we're to be found; that's why he's coming by way of the ravine, to surprise us from the sides. Boys!

ALL: We're all here, captain.

KATSANDONIS: Yiusuf Arapis is coming with his army; I don't want any one to shoot at Yiusuf, I want him for bait. Kostas, watch that nothing happens to Yiusuf; if we kill him, as we did Veli, Ali won't have anyone to lead an army against us. So keep your eyes open; Yiusuf is the bait who brings the sheep to the slaughter.

KOSTAS: All right, captain; as you command.

KATSANDONIS: Now, eat bread, sharpen your swords, and be ready. As for Kentron, give him arms to fight, too; give him Vasilis's kilt, may he rest in peace.

KENTRON: I guess it's just my luck to wear "may-he-rest-in-peace" hand-me-downs.

ACT II, SCENE 5.

YIUSUF ARAPIS: [*To the soldiers*] Hey, from here, put them in middle, catch all, that Katsandonis catch alive, you hear, alive!

SEMBSEDIN BREMETIS: Phew! Alright, agas, phew, we catch alive.

[*They all approach and enter Katsandonis's hideout.*]

KENTRON: [*Hiding, speaks softly*] Captain, there they are. Wow! Look how many there are!

KATSANDONIS: Quiet, you, I see them. Boys, keep your minds on

your work. I'll fire first, and on my shot we'll all attack together. I
want a body for each bullet.

UNCLE GEORGE: Hey, ya, shush. I gots th' scythe.

KENTRON: My uncle is going for a harvest.

UNCLE GEORGE: Shush, ya worthl'ss thing!

KENTRON: I shouldn't even laugh? Do I have the scabies?

KATSANDONIS: Come on George pipe down now; they're coming
closer. Keep your eyes peeled.

YIUSUF ARAPIS: [*Quietly*] Phew, over here, you. Get going from
here.

[*The soldiers draw near.*]

KENTRON: Will you look at that? He'll step on me, damn his hide!
What, is he blind? Look how close he's coming?

UNCLE GEORGE: Looks at 'em, lazy bums, looks at 'ow 'em lazy
bastards is comin.

KATSANDONIS: [*Standing up, he shoots.*] Charge boys, charge
lads; get those infidels!

[*The battle begins in which Yiusuf Arapis's rabble are decimated.
Yiusuf Arapis retreats with half his soldiers and flees, leaving many
dead, among them his godson Sembsedin Bremetis.*]

YIUSUF ARAPIS; [*Retreating*] Phew! Phew! What happen to me?
Phew! Phew! Hey, what they do to me, the lions? [*He leaves.*]

KATSANDONIS: That's enough. Thank God that this battle, too,
was in our favor.

KOSTAS: Glory be to God who is in Heaven.

KENTRON: And hollow be his name, amen.[88]

UNCLE GEORGE: Praiz' th' Lord!

KATSANDONIS: What is it, George?

UNCLE GEORGE: Looks at th' spit with th' tripe, cap'n; looks,
som'one ates th' tripe and wrapped shoe-leather on th' spit with laces.
I went to bites it and almost lost m' teeth.

KATSANDONIS: Say, who did this?

UNCLE GEORGE: Who else, but m'nephew?

KATSANDONIS: Hey, you, Kentron?

KENTRON: Me .. m .. m.

UNCLE GEORGE: Ah, ah, a fit's got 'm; he ates it.

KATSANDONIS: Let him go this time, George; next time he won't
do it or he'll go without food for five days.

KENTRON: All right, I won't bother next time, captain.

KATSANDONIS: Kostas.

KOSTAS: Here I am, captain.

KATSANDONIS: Gather the boys and let's get going; we can't stay here any longer; the hideout has been discovered. We'll hide out near Panos Tsaros's Inn.[89] Keep an eye on Theodore.

KOSTAS: Don't worry, captain.

[*He whistles, and they all depart except Theodore.*]

YIUSUF ARAPIS: [*He comes out.*] Phew, the klephts leave. Hey, phew, what they up to? [*He notices Theodore and hides.*]

THEODORE: [*Coming out*] Hey, look at that? They all left, and I didn't even know it.

[*He approaches but Yiusuf captures him with some soldiers.*]

YIUSUF ARAPIS: [*To Theodore*] Phew! Shush, klepht.

THEODORE: [*Trying to whistle*] Hey, wait a minute, you looters.

YIUSUF ARAPIS: Get moving, you.

[*They leave.*]

ACT III, SCENE I.

[*To the left, Panos Tsaros's Inn; to the right, Katsandonis's hideout.*]

KOSTAS: Everyone is accounted for captain except Theodore.

KATSANDONIS: Are you sure, Kostas?

KOSTAS: He's missing; I don't know what happened to him.

KATSANDONIS: Didn't the boy follow us?

KOSTAS: I don't know, captain.

KATSANDONIS: Send the boys to look around; it looks like Theodore has been captured.

[*Kostas leaves, and they all scatter searching for Theodore; in a short while they return.*]

KOSTAS: We can't find the boy anywhere, captain.

KATSANDONIS: Yiusuf's got him prisoner. Hey, Kostas, you disappointed us.

KOSTAS: Don't worry captain. We'll get him back.

KATSANDONIS: How are we going to do that?

KOSTAS: This morning in the battle, I killed Yiusuf Arapis's godson, Sembsedin Bremetis.

KATSANDONIS: So, what's the point?

KOSTAS: Here's the point. We send a soldier to bring Sembsedin's head here; then, send a villager to Yiusuf Arapis to make a trade:

Theodore for the head. Otherwise, he'll be disgraced. You know the Albanians consider it a disgrace to dishonor the dead. That way we'll get Theodore.

KATSANDONIS: Good, let's do it that way, Kostas. Send Uncle George for the head.

KOSTAS: At your command, captain. [*He leaves.*]

ACT III, SCENE 2.

KOSTAS: Hey, George, where are you?

UNCLE GEORGE: 'Ere I'm.

KOSTAS: Listen, go to the battle site; you'll find Sembsedin Bremetis's dead body. Get his head and bring it. We need it.

UNCLE GEORGE: Ah, I go's. [*He leaves.*]

KATSANDONIS: Say, Kostas, did you send him?

KOSTAS: He's on his way, captain.

UNCLE GEORGE: [*Returning without the head, frightened*] Praiz' th' Lord!

KATSANDONIS: What's wrong?

UNCLE GEORGE: What can I tells ya, cap'n, th' soul of th' Turk turn'd into a dog and sits on 'is head; I saw th' dog with m' own eyes.

KATSANDONIS: What the hell are you saying, George? I won't call you a coward, because I know you better, but the dog you saw is Sembsedin's! He sees his master's dead, and he won't leave his side. Hey, Kostas, go ahead, you bring us the head.

[*Kostas leaves and in a little while returns with the head, followed by the dog.*]

KATSANDONIS: Hey, George, do you see the dog?

UNCLE GEORGE: Praiz' th' Lord; would ya looks at that, but I'm not goin close.

KATSANDONIS: Hey, Kentron, where are you?

KENTRON: Here, captain.

KATSANDONIS: Take off your kilt and come here; I have a job for you.

KENTRON: Right away. [*He takes off the kilt.*] Here I am!

KATSANDONIS: Good. Go to Panos Tsaros's Inn where Yiusuf Arapis is staying with his army. Greet him for me and tell him that since he's holding Theodore prisoner, I have the head of his godson Sembsedin Bremetis. If he wants to make a trade, he's to give me Theodore, and I'll give him the head. If he doesn't agree, I'll hang the head at Five Wells, so whoever passes can spit on it and mutilate it; then, if he wants, he can come and get it.[90]

KENTRON: I'm going to tell him all this?

KATSANDONIS: Yes.

KENTRON: Oh, no! He'll roast me.

KATSANDONIS: Don't be scared; you'll tell him you were going to Yiannina with your wife and child to greet Ali and pay him your head-tax, and that I caught you and held your family; if you hadn't gone I would have killed them. Then, he won't bother you.

KENTRON: Holy Mother!⁹¹

KATSANDONIS: Also, tell him the two of us can talk better face-to-face. He has my word it's safe; let him come out of the inn and I'll come out to the cowshed.

KENTRON: All right, captain, I'm going; if I'm late, boil some wheat in my memory; if you don't mind, boil it now and give me some too so I can forgive myself. [*He leaves.*]

ACT III, SCENE 3.

KENTRON: [*Approaching, crossing himself*] Oh my God save me.

SOLDIER: Phew, halt, you.

KENTRON: Halt!

SOLDIER: What you want, you?

KENTRON: I want the aga.

SOLDIER: Phew, wait.

[*He leaves, and Yiusuf comes out.*]

YIUSUF ARAPIS: What you want, you?

KENTRON: Aga, listen; I poor fool am not to blame; it's that rascal Katsandonis, that donkey.

YIUSUF ARAPIS: What Katsandonis do, you?

KENTRON: He captured me and my family and stole ten lira I was taking as head-tax to the master at Yiannina; he sent me here to set up a trade. You have Theodore, he has your godson's head. If you agree, give him his nephew Theodore, and he'll give you the head; otherwise, he'll hang it at Five Wells to be mutilated.

YIUSUF ARAPIS: You tell him cook it and eat it. [*He leaves.*]

KENTRON: I'll tell him.

PANOS TSAROS: What is it, Yiusuf Agas? What did I hear?

YIUSUF ARAPIS: Katsandonis say me give him klepht.

PANOS TSAROS: Turn him over, Yiusuf. You'll be disgraced if Katsandonis dishonors your godson. What will people say?

YIUSUF ARAPIS: What if master learn I catch klepht and let go, hey Panos? He be furious.

SOLDIER: Phew. We tell nobody, Yiusuf Agas.

PANOS TSAROS: You know your soldiers won't say a thing.

YIUSUF ARAPIS: Phew, all right. [*He goes out.*] Phew, hey you!

KENTRON: Here I am.

YIUSUF ARAPIS: Phew, you tell Katsandonis we fix trade; but how we do it?

KENTRON: If you agree, he said protect yourself and stand here at the inn, he'll be across at the cowshed. Just give me the say so; give me your word for his word.

YIUSUF ARAPIS: Go, my word for his word; tell him come out.

KENTRON: I'll tell him; wait here.

[*He leaves. Kentron tells Katsandonis what went on.*]

KATSANDONIS: [*Coming out*] Greetings Yiusuf.

YIUSUF ARAPIS: Greetings to you, Captain Andonis. My word for your word, Captain Andonis.

KATSANDONIS: So, what do you say; do we make the trade?

YIUSUF ARAPIS: We do it, Captain Andonis.

KATSANDONIS: Listen, you send a soldier with my nephew Theodore at the same time that I send you your godson's head.

YIUSUF ARAPIS: Phew, all right, Captain Andonis, all right.

KATSANDONIS: Hey, Yiusuf, is there anything else?

YIUSUF ARAPIS: Phew, me tell you, phew, is shame soldier like you roam mountains. Phew, shame, Captain Andonis. Phew, you obey master, he make you Dervenagas of Agrafa.[92]

KATSANDONIS: Listen, Yiusuf, if you value our friendship, don't talk to me about Ali; I know him well. His estates are notches on my sword; I get what I want when I want it. I don't need Ali to give me anything.

YIUSUF ARAPIS: Phew, shame, Captain Andonis, phew. Obey him!

KATSANDONIS: What? Obey Ali? Obey and make it easier for him to roast me, to boil me in oil. Ah! Yiusuf, I know this rotten Ali too well.

YIUSUF ARAPIS: Phew, shame, Captain Andonis; curse Ali to my face.

KATSANDONIS: Hey, Yiusuf, if I embarrass you, here's your sword and here's mine; if you want, come and cut out the embarrassment.

YIUSUF ARAPIS: Phew, no, Captain Andonis, we friends, we friends.

KATSANDONIS: Well, then, the trade will go on just as we said. Our pact is done; from here on, wherever you find me, attack; and I will do the same. [*He leaves.*]

YIUSUF ARAPIS: Phew, phew. Hey, what this? He say one thing and mean other, phew, phew. He demon, lion.

[He leaves. Uncle George comes out holding the head, again followed by the dog, and an Albanian comes out with Theodore; they make the exchange. The soldier takes the head and leaves, while Uncle George takes Theodore.]

UNCLE GEORGE: Com' Ted, m'boy. Com', now, m'boy, don't act like that.

THEODORE: How can I face my uncle, George? I've disgraced the whole gang.

KATSANDONIS: [Coming out] Hey, Theodore, don't be embarrassed. That's war; you'll be wounded, you'll be killed, you'll be taken captive. You've got to expect all this in battle. Don't be discouraged. Come in. [He leaves.]

KOSTAS: Welcome, Theodore. How are you? Did this dumb Arab get you? Hey, just wait till I get my hands on him; I'll cut him to shreds. He'll learn not to take captives from Katsandonis's gang!

THEODORE: We've been dishonored, Captain Kostas.

KOSTAS: Hush, I'll take care of this dishonor.

YIUSUF ARAPIS: [Alone] You, Katsandonis, if I get hands on you, fool; ah, you see what I do you.

KOSTAS: [Coming out, he notices Yiusuf.] Hey, Yiusuf, I've come to kill you.

YIUSUF ARAPIS: [Taken by surprise] Phew! Captain Kostas.

KOSTAS: Hey, you, you think you know how to take captives? Now you'll really see how it's done. [Rushes toward him]

YIUSUF ARAPIS: [Running from him] Phew, truce! Hey, Kostas, truce.

KOSTAS: [Running toward him] I'll show you truce.

[They begin a frightful chase. Katsandonis, seeing Kostas, rushes toward him to restrain him.]

KATSANDONIS: Stop, Kostas, stop, leave him alone, you.

[Kostas continues to chase Yiusuf.]

KOSTAS: Stop, you dumb Arab, and see what I'll do to you.

YIUSUF ARAPIS: [Running] Truce, hey, Kostas, truce.

KATSANDONIS: Let him go, Kostas, don't bother him.

KOSTAS: [Restrained] For God's sake, captain, what's the matter?

KATSANDONIS: Hey, Kostas, I was telling you not to run; I can't run. My legs ache, I'm out of breath; I can't, hold me up.

KOSTAS: For God's sake, captain, what's the matter?

UNCLE GEORGE: Praiz' th' Lord, hey, what's th' matt'r with th' cap'n?

KATSANDONIS: I've broken out in a cold sweat all over my body. I have chills. Hey, Kostas, I'm thirsty; I want water.

KOSTAS: You can't drink, captain, you're tired; if you drink water, you'll get worse. Look there, on your chest, you've broken out in spots.

UNCLE GEORGE: [Spits on him] Phtou, phtou, lest I bewitch ya, m'boy; ke'p still, ther's nothing wrong with ya, ke'p still, m'littl' one, ke'p still.

KATSANDONIS: Take me inside, Kostas; I'm very tired here.

[They lift him by the hands and take him in.]

UNCLE GEORGE: Oh, Holy Virg'n, it's th' end of m'boy; it's th' end of th' cap'n.

KATSANDONIS: George, where are you?

UNCLE GEORGE: 'Ere I'm, cap'n.

KATSANDONIS: Take this letter and go to Saint John of the Lice; find the abbot. Give him the letter and get an answer right away.

UNCLE GEORGE: Watch m' dust! [He puts the letter in his shoe and leaves.]

ACT IV, SCENE I.

[Saint John's monastery to the right.]

UNCLE GEORGE:]Coming out, he approaches the monastery.] Praiz' th' Lord, I wasn't stung by 'em wasps that attacks th' mules and makes 'em falls down. [He knocks at the monastery.]

ABBOT: [Coming out] What do you want, my child?

UNCLE GEORGE: Ya th' abbot?

ABBOT: I am, my child.

UNCLE GEORGE: [Taking the letter from his shoe] 'Ere, tak' th' lett'r, reads it and gives m' an answer.

ABBOT: [Takes the letter and reads] "Holy Abbot, I've got chicken-pox; can I stay at the monastery for ten days? Greetings." [To Uncle George] My boy, who gave you this letter to bring to me?

UNCLE GEORGE: Don't know.

ABBOT: Who wrote it?

UNCLE GEORGE: Don't know.

ABBOT: Good soldier. I know who wrote the letter. From the handwriting, Katsandonis wrote it; go tell him the monastery is his as long as he wants, not just for ten days. Go.[93]

UNCLE GEORGE: S'long, priest. [*He leaves.*]

ACT IV, SCENE 2.

ABBOT: Come here, my child.

KARDERINIS: What do you want, Holy Father.

ABBOT: Why have you left the livestock, my son? You must guard them; you know evil men are about; we could lose them. Go, my son. [*He leaves.*]

KARDERINIS: [*Alone*] The abbot always sends me into the fields. I don't know what's going on here, lately; he doesn't let me stay at the monastery, at all. What's going on?

ACT IV, SCENE 3.

YIUSUF ARAPIS: [*Coming out*] Phew, hey, you, little kid-monk.

KARDERINIS: Welcome, agas.

YIUSUF ARAPIS: Phew, hey, little monk, you know me?

KARDERINIS: Don't I know the Agas of Epirus?

YIUSUF ARAPIS: Phew, hey you, what you doing here?

KARDERINIS: What would I be doing? I'm a goatherd at the monastery.

YIUSUF ARAPIS: Phew, hey, you son of bey, not goatherd.

KARDERINIS: Me, the son of a bey, Yiusuf? You're making fun of me.

YIUSUF ARAPIS: I give you this, you see? [*He gives him a letter.*] Read.

KARDERINIS: [*Takes the letter and reads*] "Yiusuf Agas, if you happen to pass by Saint John of the Lice, please do me a great favor. You'll find there a small monk; he is my child. He bears a red mark on his forehead; they call him Karderinis. I had him with a Christian widow, and I abandoned him in the monastery. Bring him to me, and give him this sack full of florins. I greet you, Moustafa Bey of Artas." So, I'm the son of a bey, and I didn't even know it. Take me to my father, Yiusuf.

YIUSUF ARAPIS: I take you, first must catch Katsandonis; he come this way?

KARDERINIS: It's been fifteen days since he passed by here; he took bread and left.

YIUSUF ARAPIS: Phew, if see him, you come tell me, and I give you florins and take to your father. So long now. [*He leaves.*]

KARDERINIS: Would you believe I'm the son of a bey? If I see Katsandonis, I'll turn him in, so I can go to my father. [*He goes into the monastery.*]

ACT IV, SCENE 4.

[*Uncle George comes out with Kostas, carrying Katsandonis on their shoulders.*]

KATSANDONIS: Slow, boys; I can't take it, slow.

UNCLE GEORGE: Hush, m'cap'n, ther's nothin wrong with ya, hush.

KATSANDONIS: Put me down slowly, slowly, and you, George, call the abbot.

[*They put him down very slowly; while Kostas holds him by the shoulders, Uncle George knocks at the monastery.*]

ABBOT: [*Coming out*] Welcome, boys. What is it, Andonis, my son?

KATSANDONIS: I'm weak all over, Holy Abbot; my whole body is dripping in a cold sweat.[94]

ABBOT: It's nothing, Andonis, my son. Have courage; Almighty God would not take the protector of Epirus from us. Courage, my son.

UNCLE GEORGE: Hey, priest, shush; why should God tak' 'em? If he tak's 'em, he'll hav' to deal with me.

KATSANDONIS: Quiet, George. Don't cuss.

ABBOT: Bring him inside, my sons; don't tire him any more.

[*All go inside the monastery and put Katsandonis down in the abbot's cell.*]

KATSANDONIS: Now, boys you can't stay here; you've got to get back to the gang, Kostas; the boys need you. They have no one but you, now that I'm missing.

UNCLE GEORGE: What're ya talkin' about, cap'n? We'll stay 'ere; if we leav', wh'll guards ya?

KATSANDONIS: Boys, you can't stay here; your kilts will betray us; that's bad for me and the monastery.

KOSTAS: Let's kiss you, captain, and we're off.

KATSANDONIS: No, boys, my illness won't allow it.

UNCLE GEORGE: What's that ya says? Th' illness won't allow it? As for me, I'm gonna kiss ya, and sh' can com' deal with me if sh' wants.

KATSANDONIS: Quiet George, I told you it can't be.

UNCLE GEORGE: [*He kisses him.*] I kisses ya and wh'ever wants, let 'em com' deal with me.

ABBOT: Go, dear friends; you can't stay here; you'll endanger your captain.

KATSANDONIS: Get going, boys, good luck. You, Kostas, watch after the boys as much as you can.

KOSTAS: We salute you, captain; get well soon.

UNCLE GEORGE: Adios, cap'n, and gets well.

[*Uncle George and Kostas leave.*]

KATSANDONIS: Good-bye boys, good-bye.

ACT IV, SCENE 5.

ABBOT: Katsandonis, my son, you need rest and quiet.

KATSANDONIS: Water, Holy Abbot, water. I'm on fire.

ABBOT: You shouldn't drink water, my child; I'll make you some soup to drink, now.

KARDERINIS: [*Coming out of the monastery*] The abbot has someone inside the monastery. He told us he's possessed by a demon, but how can he talk to him? I'll take a ladder and look in his cell through the skylight. [*He takes a ladder, mounts it, and eavesdrops.*]

ABBOT: You musn't worry, my son; worry is man's worst enemy.

KATSANDONIS: Are there any letters for me?

ABBOT: No, my son, the one you had the day before yesterday, I sent with your godfather.

KATSANDONIS: I don't think I'll be in bed too long, Holy Abbot.

ABBOT: No, Katsandonis, my son, you'll be up in ten to fifteen days.[95]

KARDERINIS: Ah, it's Katsandonis; now, I'll tell Yiusuf so he can catch him and take me to my father.

[*He gets down, puts the ladder in the monastery, departs, and finds Yiusuf.*]

YIUSUF ARAPIS: Phew, hey, little monk, where going?

KARDERINIS: Yiusuf Agas, Katsandonis is sick inside the monastery; the abbot has him inside his cell.

YIUSUF ARAPIS: How's that, you?

KARDERINIS: Yes, Yiusuf Agas.

YIUSUF ARAPIS: Phew, stay here; I come back to take to your father.

[*Yiusuf takes the troops and surrounds the monastery. Knocks on the door.*] Phew, hey, abbot, abbot!

ABBOT: [*Coming out*] What do you want, my son?

YIUSUF ARAPIS: Phew, hey, you, you have Katsandonis hid inside, alas; go, say it, or devil take you.

ABBOT: What Katsandonis, my son? I know nothing.

YIUSUF ARAPIS: Now, I show you! [*He beats him.*]

ABBOT: Wait, let me check, my son, let me check. [*He goes in to Katsandonis.*] Andonis, my son, Yiusuf Agas is asking for you.

KATSANDONIS: I've been betrayed, abbot![96]

ABBOT: I don't know, my son. [*He comes out.*] There's no Katsandonis here, my child; he isn't here; would I lie to you?

YIUSUF ARAPIS: [*Beats him mercilessly*] Hey, you, where Katsandonis?

ABBOT: Ouch, ouch, Lord, I don't know, I . . . don't . . . know.

YIUSUF ARAPIS: Phew, I kill you, if not confess.

KATSANDONIS: [*From within*] Wait, hey, Yiusuf!

YIUSUF ARAPIS: [*Frightened*] Captain Andonis!

SOLDIERS: Captain Andonis!

KATSANDONIS: Hey, Yiusuf, I never beat a priest of yours; how dare you beat mine? Why do you do it, you?

YIUSUF ARAPIS: Phew, surrender, Captain Andonis.

KATSANDONIS: I'm sick; come and get me.

YIUSUF ARAPIS: Surrender weapons.

KATSANDONIS: Katsandonis doesn't surrender his weapons; he breaks them. [*He breaks them.*]

YIUSUF ARAPIS: Phew, phew, phew, hey, what he, lion?

KATSANDONIS: Hey, how will you take me to Yiannina when you get me?

YIUSUF ARAPIS: Tie up and take like klepht.

SOLDIER: If you tie, we not come; phew, Katsandonis give us word, and we take that way.

YIUSUF ARAPIS: Phew, all right, you. Go in.

[*They go in, seize him, and get on their horses with Katsandonis in the middle. They depart toward Yiannina, behind them two soldiers bring the abbot.*][97]

KATSANDONIS: [*As they travel, he sings*][98]

Turks, reign in the horses just a bit and let me catch my breath.
I want to say good-bye to the hills and to the rocks up high.
I want to leave orders for my lads, for Kostas Lepeniotis.[99]

Set fire to Agrafas and burn the monastery;[100]
then let the abbot burn and also Karderinis.[101]

ACT V, SCENE I.

[To the right, the hut; to the left, the serai. In the middle, a single an-vil; right and left of the anvil, two torturers with hammers in their hands.] [102]

ALI PASHA: Hey, Yiusuf, what you say? You caught this wolf?

YIUSUF ARAPIS: Phew, I catch, sir.

ALI PASHA: Tie him good and bring him here, so I see him, to see what mug he has.

YIUSUF ARAPIS: Phew, all right, I bring.

[He leaves; he comes out with Katsandonis, tied in chains.]

ALI PASHA: *[Seeing Katsandonis]* Ah!

KATSANDONIS: You'll be saying "ah" during the hour of judg-ment, you villain.

ALI PASHA: You wolf who eat my sheep?

KATSANDONIS: You're the wolf; you're like all-devouring Hades.

ALI PASHA: Obey me, Katsandonis; obey.

KATSANDONIS: Katsandonis doesn't obey dogs; whatever you have to do, do it an hour sooner, villain.

ALI PASHA: You not obey me, you? I smash your ankles to scatter on road.

KATSANDONIS: The ankles you scatter, Ali, will one day take root, they'll sprout and grow many Katsandonians to crush your empty head.

ALI PASHA: Phew, phew, phew, phew, phew. Obey, Katsandonis. I make you dervenagas of all Epirus.

KATSANDONIS: I make a gift of your lands to others, Ali; Katsan-donis doesn't want your lands; if he did, he'd take them with his sword. I told you, whatever you have to do, do it an hour sooner so I can surrender my soul to the Highest.

ALI PASHA: Hey, now you see what I do to you. Now you see. Hey, take him; put him on anvil, break his ankles, very slowly so it hurt; hey, so it hurt.

[The torturers take him and put his feet on the anvil. [103]

ALI PASHA: Will you obey, Katsandonis, yes or no?

KATSANDONIS: You don't frighten me, Ali Pasha. Go ahead, fire and anvil, beat me, kill the hero Katsandonis.

ALI PASHA: Strike, you, strike.

[The torturers strike his feet with hammers.]

ALI PASHA: Ouch, you, won't you say ouch? Won't you ask for water? [104]

KATSANDONIS: You're the one who will ask for water, Ali, with your last breath; but you won't find it, villain.

ALI PASHA: Strike, you, strike.

KATSANDONIS: The harder they strike, Ali, the more pleasure they give me.

ALI PASHA: Stop torturers.

[*The torturers stop.*]

ALI PASHA: Obey and I make you well.

KATSANDONIS:

I say good-bye to you tall hills and to you rocks on high,
good-bye Tzoukerkas and Agrafas, where soldiers lay in hiding.
I hold you as my witnesses, and you must in turn to all acknowledge
how, with but a handful of soldiers, I put thousands to flight.
And should you come upon my wife and my little boy,
tell them how they laid their hands on me through treachery and
    cunning;
in ill health they found me, an infant in its cradle
wrapped in swaddling clothes.

ALI PASHA: Break him in pieces, you, break him in pieces!

[*The torturers strike him until they leave him breathless.*]

KATSANDONIS: [*Expiring*] Good . . . bye . . . swee . . t . . . na . . . tion. [*He falls dead.*] [105]

ALI PASHA: Phew, phew, what I do. [*Enraged*] Leave me all of you, all of you.

[*They all leave.*]

ALI PASHA: Phew! phew! phew! phew! Great outrage, set the traitor on fire, on fire. [*He leaves.*]

[*Two angels with Greece between them descend and take the soul of the hero. Greece speaks the following poem.*] [106]

GREECE:

> Before I recite my song
> "Heroes of the Greeks,"
> let all music cease,
> so I can chant my poem.

From eighteen-o-four
to eighteen twenty-one,
our fathers spilled
much blood for us, my brothers.
We're startled by the shade
of Makos Botsaris [107]
or the spit of Lamia
on which they skewered Diakos. [108]
We're startled by the shade
of Lampros Katsonis [109]
or the voice of Agrafas—
that of the hero Katsandonis.
Well done, you heroes of the sea,
Kanaris [110] and Miaulis; [111]
you set entire fleets to flame
in order not to live as slaves.

[*They leave.*]

THE END

CHAPTER 3

THE SEVEN BEASTS AND KARAGIOZIS

THE ALEXANDER TEXT

Unique among the plays of the Karagiozis repertoire, the *Alexander* text shows traces of ancient, vintage festivals wedded to Christian values. We find such vestiges, for example, in the characterization of the barrenness of the land as monstrous and therefore unnatural, in the prohibition of the life-giving waters of the spring, in the association of the monster with darkness, death, and the breakdown of social order, and in the ritual sacrifice of children. In the Karagiozis *Alexander* hero, a Christian warrior who slays a dragon to rid the land of a menace or to win the hand of his lady, we find a hero who, like the Christian monster-slayer Saint George, is a rectifier of evil deeds, a divine champion identified with fertility and life—eros, the force of creation. In the dragon's protean manifestations as a many-headed beast, like the hydra of Heracles or the beast of Saint John's *Apocalypse,* he is untamed and self-restoring. A chthonic agent, the dragon is identified with chaos or death—thanatos, the force of destruction.[1] Alexander reestablishes balance as he brings stability and the new kingdom.

Markos Ksanthos's version of the *Alexander* performance offers not only prototypical elements of the Karagiozis text (the offer of a reward for slaying the dragon who guards the spring, a procession of characters who fail in attempts against the dragon, and the final, successful attempt by Alexander), but exhibits the various influences that have affected the performance (from the classical to the Christian, from the world of romance to that of folklore). Ksanthos's work excludes certain folktale influences that show up in later performances (the hero cutting the tongues of the beast, Karagiozis posing as the dragon-slayer, and the exposure of Karagiozis by means of the tongues) but includes folklore motifs that later died out (the conflict between a grandmother and her beautiful granddaughter and the attempt to poison the successful suitor with an apple). Focusing on an erotic motif brought to the performance by myth (reinforced by Hellenistic romance and persistent through the Middle Ages), Ksanthos borrows his conclusion (the death of Alexander's love and the hero's suicide) from the Alexandrian world of romance. Both the love interest and the suicide disappear from later versions of the text.[2] The latter falls victim not only to Greek Orthodox proscriptions against suicide but to popular resistance to the idea that a cultural hero would submit to such defeatism. The earliest preserved Karagiozis *Alexander* text, Ksanthos's version thus responds to folk ideas and archetypal themes that spread across Greek, Balkan, and Turkish lands, demonstrating at the same time the variance that results from oral traditional transmission.

The *Alexander* text is important not only for its ideological statement but for its ideally suited position for serving as a transitional form between the inherited Turkish comedies and the later Greek heroic texts. The *Adiohus, Riddle,* and *Alexander* texts are about a figure performing an unusual or heroic labor, feat, or deed. The *Alexander* variant *Adiohus and the Lions,* for example, is referred to by the player Yiorgos Haridimos[3] as an abduction text of the type identified as a *listi,* or brigand text. The *listi* text is an antiheroic text that, like the heroic texts based on events in the lives of the klephts, has an historical basis. On the other hand, the *Alexander* text and the *Riddle* text, in which Alexander is used as a hero, share a common central theme with the comic Turkish text, *The Urn,* for all three texts contain a contest of suitors for the hand of the pasha's daughter.

The Karagiozis *Alexander* text has survived in ten players texts spanning the period from 1924 (Ksanthos's print text) to 1974 (a taped performance by Yiorgos Haridimos).[4] No other work in the Karagiozis repertoire has survived in so many variants, providing a rare opportunity to trace influences on the text. Of these ten, four are taped performances (Avraam, Karambalis, and two by Haridimos), four are print texts (Ksanthos, Spatharis, Mihopulos, and Mustakas), one is a dictation (Papanikolaos), and one a performance synopsis (A. Mollas).[5]

Ksanthos's work, as the earliest of the printed texts, serves as a bridge between Karagiozis texts of the late nineteenth century and those of the second half of the twentieth century. His version begins with a conversation between Hatziavatis and a bey, a scene that opens most Karagiozis texts. In this conversation, Hatziavatis discovers that the pasha's mother has become the ruling pashina. She has announced that her beautiful granddaughter, Sirene, whom she considers her rival, must wed whoever slays the seven-headed beast of the cave, and that the slayer may then accede to the throne; she is confident, however, that no one can achieve such a feat. A series of suitors arrive to challenge the beast, among them an old bey, Dionisios, Omorfonios, Stavrakas, Barba Yiorgos, and Manusos. Each escapes harm, some with Karagiozis's help, but none manage to defeat the beast. Alexander then enters and is almost killed in an extended battle with the monster. Caught by the beast, Alexander convinces the reluctant Karagiozis to release him; he then calls on the saints and slays the beast. Karagiozis poses unsuccessfully as the slayer at the pashina's palace and is exposed by Alexander (though not, in this version, by displaying the tongues of the beast). Fearful of losing her throne, the pashina refuses Alexander's claim to Sirene and orders the girl killed by two guards. The murder is avenged by Alexander who kills the two assassins and then takes his own life. When Karagiozis discovers the hero's suicide, he murders the pashina and then buries the bodies of the two lovers to prevent their being eaten by dogs.

Ksanthos's text is distinctive for its hero's erotic involvement and for its attempt to complicate the plot in the manner of a romance. The latter is accomplished through the performance of a labor to win the hand of a fair maiden and the inclusion of the interpolated suicide. Ksanthos focuses more on the slaying of the monster as a means of winning a beautiful prize rather than of saving the countryside from the catastrophe inflicted upon it by the beast.

Mustakas's *Alexander* text, by contrast, develops the terrors wrought by the beast as a moral comment on the sins of the ruler whose reign has brought with it disaster, a theme as ancient as the myth of Oedipus. Neither his version, nor that of Mihopulos, permits any question of the hero actually accepting the prize that has been won, for the feat has been undertaken as a patriotic act to free the land of evil, to demonstrate the superiority of Greek over Turk, and to affirm the virginal innocence of the Greek spirit, which alone can defeat the chaos threatening to overwhelm the land. The refusal of Alexander to wed the pasha's daughter is presented by both Mustakas and Mihopulos as the saintly self-denial of a Christian hero, who calls on Christ, Mary, and the saints to aid him in his fight against a demonic antagonist. In his variation of the text, Mihopulos makes Alexander a roving cavalier who travels the world in search of wrongs to right; he consciously ties the hero to Pseudo-Callisthenes's romance in his narration of Alexander's deeds.

Walter Puchner[6] suggests there could not have been merely one type of *Alexander* text in the 1900 repertoire; rather, given the influence of the Alexander *filladia* (popular or demoticized versions of the Pseudo-Callisthenes *History of Alexander the Great*), several must have arisen. That they later joined together into one text would have represented the first step of a substantive assimilation of Asiatic theater into Greek culture. He identifies three different streams of Karagiozis performances: the vulgar Anatolian performance, the Epirote school, and the works of Mimaros, representing, respectively, a performance type, a school of players, and a master performer. According to Puchner, this assimilation of thematic networks or braids arises under the influence of the laic culture of the Turkish occupation and not, like other assimilations, from the pantomimes, Fasuli, newspapers, comic idylls, and reviews.

Yiorgos Veludis[7] identifies a set of three themes representing the different streams of influence in related *Alexander* texts: the slaying of a dragon to free the vizir or pasha's daughter (the *Alexander* text); the unraveling of riddles posed by the vizir's daughter (the *Riddle* text); and the marriage of the vizir's daughter (the *Adiohus* text).

The *Riddle* text itself has several possible origins. Alexander not only had a reputation in popular tradition for being able to undo riddles (possibly influenced by his cutting of the Gordian knot in the course of his conquests), but he was credited in the Alexander *filladia* with solving a riddle to win the Queen of Syria, whom he later married to become king.[8] Yiorgos Haridimos[9] describes Alexander the riddle-solver as a surrogate for Oedipus (in this sense, the pasha's daughter, as poser of the riddles, is a surrogate for the sphinx), since classical figures had, in his view, no place in the Karagiozis performance tradition. Resolution of the riddles is balanced by Alexander's function in tying together Greek history across its various periods to create a metahistorical statement about the nature of the struggle of the Greek people.

As a resolver of events, Alexander is seen in popular tradition as one who continues to "live and rule." Thus, Haridimos explains, Alexander is considered too important a figure to use in the related *Alexander* text *Adiohus and the Lions*. Instead, a minor luminary (Adiohus, one of Alexander's generals) is chosen to be featured. The *Alexander* text, by contrast, carries a deeper meaning and so uses Alexander as its hero. According to Veludis,[10] the use of Adiohus as an Alexander surrogate is facilitated by the special role he plays in the Alexander *fil-ladia* in the palace of Kandakis, where Alexander disguises himself as Adiohus while Adiohus takes his place back at the camp.

The ritual quality of the *Alexander* text constitutes its fundamental aspect in the two different versions noted by Haridimos and the ten variants in our sample. Elements are balanced against one another to create primary contrasts. The most highly generalized oppositions oc-cur by pitting Christian against pagan, the Orthodox West against the Islamic East, and Greek against Turk. On a lower level, overreachers attempt an unjust assertion of power and fail because of some higher law or moral order; the dragon in its attempt to achieve dominion over the princess, and the queen, over Alexander. Karagiozis and the suitors fail too, but their failure is not an index of their corruption; it occurs instead because of a lapse in judgment that results in a vain assertion of power. Elsewhere, failures are based on an inadequate evaluation of the nature of events. The submission of the princess to the snake and the suicide of the disappointed Alexander result from underestimating human value and giving in to the monstrous in life. A just balance or return to order is effected by the princess's exposure of the poisoned apples and Alexander's unmasking of Karagiozis as a pretender. A lit-eral overcoming of the monstrous occurs in Alexander's slaying of the dragon and Karagiozis's revenge on the unnatural queen.

The Saint George legend provides perhaps the most fertile ritual in-fluence on the Karagiozis *Alexander*. The legend as it appears in mod-ern Greek ballads depicts the saint as a Christian knight, whose mis-sion is to liberate a city of Christians being persecuted by a dragon, itself a divine agent. Controlling a village spring, the dragon will not permit water to be drawn until a child is sacrificed. The sacrifice takes place by lot until the lot falls to the king's daughter. Saint George ar-rives to rescue the princess who warns him to flee the monster. The saint remains to wrestle with evil, and, with the sign of the cross and an appeal to God, he slays the dragon. The ballads conclude with the saint's refusal of the girl as a reward for a labor that he has undertaken in the service of the Lord.[11] The major elements of the legend as they appear in the ballads are central to the Karagiozis *Alexander* texts— the liberating mission, the dragon guarding the spring, child sacrifice, the princess's warning, the saint's appeal to God, and the denial of a reward.

The Saint George legend also appears in a rare Greek folk tale in which occur a series of events not found in the ballads. These events reflect the influence of the folk-tale tradition—particularly that of the popular Greek folk tale, "Faithful John"[12]—rather than an idio-syncratic version of the legend. A wretch appears in this tale and claims to have killed the dragon. Too frightened to reveal the true slayer of the beast, the princess awaits the arrival of Saint George, who exposes the pretender by producing the tongues of the monster that he had severed in battle. The princess in this folk-tale version is married in the end to a commoner.[13] These events are presented by A. Mollas, Mustakas, Papanikolaos, Haridimos, and Mihopulos in their *Alexander* texts.[14]

The influence of the Saint George legend on the Karagiozis *Alexander* text emanates largely from the nonecclesiastical popular tradition of the Balkans and the Eastern Mediterranean. In this tradition, the saint represents a natural rather than a moral force, a hero who serves the community more than God. Carrying ecclesiastical overtones of the victory of God over Satan and of Christianity over paganism, the saint's battle, nevertheless, is more clearly tied in the folk tradition to archetypal themes of life over death and fertility over sterility. The popular tradition thus exerts an influence that the ecclesiastical tradition tried to suppress.[15]

The significance of Saint George to the development of the Karagiozis *Alexander* is testified to by Agiomavritis, a Karagiozis player who performed in Patras c. 1890. He viewed a Karagiozis performance in Stilida, when he was not yet ten years old, that presented Saint George slaying a dragon and rescuing a princess.[16] According to this eyewitness, the representation of a saint on stage, especially in a situation that threatened an erotic involvement, was considered an affront to the church. Saint George was thus gradually replaced by the legendary Alexander in the Karagiozis performance. The anachronistic cross at the top of Alexander's lance remains a vestige of Saint George's continued presence in the performance, according to the player Yiorgos Haridimos.[17]

Puchner[18] and Sifakis[19] follow Veludis's hypothesis[20] that Alexander was chosen over St. George because he is more widely known in popular tradition and folk tales as well as through the Pseudo-Callisthenes *History of Alexander the Great* and its laic offshoots, the Alexander *filladia*. Sifakis[21] notes that the Alexander of the *filladia* is a Christian monster-slayer, which would have facilitated his assimilation into the Karagiozis text.

Veludis's thesis begins with his contention that the Pseudo-Callisthenes *History* was demoticized among the people of the various lands of Byzantium through the popular manuscripts or *filladia* dealing with the Alexander legend. These *filladia* surfaced at the end of the seventeenth century (when the first laic version of the *History* was printed in Greek in Venice); they arose out of popular Greek cultural traditions of the Byzantine period and went through numerous changes throughout Ottoman rule. In Veludis's view, the dispersion of these Alexander materials makes the laic Alexander *filladia,* together with laic folk tales, folk songs, and traditions, the natural source for the *Alexander* text of the Karagiozis performance.[22]

Veludis, in sum, sees St. George as merely an incidental influence on the Karagiozis *Alexander* text, an influence superseded by the laic and ethnic patriotism of the Alexander tradition. Alexander is taken as a man of the people, so well known that he served as a "passe partout" for the entry of ancient myth into modern folklore. St. George's contribution, in his view, is to add the symbolic element of a battle against Satan, death, and sin.

In support of his thesis, Veludis introduces four interesting pieces of evidence. First is a folk tale[23] reported in 1877 and told by a shepherd from the Parnassos area. In this tale, Alexander liberates the land from a king who has enslaved the shepherd's ancestors; he conquers a king who fought with the aid of an animal; and he visits a cave. The tale seems to be influenced by the laic *filladia* of the Pseudo-Callisthenes *History.*

Second is a folk tale from Sparta[24] in which a king invites princes to compete in contests to win the hand of his daughter. Alexander enters, wins, and leaves, and the princess draws him back with the aid of a snake that Alexander has rescued.

Third is a tale[25] told in Crete that Alexander went to ask for the hand of *orea* or "beautiful" Eleni who proposed a feat that he successfully completed. Frightened to receive Alexander as her spouse, she died of fear. This tale is used as an explanation for Alexander's opening of the Bosphorous Straits. It is also told in a somewhat different form[26] in which Eleni (or Helen) is clearly the mythic heroine of the Trojan War and Alexander is Alexander (Paris) of Troy.

Fourth, Veludis refers to versions of "Erriko tis Flandras"[27] in which Alexander is used in place of Erriko. The song tells of a king's daughter (Eleni) who refuses to wed a king. In addition, Veludis[28] cites several instances in which Alexander is seen as a dragon-slayer in oral tradition. Veludis discusses as well the representation in iconic art of Alexander, St. George, Digenes, and Erotocritos in soldier saint costumes with crosses, slaying a beast or a dragon.

What Veludis's thesis does not, however, take into account is the overwhelming influence St. George has had on the widely distributed monster-slaying tradition, a tradition capable of swallowing up heroes as diverse as Perseus, Heracles, Digenes, Alexander, and St. George. Alexander, by contrast, is only tenuously associated with monster-slaying, the critically central event of the Karagiozis *Alexander* text.[29]

Although the extent of Saint George's direct association in popular accounts with monster-slaying is not shared by Alexander, the Alexander legend itself is fed primarily by the *History of Alexander the Great,* a fictionalized biography by Pseudo-Callisthenes variously dated from the second to the fifth centuries.[30] Pseudo-Callisthenes's work, however, does not include the contest for the hand of a maiden, a monster who guards a cave or spring, the character Sirene, the refusal of the maiden as a reward, the cutting of the tongues of the beast, the appearance of a pretender and his exposure, or the calling upon God on the hero's behalf; the *History of Alexander the Great,* in other words, has none of the standard features of the Karagiozis *Alexander* text. There are, nevertheless, several suggestive parallels to the Karagiozis texts in this epic romance. Alexander married Roxanne, daughter of Darius, ruler of Persia. She, like Sirene, was the heir to a king's throne, and her union with Alexander was resisted by her father.[31] Further, in Alexander's travels the hero came upon such fantastic animals as the wild beasts of the army of Porus, the animal that drowned Philon, and the four-headed monster that prophesied Alexander's death.[32] One beast encountered was a dragon who lived upon a mountain top, of whom the Alexander of the romance writes, "I caused him to be slain."[33] Of his return to Babylon from the East, Alexander writes, "I arrived at the cave of Heracles. From there we arrived at a land of darkness where beautiful women lived."[34] This land of darkness with its beautiful women, this cave of Heracles, and this dragon of the mountain top may have legitimized the association of dragon-slaying with the Alexander figure in the Karagiozis texts; it may, as well, have reinforced the dark atmosphere of the texts in which a beautiful woman is forced to dwell in the shadowy realm of the monster, a realm physically represented by a cave commonly used in Karagiozis performances as part of the setting for the spring. In addition, the Alexander of the *History* is represented as engaged in great labors, as a scourge of evil, a righter of wrongs—as he saw a wrong—and a model of Aristotelian ethics. Finally, the anachronism of placing Alexander in the *History* in the post–Hellenistic world of Pseudo-Callisthenes is matched by the garbing of Karagiozis in the costume of a Byzantine border guard.

The confluence of the Saint George legend, which can be traced to the twelfth century (although his martyrdom occurred in the fourth), and the earlier Alexander romance was aided by medieval additions to the Alexander legend. In holy writings, he was depicted in the garb of the soldier saints[35] and portrayed as a pious Christian emperor.[36] The Christian coloring given to the pagan hero and the continuing secularization of Saint George in ballad and folk tale led to an assimilation of details from the Saint George legend in the popular tradition and to a close identification of the two heroes.

A popular Byzantine Christian hero, Digenes Akritas (a border guard), may have aided the assimilation of details, for he, too, was known as a dragon-slayer. The account in the ninth to eleventh century A.D. Greek Akritic Romance (as Mavrogordato labels it)[37] conforms in basic details to the configuration of the dragon-slayer tale of the Karagiozis performance: it involves the rescue of a lady from a three-headed dragon at a spring and the slaying of the monster with a sword. Itself based on floating folk tales, the Akritic Romance presents a monster that is no mere serpent or snake but is well on its way to becoming the *drakos* or supernatural ogre of modern Greek folk tale, the very beast specified in many Karagiozis performances (the snake is featured in others). Digenes is of double descent—Moslem and Christian—a characteristic he shares with the Alexander hero,[38] and though not primarily viewed as a dragon-slayer, he has been identified as the figure of a dragon-slayer on thirteenth-century Athenian pottery fragments.[39] The same figure has equally been identified as Saint George, an indication of the shared characteristics of the legends of these two heroes and a demonstration that Digenes provides an ideal transition from the Hellenistic world of Alexander to the twelfth-century legend of Saint George.

The legend of the dragon-slayer becomes more diffuse in the post–Byzantine world. We find, for example, in *The Saltukname*, a book of Turkish adventures gathered between 1473 and 1780, a dervish hero, Sari Saltuk, who dresses as a Christian monk and slays a dragon. Indeed, it is difficult to distinguish this figure from a Christian saint.[40] The diffusion of this tale is indicated by the mixed Anatolian and Balkan, Christian and pagan traditions from which it draws even though its activities are centered in Anatolia, Dobrudia, and the Crimea.

This same tale, or one very much like it, seems to have survived in a Turkish dragon-slaying legend current in early twentieth-century Rhodes.[41] In this version, a dervish kills a dragon by inducing it to eat forty asses loaded with quicklime. Rhodes had its own dragon-slaying tradition that dates from at least 1521, 170 years after the death of the historical figure Dieudonne de Gozon, third Grand Master of the Knights of Saint John at Rhodes, the hero of the tale. Of particular interest in the de Gozon legend are the following elements: the hero killed the dragon with the help of two dogs and a horse; he cut off a piece of its tongue as evidence of the slaying and told no one of his labor; a Greek, discovering the carcass, claimed to be its slayer; the hero refuted the pretender by showing the tongue, only to be imprisoned for disobedience rather than rewarded. The historian of the Order of Saint John, Bosio, wrote down the legend in 1612, deleting the incident about the Greek and his false claim but adding a cave from which a spring flowed as the dragon's lair and an incident in which the dragon fell upon the hero, who had to be rescued from under it by his servants. The similarities between the de Gozon legend and the Karagiozis text deserve note.

The emergence of the Saint George legend in the twelfth century and the appearance within a century of each other of the de Gozon and Sari Saltuk legends in the fifteenth and sixteenth centuries, together with the differing sources (Greek, Frankish, and Ottoman) and the geographical distribution of the legends (the eastern, central, and southern extents of Byzantine lands) indicate how diffused the dragon-slaying adventure was and how deeply impregnated it was in the fabric of Greek life throughout its Byzantine, Frankish, and Ottoman history.

Several other tales or myths aided in the transition or provided the Karagiozis *Alexander* text with certain details. The myth of Odysseus, for example, may have been the original source of the heroine's name "Sirene." Veludis,[42] here followed by Puchner,[43] sees the origin of the name in an erotic episode in the Alexander *filladia*, in which Alexander undergoes danger and resolves riddles for the favor of Semirami, Queen of Syria; he marries her and becomes king. A third possibility is discussed by Sifakis[44]—the Turkish Karagoz text *Ferhat and Sirene*.[45] The Turkish play contains the folk-tale themes of a wicked mother, a lover put to trial, and a murder of an evil agent. It relates a tale in which the widowed mother of Sirene resists the lovers' union, imposes tasks on the hero, and employs a witch to murder the lover. An extension of this influence in the Karagiozis repertoire appears in A. Mollas's *Alexander*-like text, *Adiohus and the Lion*, in which the use of poisoned apples is again introduced, presumably a borrowing from the widely spread Indo-European "Snow White" folk tale.[46]

Puchner[47] argues that the task performed in the *Ferhat and Sirene* text (getting water from a rock) recalls the motif of the *ofis* who controls the life-giving source of water, a motif brought into the Karagiozis text through the Saint George tradition. Ioannos[48] and Melas[49] accept *Ferhat and Sirene* as a Karagiozis *Alexander* source, but Sifakis[50] is unreceptive on the premise that *Ferhat* has no relation to dragon-slaying. He identifies *Ferhat* as an erotic history by the Persian poet Niznami who died in the beginning of the thirteenth century. Sifakis nevertheless acknowledges that Karagiozis players borrowed the form of the Turkish snake that appears to Karagoz in *Ferhat* (when Karagoz is on a trip on his donkey, the snake appears and speaks, demanding money; the snake seizes the head of the donkey and disappears). Karagiozis adopted the form of the Turkish snake over that of the *drakos* and *thirio* of Greek folk tales and the *ofis* of Greek iconography.[51]

The legend of Perseus, in which the hero rescues a princess from a monster, possibly provided the original erotic motif of the play, a motif muted in the Saint George legend,[52] present in the Alexander romance, and carried in *Ferhat and Sirene*. The love motif occurs side by side in the folklore stream with the presentation of classical heroes as worthy Christian warriors, although the Christian influence of the Middle Ages inhibited the presentation of physical love as the driving force of legends dealing with saints.

We thus find in the Karagiozis *Alexander* text an expression of the influence of the past on the present, but an expression rooted not in the classical so much as in the Byzantine past.[53] The influence is embodied in a broadly diffused expression characteristic of the mixed influences on Greek folk thought in the Ottoman period. Vestiges of vintage festivals and themes from the myths of classical Greece were only known through folk motifs found in popular traditions of the Byzantine and Ottoman periods and widely distributed throughout Greece, the Balkans, and Anatolia. Alexander, Saint George, and the heroes of Romance and Greek folk tales mixed indiscriminately to create an ideal hero whose ultimate reference was Saint George rather than Alexander the Great, whose ultimate virtue was civic rather than ecclesiastical, and whose motivation was more erotic than disinterested.

THE PERFORMER MARKOS KSANTHOS

Markos Ksanthos, a Cretan, carried the family name Ksanthakis. He is credited with having developed the Cretan type, Manusos Kritikos, that Andonios Mollas brought to the performance. Like his teacher Mollas and his own student Kostas Manos, Ksanthos followed the playing tradition of Yiannis Rulias, a tradition that attracted the largest number of players during the 1920s and 1930s. Whereas Manos branched off to represent the Peloponnesean tradition of mixed touring and town performances, Ksanthos came to represent the urban tradition of Attica. He based his performances in Athens where he played during the early decades of the twentieth century. Having graduated from secondary school, Ksanthos was one of a handful of literate Karagiozis players. Indeed, the fact that a number of Karagiozis players could read and write and that several had graduated from grammar school has led to a debate over whether the Karagiozis texts were purely oral compositions. Nevertheless, a player with both hands and eyes occupied is unlikely to find recourse to a written text possible, unless it is memorized or tacked to the screen in an outline version. Although references have been made to them, there is no physical evidence of outlines tacked to the screen. Moreover, most players have been at best semiliterate, and the use of prepared materials of this sort, or notebooks, while tolerated, is considered untraditional among the widest body of players.

As for memorization, it would have required the concept of a fixed oral text among players of the tradition or the existence of print texts to serve as master texts, as well as the actual use of such texts by players. There is virtually no evidence of a concept of fixed texts; as well, there is little evidence among players of the formal use of mnemonic techniques or aids.[54]

Ksanthos performed in Athens during a period when players could attract a crowd averaging from four to six hundred, while a weekend or special performance, for charity or celebrating a player's anniversary, could attract from twelve hundred to two thousand spectators. The size of the audience depended on whether a player performed on a daily basis (as he generally did in the summer), when an audience of four hundred was considered reasonable, or on weekends (as occurred during bad years and during the winters), when he could attract a thousand or more a night.

The admission price for a performance varied widely. In the villages, a collection plate might be passed around or the price of a drink increased from ten to fifteen lepta (one hundred lepta to the drachma). Often a player performed for goods, especially during war years, when money had little real value, and in the provinces, where barter was a common practice. In the cities, by contrast, tickets were used. In 1910, a ticket would cost between twenty and thirty lepta, and in 1930, about two drachmae. A popular player in the 1920s could make as much as 2500 drachmae a week after expenses, while modern players can barely make a living. Fantastic stories have arisen about the money-making abilities of famous city players. Mimaros in Patras, for instance, was supposed to have accumulated as much as half a million drachmae by 1897, while Manolopulos in Athens was reported to have amassed a million by 1926.

Known for his ability to improvise[55] as well as to perform a variety of Karagiozis plots, Ksanthos was the first player to commit his oral texts to print. He oversaw the publication of forty-six of them between 1924 and 1926. Ksanthos died of heart failure in Karistos in 1932 while on tour. His fellow player Sotiris Spatharis related that Ksanthos died while he was playing and that "all the people of Karistos went to his funeral for he had entertained them for years."

THE SEVEN BEASTS AND KARAGIOZIS[1]
A COMEDY IN FOUR ACTS[2]

BY MARKOS KSANTHOS

CHARACTERS

Karagiozis
Hatziavatis
Tahir, a rich bey[3] and member of
    the palace retinue
Emine, the pashina[4]
Serini, granddaughter of the pashina
Mustafas, an old bey
Dionisios (Nionios)
Manusos, a Cretan Greek
Stavrakas
Omorfonios
Uncle George
Kolitiris
Alexander the Great[5]
Veli Gekas (Dervenagas)[6]
Hasan, soldier
Gusas, soldier

[*The scene shows the serai, or pasha's palace, on the right and Kara-giozis's hut on the left.*]

HATZIAVATIS:[7] [*Singing,*[8] *he moves forward to meet Tahir, a rich Turkish gentleman.*]

> I'll don black robes
> and a dervish[9] be
> to roam the desert
> for love's ecstasy.[10]

TAHIR: [*Continuing from the other side*]

> The world consoles me
> and the mountains weep
> while the muted stones
> my patience seek.[11]

HATZIAVATIS:[12] [*Stops Tahir and bows to him*] I bow, effendi[13] Tahir, first to God the Highest and then to your highness.

TAHIR: Welcome, friend Hatziavatis. In heaven I would seek you but on earth I greet you.[14]

HATZIAVATIS: I'm at your service, effendi.

TAHIR: Since you don't have to work, why don't you come by the serai at least so we can see you? Or do you have a complaint against some officer?

HATZIAVATIS: What's that you say, effendi, a complaint? May lightning strike me if I have a complaint against you or any other officer.

TAHIR: So why, then? But I think I know what's going on, Hatziavatis; since the late vizir died, you haven't been interested in stopping by the serai.

HATZIAVATIS: No, effendi, it's not that! You know how it is; every morning I go to the marketplace looking for work. That's why I don't have time to come to the serai.

TAHIR: In that case, you're forgiven. Listen, then, Hatziavatis, I'll tell you what I want. I've been looking for you at her Highness's request.

HATZIAVATIS: Forgive me for interrupting you, but what Highness do you mean?

TAHIR: Ah, yes, I forgot to tell you. Well, then, when the pasha died, he left a daughter called Serini as well as his mother Emine. On his death, his mother ascended to the throne, taking the title pashina.

HATZIAVATIS: Why didn't his daughter Serini take the throne, effendi?

TAHIR: That I don't know. All I know is that the pasha's mother rules our city now. So, by her command, Hatziavatis, you're to announce throughout the city, in both Greek and Ottoman quarters, that whoever can kill the seven beasts of the deserted cave will take the lovely Serini for his wife. On the death of the grandmother, he will also ascend to the throne. What do you say; can you do it, or have you other work?

HATZIAVATIS: Are you kidding me, effendi? I'm off.

TAHIR: Very good; when you finish, come by and I'll pay you.

HATZIAVATIS: O.K., I'll be there, effendi. So long.

TAHIR: Good luck, Hatziavatis.

ACT I, SCENE 2.[15]

HATZIAVATIS: There you have it, friend; as soon as I finish my work, I'll get something, no matter how small; at least a lira probably. Who knows, it might even be two, three, or five; anyway, it doesn't matter. Thank God, no one should ever despair. But why don't I get started instead of sitting here, so I can finish down at the marketplace? Let me get started, then: "Hear ye, beys, agas, pashas, dervishes, Englishmen, Frenchmen, Russians, Italians, Austrians, Chinese, Americans, Greeks, and Ottomansssss. . . ."

KARAGIOZIS:[16] [*Inside the hut*][17] What the devil got into him, howling like a dog?[18]

HATZIAVATIS: "Hear ye, beys, agas. . . ."

KARAGIOZIS: Damn it, may your mouth rot, may you be stricken by scarlet fever, by rickets of the neck.

HATZIAVATIS: [*Continuing*] ". . . dervishes, Englishmen, Frenchmen, Russians. . . ."

KARAGIOZIS: May you grow calluses on your teeth; may nausea overtake your fingers; may your eyes go white and turn to chalk, and may you be protected from evil, amen. [*He comes out slowly, hunched over.*]

HATZIAVATIS: ". . . Italians, Americans, Greeks, and Ottomans. . . ."

KARAGIOZIS: [*Hits him*] Take that, God damn your mouth.

HATZIAVATIS: [*Angry*] What are you hitting for? Damn you! I bit my tongue.

KARAGIOZIS: You good-for-nothing, I'll make you bite your eye; I'll make a pit of your mouth.

HATZIAVATIS: But why, what for?

KARAGIOZIS: You smart aleck, Hatziavatis; what do you think I turned my house into that you're calling in the British, Gauls, ducks, geese, and hens? Where will I find the corn to feed them? And then, what if they get into some argument or other and destroy my hut! Don't you understand, you crafty rascal—I've tied it together with rushes!

HATZIAVATIS: My good fellow, come to your senses. I'm only making an announcement.

KARAGIOZIS: Why? Are you a cock that you should crow?

HATZIAVATIS: Damn it, I have a decree from Grandma herself to cry out.

KARAGIOZIS: And what does this decree say? Read it, so I can hear.

HATZIAVATIS: All right, but ask me politely; don't whop me right off the bat.

KARAGIOZIS: But that's my habit, you see; besides, is this the first time I ever hit you?

HATZIAVATIS: No, it's not the first; there've been many.

KARAGIOZIS: Well, since it's not the first, you shouldn't be picky. You know that when I see you I give you what's coming to you, just as Veli Gekas gives it to me. Come on, read the degree.[19]

HATZIAVATIS: So, listen to what it says: "I permit this person, Hatziavatis Tselepis, to proclaim freely throughout the city—Pashina Emine."

KARAGIOZIS: [Hits him] Why, you worthless good-for-nothing, you dare comply with decrees that don't bear my signature?

HATZIAVATIS: [Laughing] Ha, ha, ha.

KARAGIOZIS: [Hits him] Take that, and that, and that; each haw-haw costs a blow.

HATZIAVATIS: O.K., forget it, but now that you've frittered away my time, and I won't be able to make my announcement, what's to be done? Go ahead tell me.

KARAGIOZIS: Why not take me along, Hatziavatis, to announce together?

HATZIAVATIS: Bravo, Karagiozis, come on.

KARAGIOZIS: O.K., I'll come. But I divide whatever we get myself.

HATZIAVATIS: It's all the same, whether it's you or me.

KARAGIOZIS: Oh, no, you're mistaken.

HATZIAVATIS: All right. But I don't know if you have the voice.

KARAGIOZIS: Voice you say? A voice like you wouldn't believe.

HATZIAVATIS: Let's rehearse, Karagiozis.

KARAGIOZIS: [Shouts loudly] Ah, ah, ah!

HATZIAVATIS: No! Damn you!

KARAGIOZIS: What, louder?

HATZIAVATIS: No, higher.

KARAGIOZIS: Wait. [*Walks off*]

HATZIAVATIS: Come back here; where are you going?

KARAGIOZIS: Didn't you say higher? I'm going to climb the hut.

HATZIAVATIS: Not up high, dummy, but higher in the voice, that is "minion."[20]

KARAGIOZIS: Ah, I understand, "delicatsion."[21]

HATZIAVATIS: Yes, yes, bravo, cry out.

KARAGIOZIS: [*Calls out*] Oh, oh, oh.

HATZIAVATIS: No, higher.

KARAGIOZIS: Ei, ei, ei.

HATZIAVATIS: Good, that's fine. That's the way, now you've got it.

KARAGIOZIS: Of course! So long.

HATZIAVATIS: Come back here.

KARAGIOZIS: What is it?

HATZIAVATIS: Where are you going?

KARAGIOZIS: I'm going to warble.

HATZIAVATIS: And do you know what you're going to say?

KARAGIOZIS: I'll say, "oh, oh, oh."

HATZIAVATIS: Listen to me, pay attention; whatever I say, you say.

KARAGIOZIS: Speak, I'm all ears.

HATZIAVATIS: "Hear ye. . . ."

KARAGIOZIS: "We heard. . . ."

HATZIAVATIS: Not "We heard." "Hear ye."

KARAGIOZIS: Oh, come on, it's the same thing.

HATZIAVATIS: "Hear ye. . . ."

KARAGIOZIS: "We heard. . . ."

HATZIAVATIS: Damn you! "Hear ye. . . ."

KARAGIOZIS: "We heard. . . ."

HATZIAVATIS: God damn it, say it any way you like. Why should I bust my head to fill yours?

KARAGIOZIS: That's what I say. Continue.

HATZIAVATIS: "Beys. . . ."

KARAGIOZIS: "Lazy days. . . ."[22]

HATZIAVATIS: "Agas. . . ."

KARAGIOZIS: "Asparagus. . . ."[23]

HATZIAVATIS: "Pashas. . . ."

KARAGIOZIS: "Pasta. . . ."[24]

HATZIAVATIS: "Dervishes. . . ."

KARAGIOZIS: "Beverages. . . ."[25]

HATZIAVATIS: "Chinese. . . ."

KARAGIOZIS: "Grated cheese. . . ."[26]

HATZIAVATIS: "Englishmen, Frenchmen, Russians. . . ."

KARAGIOZIS: "Kidney bean, nectarine, scallions. . . ."[27]

HATZIAVATIS: "Italians, Austrians. . . ."

KARAGIOZIS: "Carpenters, grocers, butchers, kettle makers, aristocrats, and paupers. . . ." Are there any others? "Good salty fish eggs, sardines caught by sponge divers."

HATZIAVATIS: What sardines and fish eggs are you talking about?

KARAGIOZIS: How do I know? Continue.

HATZIAVATIS: "Whoever finds and kills. . . ."

KARAGIOZIS: "Dines and his stomach fills. . . ."[28]

HATZIAVATIS: "The seven beasts of the deserted cave. . . ."

KARAGIOZIS: "The many feasts of the chocolate covered cave. . . ."[29]

HATZIAVATIS: "Will take the beautiful Serini for a spouse and, after the death of the grandmother, the throne." Go quickly, without hesitation!

KARAGIOZIS: "Will take Zerzerini and afterwards, if he wants, can read the newspaper *The Ice Cream Cone*.[30] Go quickly and no dozing, and if you get drowsy, sleep on the road." O.K., now you can go, Hatziavatis. I know it by heart.

HATZIAVATIS: Yes, but where shall we meet to make our split?

KARAGIOZIS: You'll come here to get paid.

HATZIAVATIS: O.K. Good luck, Karagiozis. [*He leaves and cries out*] "Hear ye. . . ."

ACT I, SCENE 3.

KARAGIOZIS: [*Calling out to him*] Hey you! Shove off a bit, dammit, before the Karagiozis clan wakes up and starts asking for bread! All right, now let's get on with the announcing. Oh, oh. I forgot everything. Let's see, how did he put the first part? I just can't remember the first and last parts; all the in between slipped my mind. Let's see, how did he put it? [*He approaches the front of the serai.*] Ah, ah, I've got it. Hear ye, hear ye, hear ye, and whoever didn't hear, what do I care! Where was Pussyrini and the piastres with the carpenters who will be sleeping and in their sleep will be reading *The Ice Cream Cone*? And the grated cheese with the asparagus which will go in the pasta? Hear ye! The steamer *Mizizippi*[31] departs tomorrow on the day of 12:30, the hour of Saturday, in the year October, for Sparta, Volos, Larissa,

Mitilini, Menidi, Tripoli, Karditsa, Yiannina, Evalim, America! Who has tubs for plastering, hats to be baptized? Come, come! Who's next? Here's your knife grinder. Who has razors, scissors, penknives, knives, cannons, machine guns for sharpening? Get yours right here! Here's your good pretzel vendor, glasses for sale. [*He stops.*] What the hell am I saying?

[*While he speaks, Veli Gekas stands above and watches him.*]

KARAGIOZIS: Buy a jar of sweets. [*He sees Veli Gekas's pom-pom-tipped shoe*[32] *and sings.*]

I see a boot
someone is going to get a foot
and sail away from all the kicking

What could this be? Could it be a fishing boat? No, it couldn't be, it's an airplane. [*He feels Veli Gekas.*] Holy Mother, save me! [*He falls down.*]

VELI GEKAS: Huh! Straighten up, pimp.

KARAGIOZIS: [*Trembling*] Yes, yes, so was Demosthenes.[33]

VELI GEKAS: Huh! Why you here, you, huh? To make racket?

KARAGIOZIS: I didn't take the racquet.[34]

VELI GEKAS: This time you bouzouki,[35] huh? I'll let you go. Huh? So next time, huh? You'll know you'll get it.

KARAGIOZIS: I know, there's no need to hold a tryout.

VELI GEKAS: [*Hits him*] Huh? That's how you'll get it. Huh? Take that, and that, and that, and that!

KARAGIOZIS: Ouch, ouch, I'll puke, may your dead be forgiven and your living decrease. No more, enough.

VELI GEKAS: Huh? Hey you, you like that?

KARAGIOZIS: Why? Did anyone complain? It was fine, next time add more sauce, you hear?

VELI GEKAS: Huh? Next time I'll beat you till you ripen.

KARAGIOZIS: Of course, because this time you beat me green.

VELI GEKAS: Huh? Right, right. [*He leaves.*]

KARAGIOZIS: May you come to a good end, as they say, you dumbbell. No sir, I take his as a case of disrespect. I'll go demand his apology.

[*He approaches the serai and calls. With his cries, Hatziavatis comes out.*]

HATZIAVATIS: [*Calls to him*] Karagiozis, friend, what happened to you?

KARAGIOZIS: Is that you, Hatziavatis?

HATZIAVATIS: Yes, sweetheart, it's me; get up.

KARAGIOZIS: [*Makes a vulgar sign with his hand*] There, take that for your sweetness, you no-account. Is that any way to sneak up on me? I thought it was thieves wanting to take my money.

HATZIAVATIS: What, do you have money, Karagiozis?

KARAGIOZIS: Money and then some.

HATZIAVATIS: Where did you find it?

KARAGIOZIS: It's this way, my boy. I say to myself, why run around proclaiming in the streets, and I decided it's best to come and announce outside the serai; so I did. I just began to warble, when I hear from Tahini.[36]

HATZIAVATIS: Master Tahir?

KARAGIOZIS: Yes, yes, and he says, "What fine-fleshy-devil-forged-youth is he who cries out so sweetly?" He calls the cashier and says, "Give this warbler fifty lira." And the cashier, Hatziavatis, my friend, descends and starting here [*he shows him the ground*] he counted for me up to here. From here on he had no more to hand out and he left; in other words, I learned to tango, fox trot, polka, and waltz.

HATZIAVATIS: Could it be you were beaten?

KARAGIOZIS: It seems you got it.

HATZIAVATIS: Come on, let's go up, get paid, and divide our shares.

KARAGIOZIS: It's not necessary.

HATZIAVATIS: Then wait right here. I'll go get paid myself and come back.

KARAGIOZIS: O.K., go; you'll be treated well.

[*Hatziavatis goes up, while Karagiozis waits below.*]

VELI GEKAS: Huh? Halt, you. Huh? Where you off to?

KARAGIOZIS: Give it to him, dummy!

HATZIAVATIS: It's me, gallant one, me, brave one, me, my dervish, me Hatziavatis.

KARAGIOZIS: Will you listen to that sly dog, that greasy spoon; by mincing about, he saves his skin. I wouldn't have had a chance of getting upstairs without a reception.

TAHIR: Who is it?

HATZIAVATIS: Me, long-lived-one.

TAHIR: Welcome, come in, Hatziavatis. Don't be shy.

KARAGIOZIS: No, I'm not shy. What profit is there in being shy?

TAHIR: Give Mr. Hatziavatis a piece of halva. Like it, Hatziavatis, is it good?

KARAGIOZIS: Good? Great! Boy, oh, boy, halva! I'll have some more; I like it, you know.

TAHIR: If you want anything else, don't be bashful.

KARAGIOZIS: Not at all, I'm not bashful.

TAHIR: There, take four pounds-sterling, and God be with you. Come by once in a while.

HATZIAVATIS: My respects, effendi; thank you very much. May no evil ever befall you.

KARAGIOZIS: What the hell, doesn't he ever get tired of saying such things!

HATZIAVATIS: (*Comes down*) Karagiozis, my friend, we're saved. We got four pounds-sterling.

KARAGIOZIS: Good, put them down, so I can split them.

HATZIAVATIS: What's there to split, friend? It's not as if there's many, just four—two for you and two for me.

KARAGIOZIS: Oh, no, not that way; they'll be divided by multiplication.

HATZIAVATIS: Come on, Karagiozis, let's not do it like last time where I didn't get a nickel.

KARAGIOZIS: [*Aside*] Think you'll get a nickel now?

HATZIAVATIS: What did you say, Karagiozis?

KARAGIOZIS: I didn't say anything. Put everything on the table now so we can begin the operation.

HATZIAVATIS: [*Puts them down*] There you are, to set you mind at ease.

KARAGIOZIS: Tell me, do you want to divide it as God would or as man?

HATZIAVATIS: Come on, Karagiozis, always like God.

KARAGIOZIS: In that case, Hatziavatis, my friend, God gives much to some, to others little, and this time he gave me a lot and you nothing.

HATZIAVATIS: [*Grabs him*] All right, put them down.

KARAGIOZIS: Down, down, all right then, Hatziavatis, down. O.K. I take one for myself, one for you. How am I doing?

HATZIAVATIS: Now, yes, bravo, Karagiozis.

KARAGIOZIS: [*Continuing*] One for me, one left over; that I'll take for my troubles.

HATZIAVATIS: Same as always. I see through you, you hustler. Phtou. [*He spits.*] Get out of here, you bootlicker. [*He leaves.*]

KARAGIOZIS: You're not to blame. Take somebody in your confidence, friend, and he'll rob you blind. But I did all right for now; next time I'll make sure he doesn't get a nickel.

ACT II, SCENE I.[37]

[*To the right of the scene is a great cave, to the left the hut; Mustafas enters singing from the left, holding a knife in his hand. He advances toward the cave.*]

KARAGIOZIS: [*Behind him*] Poor fellow, how sadly he sings. [*He bends down, so he won't be seen.*] Hey, you!

MUSTAFAS: Who is it, please? Oh, well. Probably no one there. Just seemed there was.

KARAGIOZIS: [*Strikes him*] Clap!

MUSTAFAS: By Allah! I bit my tongue. What the devil! Is someone throwing stones? Some punk, I suppose.

KARAGIOZIS: [*Aside*] You dummy, what stones? It was a full-blown fist. [*He hits him again.*] Clap! Clap!

MUSTAFAS: Ouch! Right in the mug! [*He calls out*] You punk, I saw you. If I get my hands on you. . . .

KARAGIOZIS: Why the big fibber; he thinks he saw me.

MUSTAFAS: You better watch out because if I see you, I'll take my pistol and blast your brains out.

KARAGIOZIS: [*Aside*] Let's not have any of your little jokes, you old dotard.

[*He raises his hand to hit him, but at that moment, the bey turns.*]

MUSTAFAS: Hey, you, I saw you!

KARAGIOZIS: I saw you too, how you doing?

MUSTAFAS: Hey, do you know me to play jokes on me?

KARAGIOZIS: What do you mean, do I know you? Aren't you what's-his-name?

MUSTAFAS: Mustafas Bey.

KARAGIOZIS: [*Hits him*] Why it's ol' Mooosetabombey. How you've grown. [*Hits him*] Well, will you look at that.

MUSTAFAS: All right, let's cut out the sign language.

KARAGIOZIS: So, where are you off to, old man?

MUSTAFAS: You have cataracts calling me an old man, damn you?

KARAGIOZIS: [*Observes him, surprised*] What the devil! Am I blind? No friend, I'm awake. Hey you, you're not old, you haven't even begun to teethe yet. How are things, Mr. Child?

MUSTAFAS: Well, my dear.

KARAGIOZIS: [*Laughs*] Ha, ha, ha. Can you believe it? He likes being called a child.

MUSTAFAS: But I'm not old, either, sir.

KARAGIOZIS: [*Ironically*] No, very young. As much as ten times ten. But tell me now, where are you off to?

MUSTAFAS: Don't you know anything?

KARAGIOZIS: No.

MUSTAFAS: Sunday, I'm getting married.

KARAGIOZIS: Boy is this world nutty! I suffer from hunger and he from love. And whom are you marrying, Mr. Child?

MUSTAFAS: The lovely Serini. Will you come to the wedding?

KARAGIOZIS: This guy's ready for the straight jacket. The whole world goes loony in the summer, but he gets it in the winter. Maybe he's got winter madness. Tell me, how did you arrive at the conclusion that you would marry Pussyrini?

MUSTAFAS: Simple! I'll kill the beasts, and Sunday I'll hold the wedding.

KARAGIOZIS: In other words, you're figuring on doing it without the innkeeper.

MUSTAFAS: What innkeeper?

KARAGIOZIS: [Indicates the cave] There! That one over there.

MUSTAFAS: Are the beasts big, sir?

KARAGIOZIS: Not really! As big as the knife you hold.

MUSTAFAS: By my soul, it's done. I'll be a pasha.

KARAGIOZIS: Yes, you'll become a pasha, but don't make out like you're coming from my hut or I'll blind you, I'm warning you.

MUSTAFAS: Hey, what do you mean? Have you any idea of my prowess?

KARAGIOZIS: Tell me, do you have any money on you?

MUSTAFAS: I've got five or six lira.

KARAGIOZIS: [As if afraid] Good God! What would have happened to you! You would have been lost for nothing, and so young!

MUSTAFAS: What's the problem, dearie?

KARAGIOZIS: Why, you louse, did you think of killing the beasts with money on you? Don't you know that when you have money the beast smells it and draws you into his mouth! You see, it has a magnet in it.

MUSTAFAS: Ah, then do me the favor, sir, of holding my money. I'll be indebted to you.

KARAGIOZIS: Really, it's no debt at all. Give it here.

MUSTAFAS: [Gives it to him] Here, sir, take it and upon my return you can give it back. I'm going now.

KARAGIOZIS: Yes, get going, but stay far away from the hut.

MUSTAFAS: [Approaches the cave and knocks] Bang! Come on out, cursed ones. [He hears a noise, "V-v-v-v-v-vout."] Sir, what's whistling?

KARAGIOZIS: [From inside the hut] The Kalamata Express.

[*The beast comes out whistling, "Vou, vou, vou."*]

MUSTAFAS: [*Sees it and trembles*] By Allah, Allah, oh my dear. [*Calls out*] Sir, sir, sir.

KARAGIOZIS: I don't have time now, I'm doing the wash.

MUSTAFAS: In the name of my mother and father, may you be cut to pieces with one blow of my blade!

KARAGIOZIS: Strike, strike!

MUSTAFAS: [*Strikes it*] Take that, cursed one.

[*The snake seizes him and runs to its cave.*]

KARAGIOZIS: What the devil! The commotion stopped. Don't you want to kill it? [*He comes out.*] I can't see a thing. Ah, I forgot. He's going to get Pussyrini. [*He approaches the cave from which he hears groans.*] Boy, oh boy, they're snacking on him. Dammit, if I don't kill it myself, nobody can. [*He throws a stone; a grunt is heard, "V-vout."*] Holy Mother! Let me out of here before it takes another snack. [*He runs to the hut.*]

KOLITIRIS:[38] What'z long, popzy?

KARAGIOZIS: [*Hits him*] Shut the door and don't make a sound, before it gets our scent.

ACT II, SCENE 2.

DIONISIOS:[39] [*Singing*]

Zante, my Zante
Crown of the Levant.[40]

KARAGIOZIS: [*Interrupting him*] Hey, Nionio. Howdy.

DIONISIOS: Greetings you cur. How are you Karagiozo? [*Quickly*] Y'well, y'well, y'well?

KARAGIOZIS: [*Stops up his mouth*] Stop! I'm only well once. Dammit, you slobberer. Your mouth works as fast as Father Gabriel's worry beads. Well, then, where to from here, Nionio?

DIONISIOS: Listen, so I can outline the menu for you. Go ahead and announce the "finamenta"[41] to the whole world.

KARAGIOZIS: What's this you say? Renounce the placenta?

DIONISIOS: What are you, a good-for-nothing scoundrel? Poor fellow, doesn't anything get through that head of yours? Listen, little one. I came to kill the little snakes and become a professor.

KARAGIOZIS: And I'm asking you to leave and forget about becoming a hairdresser.

DIONISIOS: And why not, Karagiozo? Are the little snakes big?

KARAGIOZIS: Not really! Little ones, about so big.

DIONISIOS: Then let me at them; I'll eat their hearts out.

KARAGIOZIS: What, am I holding you back? Eh, get going, since you, too, want a part in these sweet goings-on.

[*Dionisios approaches the cave and knocks. Knock, knock, knock. While Karagiozis talks to him, the beast comes out. It whistles "V-v-v."*]

DIONISIOS: Hey, what's doing that, Karagiozo?

KARAGIOZIS: It's the Orient Express. Turn around and see.

DIONISIOS: [*Afraid*] Save me! Saints save me! Hey, what kind of longboat is this? Like the mountain in Zante. Hey, what devil possessed me? Grab me, Karagiozo!

KARAGIOZIS: [*Grabs him and drags him to the hut.*] Run, Nionio, it got you!

DIONISIOS: [*Runs and cries out*] My hat, Karagiozo.

[*The angry snake grabs the hut and shakes it. "V-vvvv, vvv, vou! Vvvvvou!"*]

KARAGIOZIS: Holy Mother! Kolitiris, shut the door. [*Hits him*] Come on, hurry up! And throw the matches and the box with the wicks out the back!

[*Kolitiris comes out to see what it is. The snake roars "Vvvvv."*]

KOLITIRIS: Pop! Popzy!

KARAGIOZIS: What's troubling you, boy? Something take your breath away?

KOLITIRIS: Give me panz to chanze.

KARAGIOZIS: [*Laughs*] Ha, ha, ha, ha. Come on, change quickly! There goes my house! It can't possibly be saved; the beast will get it one of these times.

[*The beast leaves.*]

KARAGIOZIS: Kolitiris, go ahead, see if it left.

KOLITIRIS: What's zat, you loafer? I'm not chanzing any more.

KARAGIOZIS: Come on, let's see what'll happen. There's no other way. I'll go. I'll kill one of them. [*He calls.*] Kolitiris!

KOLITIRIS: Here I am.

KARAGIOZIS: Give me the penknife and come with me. Tonight, we must do great deeds.

KOLITIRIS: Here, take it, but I'mz leavinz.

KARAGIOZIS: [*Catches him*] Come here with me. You'll go wherever I go. Take only stones, but big ones.

KOLITIRIS: [*Bends down and takes some stones*] Popzy, I got zome.

KARAGIOZIS: Keep your mind on what you're doing; we'll attack now.

KOLITIRIS: O.K., popzy, I knowz.

[*They approach and knock on the cave. Two small snakes come out and slither toward Karagiozis.*]

KARAGIOZIS: Strike, Kolitiris, they've eaten me.

KOLITIRIS: [*Strikes one with stones.*] Get back, you blind . . . , I'll kill you.

KARAGIOZIS: Get it! You the one and I the other!

[*The two beat them off.*]

KOLITIRIS: Popzy, I killzed it!

KARAGIOZIS: Bravo, my boy, and I killed the other. Come on, now let's go. You'll become pasha and I'll get Pussyrini.

KOLITIRIS: What'z zat, you loafer? Did we killz the big onez?

KARAGIOZIS: Why, yes, you're right. We should kill the other five too. Then we'll be rolling in onions for a month.

KOLITIRIS: Come on you, before zey glab uz and make muzh of uz.

ACT II, SCENE 3.

OMORFONIOS:[42] [*Comes out of the hut*][43] I'm going to murder those little snakes, so I can become pasha.

KARAGIOZIS: [*Terrified*] What the devil! How did the beast get behind us? [*Turns and sees Omorfonios and cries out*] Holy Mother! What monster is this? We're goners now! He'll eat us for sure.

KOLITIRIS: What'z you aflaid of, it'z a manz.

KARAGIOZIS: It's a man? Good God, and my heart's in my throat, damn his ancestors. Hey, you, are you a man or the biggest viper?

OMORFONIOS: Look at me, fathead!

KARAGIOZIS: Poor wretch, where are you headed?

OMORFONIOS: I'm going to murder the snakes. Well, what do you think? Will I become pasha?

KARAGIOZIS: No doubt about it.

OMORFONIOS: How do you know, sir?

KARAGIOZIS: By revelation! As soon as the beast sees you, it'll burst its bladder, and you'll become pasha with no effort at all. I wish I had the luck to be as lovely as you. Anyway, being a pasha becomes you.

OMORFONIOS: You have my word, if I become pasha, you'll be my chief bodyguard.

KARAGIOZIS: Now I've heard everything! And when I become trash collector, everyone will fear us! Forward, my pasha, knock on the door.

[*Omorfonios approaches and knocks; from inside is heard, "Vvvv."*]

OMORFONIOS: What buzzing is that, sir?

KARAGIOZIS: Ah, here comes the Patras Express.

[*The beast comes out; the other four appear behind it.*]

OMORFONIOS: Help! Help!

[*Falls down, the beast puts its nose on Omorfonios's heart and sniffs.*]

KARAGIOZIS: What the devil, is it a doctor? [*Comes close and grabs Omorfonios by the head.*] Hey, can I have him, you drone? [*The beast roars, "Vvvvv." Karagiozis begs.*] Can I have him, yes or no? ["*Vvvvv.*"] Yes, eh? Then, I'll take him. [*He taps the beast lightly; the beast roars, "Vvvvv."*] No, O.K., I won't take him, let him be. But he's my friend. No, I have to take him. I must.

[*He pulls slowly and drags Omorfonios off. Angry, the beast seizes the hut and drags it toward its cave.*]

KOLITIRIS: Wow, popzy, our houze is zhakin.

KARAGIOZIS: A mere relocation, my boy. It'll move the hut to Stadiu Street;[44] by air mail, yet. Get out, Kolitiris, quickly.

[*The beast abandons the hut and leaves.*]

KARAGIOZIS: Praise God! Grab there, Kolitiris. Let's put it back in place.

[*They lift the hut and put it where it was.*]

KOLITIRIS: Hear zat? You loafer, you're fartin!

KARAGIOZIS: Damn your ancestors, you lazy bum; you changed your pants, now it's my turn. But since it didn't take our hut, we can't complain.

ACT II, SCENE 4.

[*Stavrakas[45] enters singing.*][46]

KARAGIOZIS: Stavro, what do I see?

STAVRAKAS: Mercy, Karagiozako; I'll come clean as a canary!

KARAGIOZIS: Could you possibly be going for the beasts?

STAVRAKAS: What else, you raspberry, since I'm to become pasha.

KARAGIOZIS: Fine, but where's your knife?

STAVRAKAS: Little brother, after I sight it, I'll hollow it out; that'll wring it out of shape. Get my drift? Come and see, if you want.

KARAGIOZIS: Yes, yes, get going. I'll be there in the cave.

STAVRAKAS: Hey, by Saint Aglea,[47] you'll see, little brother, how lions battle angry beasts. [*He approaches and throws a stone.*] Come out, you raspberries.

[*The beast comes out and roars, "Vvvvv."*]

KARAGIOZIS: Go to it, Stavro, let's see how lions battle when the beast grabs you.

STAVRAKAS: Little brother, Karagiozako, save me, I'm lost. If it lunges, it'll make a mouthful of me.

KARAGIOZIS: Flee, Stavro, quickly.

STAVRAKAS: [*He runs.*] Mercy, Saint Fasiani,[48] I'm twirling like a greenfinch. [*Calls out*] Karagiozako, my hat! Save it, little brother.

[*The beast roars in anger, "Vou, vou, vou, vou!" It spreads itself flat on the ground outside the hut.*]

KARAGIOZIS: [*Comes out and steps on top of the beast without realizing it.*] What the devil! When did they pave this road?

[*The beast roars, "Vou."*]

KARAGIOZIS: What's that, you say?

[*The beast raises its tail.*]

KARAGIOZIS: You mean I don't have the right of way? ["*Vou!*"] Now, I've seen everything. I'm caught between a hammer and a hard place. ["*Vou!*"] Well, now I'll die officially and publicly.

["*Vou." The beast turns and joins its head with its tail with Karagiozis in the loop.*]

KARAGIOZIS: In your father's memory, come on, let me go.

[*The beast moves and so Karagiozis escapes. The beast bites its tail. "Vou!"*]

KARAGIOZIS: Oh, boy, jackpot! If it catches me willingly again, forgive me and may God forgive you.

[*The beast leaves.*]

KARAGIOZIS: Did he leave? Thank God!

KOLITIRIS: Popzy, what'z long wiz zat mug of yourz? It'z red.

KARAGIOZIS: Just had some cherry preserves, my boy.

ACT III, SCENE I.

[*Manusos*[49] *approaches singing.*]

KARAGIOZIS: What's this? Welcome, Manusos. How are things, Mr. Manusos?

MANUSOS: Well, God blests me, how you doing, youngster? Well, eh?

KARAGIOZIS: I'm well, but I see you with your cane; where you headed?

MANUSOS: Well, Karatsoz, I learnts tsat over tsere are tsome tsnakes and came here to get tsem with my club and become patsha. Well, how do tsings look? Will I be able tso?

KARAGIOZIS: I say you should leave, Manusos.

MANUSOS: And why tsould I leave? Well, whats tso happen?

KARAGIOZIS: All right, Manusos, go ahead. Only, when you see them, don't dare come toward my hut, because I'm telling you, I'm not receiving visitors.

MANUSOS: Dummy, cuckhold! Whats to happen? I'll tsnuff tsem outs!

KARAGIOZIS: I'm leaving. Good luck and good dying. Get lost! [*Leaves*]

MANUSOS: He left, tse tson of a bitsch. Lets tsee, whats tso do now. [*Approaches and knocks on the cave with the club. "Tak. Tak."*] Tshow yourtself, devil-monkey and be acquainted witsh Captain Manusos.

[*They all come out together and make noise.*]

MANUSOS: [*Calls*] Oh, goodnests, whats tsis? [*Calls loudly*] Where are you, hey, you, Karatsoz? Over here, Karatsoz; hey, young buck! Goodnests, whats happened to me? Come on, you dummy.

KARAGIOZIS: [*Inside the hut*] I can't spare the time; I'm washing my feet. Become pasha by yourself.

[*The beast roars.*]

MANUSOS: Help me, Tsaint Tstyliani![50]

KARAGIOZIS: Manusos, do them in quickly, or I'll come kill them myself.

MANUSOS: Karatsoz, come here, and I'll give you two Napoleons.[51] Come on, you, young buck.

KARAGIOZIS: [*Comes out*] Why didn't you listen to me when I told you to take off? Stretch a foot, so I can grab you.

MANUSOS: Come on, gets a hold.

KARAGIOZIS: It got you, Manusos.

MANUSOS: Hey, you, no funny bitsness!

KARAGIOZIS: [*Pulls him slowly*] Manusos, the beast's upset. It says it wants to look you over. What do you say, shall I let you go?

MANUSOS: No, look, you, I'll bring you a lamb.

KARAGIOZIS: Get out of here! Eat it yourself. [*Pulls him out slowly until he gets him free.*] Get going, Manusos.

MANUSOS: [*Calls and runs*] My pants! Hey, Karatsoz!

[*The beast bites its tail, almost cutting it off, and disappears into the cave.*]

KARAGIOZIS: Oops, there goes my soul, straight to the Virgin.

KOLITIRIS: Popzy, what'z lunning flom your panz legz?

KARAGIOZIS: Quiet, you lazy bum and shut the door tight.

ACT III, SCENE 2.

[*Uncle George*[52] *enters singing and holding his clog shoe*[53] *in his hands.*][54]

KARAGIOZIS: Greetings, uncle.

UNCLE GEORGE: Hey wretch; what news, Karagioz?

KARAGIOZIS: Good news, but fearful hunger.

UNCLE GEORGE: Say, m'boy, 'em watersnakes big?

KARAGIOZIS: Another one for the watersnakes! Why're you holding a clog shoe?

UNCLE GEORGE: To mash 'em lively ones.

KARAGIOZIS: Damn, I'm always mixed up with nuts. Tell me, Uncle, are you in your right mind?

UNCLE GEORGE: Why, Karagiozis?

KARAGIOZIS: Do you think you're going to do anything with a slipper?

UNCLE GEORGE: Why, ya, I takes out m'blade and whittles 'em down. Ya bet, Karagioz. And if I becomes a great man, ya be king and I gets the filly.

KARAGIOZIS: Uncle, Uncle! Beat it! I don't want to lose you. It's a big one and it'll eat you up.

UNCLE GEORGE: Poor wretch. D'ya wants to fix me a light? I'm not leavin. I'm gonna go.

KARAGIOZIS: [*Aside*] O.K., you, come on out, now. There, it's coming. Holy Mother! Grab him, you!

UNCLE GEORGE: Ya talkin to yaself, Karagioz?

[*The beast stands upright without making a sound.*]

KARAGIOZIS: No, I didn't say a thing.

UNCLE GEORGE: What's troublin ya, wretch, ya're turnin yellow.

KARAGIOZIS: Then you'll go green. Look over there, Uncle, at what's waiting for you.

UNCLE GEORGE: [*Turns, sees it, and runs with all the strength in his legs.*] My, my, my and m'without incense ta anoint m'self. It's over, I'm lost, wretch that I'm. [*Calls out and runs*] Karagioooz! Grab m'clog shoe and kilt.[55]

KARAGIOZIS: [*Laughs*] Wow, a cadillac couldn't catch him now! Look at that, he bumped into the pretzel vendor. There go the pretzels. Look, look, he ran smack into the tram. [*He calls*] Run, Uncle, it got you!

UNCLE GEORGE: Is't comin, Karagioz?

KARAGIOZIS: Yes, yes!

UNCLE GEORGE: Shoulds I fall into the asbestos pit, too?

KARAGIOZIS: Fall, Uncle!

UNCLE GEORGE: I fell!

KARAGIOZIS: Good for you. There, you see, you'll become a great man after all. Dammit, that's enough. I'm going into the hut before all this running turns me into a motorcycle. [*Goes in.*]

ACT III, SCENE 3.

ALEXANDER THE GREAT: [*Approaches the cave with a lance in his hand and sings.*]

Sweet mother, I go my own way
to distant lands far away.
And you with your other sons must reside
and forever forget that I'm alive.

KARAGIOZIS: What devil of a junk dealer[56] is this? [*Pushes him*] Sir, with the plow?

ALEXANDER THE GREAT: Who is it, please?

KARAGIOZIS: Me, you drone.

ALEXANDER THE GREAT: Come forward, so we can take a look at you.

KARAGIOZIS: All right. [*Passes in front.*]

ALEXANDER THE GREAT: Well, I'll be. . . .

KARAGIOZIS: What's this! Wouldn't you know I'd get in trouble!

ALEXANDER THE GREAT: How are you, Karagiozis?

KARAGIOZIS: [*To himself*] What? He knows me? Eh, sure, I must have ripped off something of his and I don't remember it. Why the devil did I want to speak to him?

ALEXANDER THE GREAT: Why don't you speak, Karagiozis?

KARAGIOZIS: [*Trembles*] Yes, I speak. How come you recognize me?

ALEXANDER THE GREAT: Don't you remember me at all?

KARAGIOZIS: No, not at all. Why? Have I stolen something from you?

ALEXANDER THE GREAT: Why no, brother.

KARAGIOZIS: How the devil did I miss ripping him off? This is the first time that happened.

ALEXANDER THE GREAT: Don't you remember me, Karagiozis? The other day when the constables took you to jail and I saved you?

KARAGIOZIS: Yes, but which of all the days was it? Not a day passes without a visit to the police station.

ALEXANDER THE GREAT: Why is that?

KARAGIOZIS: It's this way, my good man, the world is evil. When I passed by Christopher's tinsmith shop, I saw a cup outside with a drachma[57] in it. As I was passing, it called to me, "Come here, sir." I say to it, "What do you want?" "I beg you," it says, "take me, I'm cold here." Ah, poor thing, I couldn't allow it to catch cold. I felt sorry for it and, to warm it up, put it in my pocket.

ALEXANDER THE GREAT: [*Laughs*] Ha, ha, ha.

KARAGIOZIS: Why, the booby is laughing. [*Hits him, but smashes his hand.*] Holy Mother, my hand's broken!

ALEXANDER THE GREAT: Stupid fellow! Why did you strike my breastplate?[58]

KARAGIOZIS: When did you develop it?

ALEXANDER THE GREAT: What, Karagiozis?

KARAGIOZIS: Breast hate.

ALEXANDER THE GREAT: Breastplate, I said.

KARAGIOZIS: By the way, what's this?

ALEXANDER THE GREAT: Ah, this is a lance.

KARAGIOZIS: And this here?

ALEXANDER THE GREAT: This is a bow.

KARAGIOZIS: What's this on your head?

ALEXANDER THE GREAT: This is called a helmet.

KARAGIOZIS: Well, now, where to from here?

ALEXANDER THE GREAT: To the beasts.

KARAGIOZIS: Listen to me. Don't go; you're young and you shouldn't die.

ALEXANDER THE GREAT: You needn't even discuss that, Karagiozis.

KARAGIOZIS: What, you'll go?

ALEXANDER THE GREAT: Certainly.

KARAGIOZIS: I was to go, but since you came, you go.

ALEXANDER THE GREAT: No, Karagiozis, I don't want to take your turn. Here you are, go.

KARAGIOZIS: Oh, no. I caught a cold, you go.

ALEXANDER THE GREAT: Karagiozis, don't leave. I will need you to accompany me to the serai.

KARAGIOZIS: Thank you, but I'll lock myself in the bungalow and rejoin you later. [Leaves.]

ALEXANDER THE GREAT: He's frightened, poor thing.

[Approaches and with his lance strikes the cave. Loud roaring is heard and all the beasts come out. Alexander strikes with skill and courage as the battle proceeds.]

KARAGIOZIS: Oh, dear Mother, they're making a snack of him.

[At last, four of the beasts are slain, and Alexander is left to battle the large one. The beast seizes him by the hand, and he beats at it mercilessly. Alexander falls down, singing.]

KARAGIOZIS: What the devil, why is it so quiet? [Comes out.] Good God, are they eating him? Didn't I tell him, poor sucker? But he wouldn't listen to me.

ALEXANDER THE GREAT: [Singing]

Jesus and Virgin Mary lend me a hand,
and you Saint Irini [59]
so I can slay the animal band
and earn the hand of Serini.

KARAGIOZIS: That son of a gun is singing. [Calls to him] Hey, Alec?

ALEXANDER THE GREAT: Who is it?

KARAGIOZIS: It's me, who else, Karagiozis.

ALEXANDER THE GREAT: Friend, Karagiozis, he has a hold of my hand.

KARAGIOZIS: Why doesn't he eat it?

ALEXANDER THE GREAT: Because it's iron. If you don't mind, Karagiozis, just throw a stone at the beast so I can get my hand free; I would be indebted.

KARAGIOZIS: What the hell are you saying? He should set you free to snatch me?

ALEXANDER THE GREAT: Don't be afraid, Karagiozis. I wouldn't allow that to happen. I'd rather be killed myself than see you killed.

KARAGIOZIS: Bless you. Watch out, now. I'll hurl a stone at it.

[*Throws a stone at the beast and then falls down. Alexander frees his hand and beats the beast; he finally slays it.*]

ALEXANDER THE GREAT: Thank you, God. All-powerful God, glory be thy name. But where is Karagiozis? [*Sees him and is surprised.*] Poor thing, he must have been struck by the spear during the battle. [*Speaks to him*] Karagiozis.

KARAGIOZIS: [*Under his breath*] I died.

ALEXANDER THE GREAT: You died!

KARAGIOZIS: Just now and once before.

ALEXANDER THE GREAT: But you are still speaking.

KARAGIOZIS: It's in style now for the dead to speak.

ALEXANDER THE GREAT: Rise, my savior.

KARAGIOZIS: Get out of here! Don't call me Xavier.

ALEXANDER THE GREAT: All right, where did the spear hit you?

KARAGIOZIS: Smack in the heart.

ALEXANDER THE GREAT: Then, where is the blood?

KARAGIOZIS: My little heart swallowed it up.

ALEXANDER THE GREAT: And where is the spear hole?

KARAGIOZIS: [*Shows him his nostril*] Here it is, right here.

ALEXANDER THE GREAT: That's your nostril.

KARAGIOZIS: Since I told you I'm dead, that's the end of it; don't we dead know better than you?

ALEXANDER THE GREAT: In that case, poor Karagiozis, let me finish you off so you won't suffer any more.

KARAGIOZIS: [*Jumps up and catches his hand*] What the hell are you saying? Can't a person even die? Hey, what happened here?

ALEXANDER THE GREAT: I killed it, go close; don't be afraid, it's dead.

KARAGIOZIS: Could it be faking?

ALEXANDER THE GREAT: No, go ahead, and then return so we can go to the serai together, do you hear?

KARAGIOZIS: You go and wait for me. I've got work now. Not much, about half an hour's worth.

ALEXANDER THE GREAT: All right, I'll go and wait for you. [*Leaves*]

KARAGIOZIS: [*Goes near the beast, opens its mouth, and puts his head inside.*] Take it, eat, eat it you, damn your ancestors.

HATZIAVATIS: [*Enters and sees Karagiozis near the beast and calls him*] Karagiozis, friend, we're saved! You killed it? If you did, you're the pasha.[60]

KARAGIOZIS: I, certainly, I, papa-shah. Here, come on; grab it from there, so we can throw it away.[61]

ACT IV, SCENE I.

[*The serai on the right and Karagiozis's hut on the left.*]

KARAGIOZIS: Why is Alec late? These crickets are driving me crazy.

HATZIAVATIS: [*Comes to meet Karagiozis.*] Karagiozis, friend, pasha, how are you?

KARAGIOZIS: Hatziavatis, why are you hanging around, what's the problem? You wouldn't come around before for the love of heaven; now that I became pasha, you're always here.

HATZIAVATIS: Wretched me, Mr. Karagiozis. I have children. I, too, need money, don't you understand?

KARAGIOZIS: All right. Go now, come back in an hour. I'll order up a bank to be loaded on your back; you can take it away.

HATZIAVATIS: Good. To your health, Mr. Karagiozis. [*Leaves.*]

KARAGIOZIS: I might as well go in myself and wait for Alec now. [*Goes inside.*]

SERINI: Now then, come close, Mr. Tahir.

TAHIR: I'm here, your Highness.

SERINI: What have you learned about the beast?

TAHIR: To tell the truth, I'm not sure.

SERINI: How can you possibly not know?

TAHIR: It's rumored that Alexander slew them, but I don't know whether that's true.

SERINI: Very well. Thank you. Go, now, Mr. Tahir, I have no further need of you.

TAHIR: I do homage to you. [*Leaves.*]

SERINI: Oh, Alexander, Alexander. You have loved me twelve years, and now the hour has come that I become a Greek, that you make me your wife. [*Leaves.*]

EMINE: Now, come here, Tahir. Tell me the truth, what did Serini say to you, my child?

TAHIR: Your Highness, she was asking who triumphed, that is, who killed the beasts; and I told her that Alexander killed them.

EMINE: I see. The little vixen loves him, that infidel. But she will not enjoy him. I'll pull her hair out by the roots. All right, go.

TAHIR: [*Leaves, soliloquizing*] What the devil is wrong with them?

Serini loves Alexander, her grandmother won't accept him because he's a Greek. I don't know what to think.

EMINE: [*Angrily*] She loves him! But she will not have him. I'll give her to whomever I wish; I'll give her to an agas, a pasha.

ALEXANDER THE GREAT: [*Calls*] Karagiozis.

KARAGIOZIS: Here I am.

ALEXANDER THE GREAT: Come with me. [*They approach the serai.*] Now, Karagiozis, go up to the serai to . . .

KARAGIOZIS: [*Interrupts him*] What? What did you say?

ALEXANDER THE GREAT: I said, go up to the serai.

KARAGIOZIS: What are you saying? You want them to beat me to a pulp?

ALEXANDER THE GREAT: [*Angrily*] If anyone bothers you, he'll pay with his life.

KARAGIOZIS: [*Takes courage*] You betcha. What did you take me for, a coward? You'll see how I soak up the punches.

ALEXANDER THE GREAT: You'll say that Alexander the Macedonian [62] has come, did you hear?

KARAGIOZIS: How did you say it, the Macaroni-man?

ALEXANDER THE GREAT: Alexander the Macedonian.

KARAGIOZIS: Alec the Macaroni-man.

ALEXANDER THE GREAT: Did you understand it?

KARAGIOZIS: Oh, sure, easy as pie.

ALEXANDER THE GREAT: Forward, then; go and be not afraid.

KARAGIOZIS: O.K., I'm going. [*Goes up and calls out*] Madam, I have something to tell you.

SERINI: What can I do for you?

KARAGIOZIS: Alec the Macaroni-man has come.

SERINI: I don't understand.

KARAGIOZIS: Look here, child, he came and he has macaroni, too.

SERINI: We don't want any macaroni; we already bought some.

KARAGIOZIS: O.K., I'll say you got some. [*Goes down.*] Alec, bad luck.

ALEXANDER THE GREAT: What luck?

KARAGIOZIS: They got some, she says, this morning. Now, they don't want any. If we'd come sooner, maybe they'd have bought some.

ALEXANDER THE GREAT: You devil, what are you talking about?

KARAGIOZIS: What you told me; that we've got macaroni.

ALEXANDER THE GREAT: Do you know you're a pain in the neck, [63] Karagiozis? Yes or no?

KARAGIOZIS: I'll say it, what do I care?

ALEXANDER THE GREAT: Come back here, where are you going?

KARAGIOZIS: Madam, I've something to tell you.

SERINI: What is it?

KARAGIOZIS: He says he has a pan-full on his back and it's good for making supper. Will you buy it, he says, yes or no?

SERINI: I don't understand anything, sir.

KARAGIOZIS: Listen, child, it's Alec the Macaroni-man.

SERINI: Could it be Alexander the Macedonian?

KARAGIOZIS: Yes, bravo, glory be to God!

SERINI: Tell him I'll be there in two seconds.

KARAGIOZIS: All right, I'll tell him. [*Descends.*] She told me she'll be down in two seconds.

ALEXANDER THE GREAT: Bravo, you did one job properly.

KARAGIOZIS: Why, did I shortchange the others?

SERINI: [*Comes down*] Oh, Alexander, welcome. How have you been, my dear Alexander?

ALEXANDER THE GREAT: Beautiful Highness, is it you?

SERINI: I don't want you to call me "Highness"; you know I'm going to be a Greek. Who's this gentleman?

ALEXANDER THE GREAT: This is Mr. Karagiozis, my distinguished friend.

KARAGIOZIS: Yes, yes, my little Pussyrini, how's tricks?

SERINI: Good, but why are you squeezing my hand?

ALEXANDER THE GREAT: For shame, Karagiozis, you're a disgrace.

KARAGIOZIS: Shame, he says! The poor sucker's blind; she's like a fresh loaf of bread.

EMINE: [*Calls*] Serini.

SERINI: I'm here, Grandma.

EMINE: Go inside.

SERINI: Yes, Grandma. [*Leaves.*]

EMINE: Who are you, my child?

ALEXANDER THE GREAT: I'm Alexander the Macedonian, who slew the beasts.

EMINE: Ah, my child. Wait a minute, my son-in-law,[64] so I can bring you some apples. Come here, Serini. [*She goes in.*]

SERINI: Here I am.

EMINE: You cannot wed this unbeliever. No! I'll give you to whomever I wish.

SERINI: But why, good Grandma, since he killed the beasts? Why can't I marry him?

EMINE: No, no, it's no good. You'll not have him; if you do, I'll pluck your eyes out. Now, I'll poison him, the infidel.

SERINI: [*Under her breath*] Alexander, Alexander.

ALEXANDER THE GREAT: What is it, my lovely Serini?

SERINI: Be careful; my grandmother will offer you apples, but don't eat them. She's poisoned them.[65]

EMINE: [*Comes out*] Here, my child, have some apples; I picked them fresh from the apple tree.

ALEXANDER THE GREAT: Thank you, good Grandma. I'm not accustomed to apples.

EMINE: But take some, child; eat them and see how sweet they are.

ALEXANDER THE GREAT: I wouldn't want to offend you. [*Takes one.*]

EMINE: Eat them, my boy.

ALEXANDER THE GREAT: Don't worry, I'll eat them. Farewell. Let's go, Karagiozis. [*They leave.*] Karagiozis, wait for me at the hut. I'll come in half an hour, do you hear?

KARAGIOZIS: O.K., get going.

[*They leave.*]

EMINE: So, you love the unbeliever?

SERINI: I love him, and I'll love him until I die.

EMINE: Now, you'll see. [*Calls*] Come here, Hasan, and you, Gusas.

HASAN: Yes'm. I'm here, mistress.

GHOUSAS: Yes'm. Yours to command.

EMINE: I'll make you officers, if you kill Serini.

HASAN: Yes'm. All right. Farewell.

GHOUSAS: Yes'm. We know, mistress.

[*They come out.*]

SERINI: Where are you going, soldiers?

HASAN: Yes'm. Come here, so we can whisper it to you, mistress.

[*Serini approaches, but has no chance to speak before they kill her with their swords.*]

SERINI: Oh, Alexander, save me! [*Stops breathing.*]

KARAGIOZIS: [*Comes out*] Seems I heard something. [*Approaches and discovers Serini dead.*] Ah, it's blood! Who would kill her? Curses on your ancestors!

ALEXANDER THE GREAT: [*Running*] What is it, Karagiozis?

KARAGIOZIS: [*Bending down, he cries out*] Little Pussyrini, who gave life to our manhood is gone.

ALEXANDER THE GREAT: [*His appearance changes.*] Get away from there, Karagiozis. [*Bends down and sees Serini dead. He cries out.*] My Serini, my beautiful Serini. Karagiozis, leave.

KARAGIOZIS: Wait a minute. Someone is coming.

HASAN: Hey there! What are you doing, you good-for-nothing?

KARAGIOZIS: What do you think? We want to know who killed this wretch so we can reward him with ten lira.

[*At the mention of money, the two soldiers cry out together, "Yes'm, me!" "Yes'm, no, it was me. I killed her."*]

ALEXANDER THE GREAT: Here, take your reward!

[*He hurls his lance through both of them at once.*]

KARAGIOZIS: Bravo, bull's eye! Two birds with one stone. It nailed them like crabs!

ALEXANDER THE GREAT: Karagiozis, here, take a drachma; get me some paper and an envelope,[66] but find a big envelope.

KARAGIOZIS: O.K., I know, but don't leave.

ALEXANDER THE GREAT: No, I won't. Wait, come here.

KARAGIOZIS: Present! Now, what do you want?

ALEXANDER THE GREAT: [*Bends and kisses him*] Go on, now, go.

KARAGIOZIS: What a mystery! Why did he kiss me? What the hell, maybe he thinks I'm Serini. [*Leaves.*]

ALEXANDER THE GREAT: My Serini, I follow you.[67]

KARAGIOZIS: [*Approaches*] I couldn't find an antelope. [*Stops abruptly and sees both dead. He cries out.*] Oh, Alexander! That's why you kissed me. Oh, true countryman, had I known I wouldn't have left. [*He mourns them.*] Women of the neighborhood. Girls. Shake a leg, bring me shrouds and earth; I'll sell them. Someone is coming.

EMINE: What are you doing here, you unbeliever?

KARAGIOZIS: [*Takes out a penknife.*] You old coffeepot, you old testament, you hag; damn your ancestors, you old witch! May the devil take your soul!

[*Emine tries to flee, but Karagiozis catches her.*]

KARAGIOZIS: No, you won't get away, you'll follow them. Take that and that! And that! [*He stabs her with his penknife in the middle of the neck.*] There, die a pig's death! I might as well take them now and dig a ditch to bury them in. And the old woman? Let the dogs eat her. [*Lifts them up.*] I'll bury them[68] with my own two hands. [*Leaves.*][69]

THE END

APPENDIX A: THE CHARACTERS

Between 1890 and 1910, the regular figures of the Karagiozis performance became established. They consisted of twenty-five figures who appeared with some regularity, twelve of whom constituted the core of the troupe. These twelve include Karagiozis, Hatziavatis, Barba Yiorgos, Kolitiris, Aglea, Stavrakas, Omorfonios, Dionisios, the Jew, Veli Gekas, the old bey, and the pasha. Each figure has a counterpart in the Turkish performance.

Members of the core Karagiozis troupe are differentiated by their social caste (the pasha as supreme authority, the Jew as middle-class merchant, Karagiozis and Hatziavatis as the oppressed common man), their function (the pasha as clement judge, Veli Gekas as the cruel force of law, Karagiozis as the disrupter of social order), and their personal characteristics (Omorfonio's grotesque physique and his vanity, Stavrakas's false bravery, Dionisios's pseudo-sophistication). Regional differences, however, as expressed in costume, diction, and song, most clearly distinguish the characters. Dialects, for example, abound (Greco-Vlah, Greco-Levantine, Italianate Greek, Judeo-Spanish Greek, argot Athenian, and high Greek or katharevusa), assigning figures to particular regions and certain regional characteristics. Individual songs (klephtic songs, Italian cantadas, Turkish amanes, satyric songs, bucolic songs, laments, nonsense songs, and topical songs), themselves regional indicators, are treated like *leitmotifs*, identifying characters when they enter and emphasizing contrasts between characters. Many minor characters are defined entirely by regional characteristics of costume, dialect, and song, an indication of the significance of those elements in the performance.

Karagiozis: The fool-hero of the performance, Karagiozis, adapted himself to the Greek environment by changing into the rags of the poor Greek and going both bareheaded and barefooted. Players eliminated the openly displayed phallic organ of the Turkish figure from which Karagiozis evolved and added instead an overly long arm articulated at several joints. The figure's head became disproportionately large and egg-shaped, and his nose, which in mid-nineteenth-century Greece had been represented as hooked, became broader. Originally bald, he grew hair on his head as well as a mustache. The transformation complete by 1910, the Karagiozis figure introduced himself on the screen as Karagiozis Karagiozopulos, the illustrious one of Grigoris and son of Deligratzia.

As the player Andonios Mollas explains, the Greek Karagiozis did not take up his Turkish occupation as a messenger, but became a thief who, moreover, is training his son in his chosen profession. The figure's preoccupations—with thoughts of food, money, sex, and revenge against those who abuse him—are those that Mollas presumes characterized the Greek under Turkish rule. Mollas describes Karagiozis further as one who is everywhere, who encompasses all social views. Wherever one wishes, there he appears; whatever one wishes, that he becomes. He appears in the jungle, on the sea, in the serai; he is a patriot, a politician, a lover; he takes on the roles of a pasha, an admiral, a cook; he is first in battles, in beatings, and in love.

The player Yiorgos Haridimos maintains that Karagiozis is a coward and a thief but, at the same time, is a model patriot. This inconsistent portrait, Haridimos claims, demonstrates Karagiozis's embodiment of the spirit of the Greek *laos,* of the people themselves in their varied phases. Moreover, as the irresistable force of the national spirit, the Greek Karagiozis is a *regisseur* of the scene, a centripetal force that pulls into its comic field the varied traditions and customs, the myriad dialects and regional lores of the fragmented areas of the country.

Hatziavatis: Karagiozis's counterpoint is his sidekick Hatziavatis Tselembis or "master"; he is referred to by Karagiozis as *Tsimblimbis* or "sleep-in-the-eye." Hatziavatis represents the acquiescent Greek and is the only Greek who wears the Turkish *sarikia* or headdress and who speaks in the elevated katharevusa or Purist Greek to deal with upper-class Turks. This use of katharevusa provides a useful foil for the colloquial dialects of the common Greek. Like the old man of mime, Hatziavatis is moral, honest, industrious, a good father and housekeeper—Karagiozis's opposite in every respect. As variants of the Greek response to Turkish rule, the one makes his way by favors, while the other creates disorder and takes what he wants. Together, the two represent a secondary opposition that comments on the major thematic conflict of the play, that between the oppressor Turk and the enslaved Greek. Although the folk audience appreciates the exploits of Karagiozis, who fulfills its escapist fantasies, it is probably Hatziavatis who embodies its most typical virtues and vices.

Kolitiris: Kolitiris is the son of Karagiozis and is physically a miniature version of his father. Added by 1910 to capitalize on the urbanization of the performance, Kolitiris represents the street urchins of Athens of the period. He lisps and is dressed in rags. His name comes from the word meaning "to stick to." Kolitiris replaces the Turkish nephew of Karagoz, Kutsutzuk Andrias. He is usually joined in the Greek performance by his brothers who resemble him in physical type: Birikokos, Svuros (meaning "spinning top"), Kopritis (referring to a low character, from the word for manure), and Pitsirikokos (a word suggesting smallness). A fourth offspring, a daughter Potula, sometimes appears as well; like Karagiozis's wife Aglea, she is a female replica of her father.

Sior Dionisios: Also called Nionios and Count d'Oro, Dionisios is a successor to the Turkish Frank, the European or Westerner. Dionisios's surname in the Greek performance, indicatively, is Frink. Dionisios is presented as an Italianate Greek from Zakynthos, or Zante, an Ionian island dominated for several centuries by the Venetians. A member of an old aristocratic family whose fortunes have fallen (he wears a high hat and tails), Dionisios plays the role of a dandy who, like the Turkish dandy Chelebi, apes Western fashions.

His spoken Greek is infused with Italian words and forms, cast in the dialect of the Ionian islands. Because Saint Dionisios (a Christian surrogate for the pagan god Dionisios) is the patron saint of Zante, many players have had difficulty using this figure in both the islands and the villages of Greece where the association of a saint with a love lead is not well received.

Omorfonios: Also called Zaharias, Omorfonios is an elegant idiot with a huge head, short body, and fat feet, a probable descendant of the grotesque Turkish dwarf, Bebe Roui. In the Greek performance, he is represented as a pseudo-intellectual fop from Corfu. Speaking in a drawn-out voice and lisping like a spoiled child, Omorfonios talks through his nose creating a noise characterized by the whistling sound "ouit." His name means "beautiful-voiced." His role is that of the vain lover, though, with his grotesque appearance, he is a ridiculous figure.

Stavrakas: Stavrakas is a vulgar braggart, who, originally modeled on a harbor character from the island of Syros, became more closely associated with Piraeus whose taverns and drug dens he frequents. He has, in fact, been a favorite character of players of the Piraeus area for over half a century. Followed by his comrade Nondas, who apes him slavishly, Stavrakas thinks himself a brave man; but he is all pretense, for he never succeeds and is constantly beaten. Stavrakas and his pack of toughs (Thimis and Mitsaras, bouzoukia players; Vangelos, an organ grinder; and Lola and Nitsa, his molls) represent a macho type called *mangas*. Several Karagiozis players, among them Spiros Bobos and Psevdotheodoros, were themselves *manges*. Stavrakas's costume is that of the working class tough; he has a false beauty mark, wears a hat cocked to one side, and carries worry beads and a knife. A round-handled pistol stuck jauntily into his belt takes on an obvious phallic character. Taking the surname Tzimis, or Jimmy, Stavrakas speaks an Athenian argot, which he flaunts. He is one of the most popular figures of the troupe. A possible prototype for the figure is the Turkish performance's Tiryaki, an opium addict.

Barba Yiorgos: A strong, honest, and fearless type, Barba Yiorgos represents the rustic mountaineer or shepherd of Rumeli. Not very bright, he is feared by all. Thinking of himself as a pure Greek, he wears the skirts of the Greek mountain fighter and is angered when Veli Gekas refers to him as a Vlah, a term for an ethnic minority speaking a Latinized language in northern Greece but that is used to indicate a hick. Barba Yiorgos carries the surname Blastaras, which suggests "one who blasphemes." An ordering force in the Greek performance, he asserts a rough mountain ethic that is highly moral and Christian compared to the arbitrary Turkish justice of the history text. A Doric type, he stands as an image of strength and stability in an era of instability and change, the perfect antidote to Karagiozis who, nevertheless, mercilessly taunts him. A possible Turkish prototype for this figure is the Anatolian woodcutter, Baba Himmet.

The Jew: Often called Solomon, Abraham, or Jacob, the Jew is a merchant from Salonika (Thessaloniki) who is known for his riches and his stinginess. Although he is clever, capricious, powerful, and arrogant with his peers, the Jew is obsequious to his betters. His costume is a one-piece gown, belted at the waist, a fez, and a long beard. His head moves and is sometimes made to fall off. The Jew speaks an incomprehensible Judeo-Spanish Greek with a long, drawn-out voice of false sweetness.

The Pasha: The Pasha is the highest member of the Turkish ruling class represented in the performance. A provincial governor, he represents authority and stability. In the comic plays, he is generally a just and moral man, although he is not above deception. In the history plays, on the contrary, he is usually a tyrant. He is not, in any case, noted for his intelligence. The pasha speaks a mixed language of Turkish and high Greek with great formality. Wearing the Turkish pantaloons, robe, and turban, which represent his class, he often carries a water pipe.

The Old Bey: The old bey, or gentleman, generally appears in the opening scene of the play, initiating the action by his search for someone to provide a service or fulfill a position. A type like the foolish old man of mime, he is sometimes replaced by an old Greek. The bey serves as the butt of Karagiozis's jokes and often has his business ruined by the latter's antics. He is usually the father of the young female love lead and is frequently gulled by those about him.

Veli Gekas: Veli Gekas is also called Dervenagas, a ruler or guard of a mountainous district or pass. He is a Christian and a Vlah, the first officer of the serai, and the enforcer of the pasha's rule. An arbitrary and cruel figure, he mistreats Karagiozis and intimidates the Greeks. Nevertheless, he fears the fool's wit and considers himself kin to Barba Yiorgos, whom he believes to be a Vlah. A simple, uncivilized man, he speaks mixed Greek and Turkish. The brutal Janissary guard of the Turkish performance, Tuzsuz deli Bekir, is the prototype for this figure.

Aglea: The wife of Karagiozis, Aglea is known as Karagiozena and is sometimes called Anga, Andrena, or Zambeta. She is infrequently identified as the mother of Karagiozis. Aglea appears irregularly and, like Karagiozis's children, is a physical replica of her husband. She takes the role of the nagging wife, an earthy and pragmatic figure. In the Turkish performance, the fool-hero Karagoz also has a nagging wife. Unlike Aglea, however, in the Turkish performance the wife does not serve as the main female type, but is overshadowed by the Zenne, a scandalous courtesan from whom Aglea borrows her sexual promiscuity in earlier Greek texts.

In both the Turkish and Greek performances, women are generally regarded as quarrelsome and sexually loose and are used less frequently than the male figures. The Greek performance adds a young girl to function as a love lead in the suitors' play. This role, while it portrays women with greater sympathy, essentially relegates them to passive objects dependent upon men.

APPENDIX B: THE STAGE

The Karagiozis puppet stage defines the player's spatial limitations. An easily dismantled booth or *skini,* it commonly appears in the shape of an elongated rectangle. Its dimensions prior to 1920 have occasionally been reported at thirteen feet high and eight and one-half feet wide, influenced by the Turkish stage that was like those of itinerant marionette or hand puppet performers. Its contemporary shape is more commonly five and one-half feet high and seventeen feet wide, its abbreviated height made possible in cafe-theaters and theaters where raised stages were available. The greater width resulted from the growth of larger audiences in the cities and the subsequent use of larger theaters, a shift away from the coffeehouses in which players performed on tour and where they used a smaller *skini.*

The *skini* is set on a small, raised platform that gives the booth as much as two or three feet additional height. The apron or *podia* of the *skini* facade is often decorated with scenes from plays or drawings of puppet figures, and the strip over the screen, the *erio* or *kambot,* often carries the player's name. Planks of wood called *kuindes* cover the sides of the *skini,* which are supported by four posts or *kandronia.* The top of the booth is open. A shelf one foot to one and one-half foot wide is set three feet off the floor of the *skini* behind and below the bottom edge of the screen, both as a walkway for the performing puppets and as a place to set the lamps used to illuminate the figures. Nine to twelve shelf lamps stand about one foot away from the screen; they are complemented by three overhanging lamps that are hung out from the top of the *skini* on projecting pieces of wood. All the lamps hang between the player and the screen. The overhanging lamps are used both to create an even wash of light and to illuminate the set pieces, which are currently attached to the screen with staples; in performances at the beginning of the century, set pieces were nailed to the bottom edge of the screen. Candles or oil lamps, sometimes with two wicks, were used until 1908 when gaslight—a ten-foot long system that had twelve pipe openings and could be dimmed—was introduced; in 1918 electric light was first used. Oil lamps were least efficient as they let off black smoke, soiling the puppets. Sometimes, in the midst of a performance, puppets were accidently dipped into the oil.

Scene changes have been accomplished since 1927 by a pulley system invented by the player Harilaos. Two screens or *tavles* are used, one already acting as a set scene and one hidden from the audience, either by the *erio* or the *podia* of the *skini,* depending on how the *skini* was constructed. Each screen has its own tracks or grooves so that when the scene change is to occur, the new screen with its pre-set screen can ascend or descend simultaneously with the ascent or descent of the old screen. The design of the *skini* was kept simple to facilitate the disassembling and reassembling that takes place when a player changes homes. The player on tour often had to set up a makeshift *skini* (in which he ate, slept, and performed) out of sack and old wood, carrying with him only his puppets and certain necessary equipment such as the screen, lamps, and sticks to manipulate the puppets.

Early puppets, drawn in profile, were nailed to a stick or *susta* twenty inches long. *Sustes* could also be inserted into a slit in the cardboard figure. Players had either to nail and unnail *sustes* repeatedly or keep two puppets of each major figure, one facing in either direction. As the performance developed, Levteris Kelarinopulos designed a hinge that attached to the shoulder of the puppet, making such adaptations unnecessary. Such a simple device avoided the need either to bend one figure backward to hold a conversation with a puppet facing in the same direction or to back the puppet off the stage when he had to reenter from the same side. Early puppets were simply articulated at the waist and were neither well differentiated, carefully designed, nor highly individualized; they borrowed their form from comparable Turkish Karagoz figures. As the performance developed, the number of puppets grew from fifteen in the basic troupe to twenty-five. They also grew in size from one foot and two inches for the largest to three feet and six inches.

Yiorgos Haridimos's troupe provides a view of a typical set of puppets. In his troupe, the Jew, Barba Yiorgos (Uncle George), the pasha, and Hatziavatis are jointed at the waist and at the top of the thigh, while Omorfonios and Dionisios are jointed only at the waist. Dionisios's hat is set on the puppet so it can fall off, while the head and one hand, both made of leather, are detachable from the puppet's cardboard body. The cardboard has been slit open to receive the leather pieces that are held by a metal pin. Stavrakas, like Dionisios, has a detachable leather hand and head. His hat, set on a metal pin, is movable. His arm, at the end of which is attached a string of worry beads, is articulated in four places. The only other figures with articulated arms are Karagiozis (five joints), Alexander the Great (three joints), and Adiohus, a figure sometimes interchangeable with Alexander. Articulated arms are moved by a *susta* attached at the hand. Supernumerary pieces, such as Albanian, Greek, and Turkish soldiers, are of one piece. A number of soldiers are often cut as a single piece and moved as a unit. The only individual figure unattached at the shoulder is the Jew. Originally fitted with a head that moved or could fall off, this puppet is still attached to the *susta* at the back of the head or neck, an arrangement that allows the player to create distinctive movements for the figure.

The size of the puppet in some instances corresponds to its function or its nature. Each player's troupe is slightly different in size, although the general range and relationship are comparable. Among special figures, the legendary hero Alexander is the largest at three feet and seven inches. Barba Yiorgos, the guardian of the Greek scene, is the largest of the regular troupe at three feet and three inches. Stavrakas and Dionisios are tall as well, just under three feet and three inches. A hunchbacked, bent figure, Karagiozis is shorter, in some troupes only one foot and eight inches. In some troupes, Veli Gekas appears at

Karagiozis's height, his short stature expressing the distaste with which he is greeted in the performance. More generally, however, he is as tall as Barba Yiorgos, providing a worthy opponent for the hardy mountaineer. The smallest figures are Karagiozis's sons, the Kolitiria, at about a foot and a half. Puppets were rarely more than a meter (thirty-nine inches) in height because of the difficulty in moving such large figures.

Early Greek puppets were made of cardboard out of which numerous details were cut. Colored paper was placed over the cut openings of some figures to add color to the design. Because cardboard figures tended to disintegrate if not well cared for, they were considered impractical. Nevertheless, both their hardiness, when made of strong cardboard, and their aesthetic appeal have been defended by many players. Avraam claims to have used some cardboard figures for as long as twenty years. Camel-leather figures were introduced from Egypt by Manolopulos in 1918. This was a major innovation in Greek puppet construction, although Turkish players had long been using leather figures. Major figures were subsequently made either of leather scraped until diaphanous or of a hard translucent plastic, the latter suggested by Dinos Theodoropulos's attempts to use a gelatinous plastic he discovered on tour in the United States in the 1920s. The leather is stretched on a wooden frame to dry, cut into shapes, and scraped with glass until diaphanous. An outline of the figure is then placed on top of the skin. Details are either drawn with black ink or cut out with a tool. A delicate art, the cutting of details—particularly for the elaborate Turkish-style puppets such as the pasha and the Jew—must be accomplished so that separate pieces of clothing, weapons, and jewelry can be seen from a distance through the visual interplay of light, shadow, color, movement, and the cut detail itself. The further away the period of cardboard figures, with their numerous and highly decorative cuts, the fewer details one finds cut into the leather figures. The leather puppets of Hristos Haridimos, for example, have none.

Tinted on both sides with translucent colors, the puppet is cut into articulated parts and the parts joined with ties or metallic eyelets. In the process of scraping, some parts of the skin remain thicker than others (depending upon which part of the animal the skin came from, the underbelly being the thinnest). Figures are, however, made indiscriminately from whatever thickness of leather is available. Plastic figures, whose details are simply painted on, give off an unfortunate glow, and colors applied to them express little warmth. Players find these lighter puppets (one hundred twenty grams as opposed to one thousand grams for an equivalent figure in leather) unsatisfactory, for they affect a player's timing. The leather figures thus still continue in use. Although they require tinting every two years to remain fresh, they can easily be passed on after a lifetime of use, as with those of the Spatharis, Mollas, and Manos families, to a second generation of players. Most troupes are made up of a mixture of leather, cardboard, and plastic puppets.

Early set pieces were minimal. The basic set, Karagiozis's hut on one side of the screen and the pasha's palace on the other, was supplemented by mountain scenes, oceans, caves, and woods, as appropriate. Though as many as a thousand pieces of scenic stock and properties came to be used, as few as two hundred were taken on tour. Players maintained, as well, a reserve of several hundred figures. This reserve included the basic troupe in various costumes and disguises, twenty to twenty-five pashas, fifty captains and soldiers, ten female figures, and numerous special figures. The multiplication of scenic units that occurred as the performance developed is exemplified by the use of various kinds of serais or palaces. Until 1918 one type was used. Players later alternated serais every two or three days for variety, the most popular being a fashionable townhouse design. Yiorgos Haridimos handled the need for variety by developing a cardboard serai that could be disassembled and reassembled in various combinations. Karagiozis's hut was retained in its original form until recent times when such players as Athineos Manthos replaced it with a more modern-looking, two-story house. Most kept the old hut unchanged, adding a television antenna to modernize it.

Many players who could not draw their figures or sets hired other players (such as Sotiris Spatharis, Kostas Manos, and Avraam) or laic designers (such as Rammos, Prosfigas, and Yiannis Diplaris, also called Vizaniaris) to design figures and sets for them. In some instances, players merely required a figure that could be laid on top of a piece of leather, cut around, and copied. Many of the laic designers were hagiographers who traveled throughout rural areas to paint icons for local churches.

The design of puppets, properties, and set pieces was often a mixed style, few players having developed an individual style of their own. Although some figures expressed a player's personal view of a figure (the Kolitiris and Omorfonios puppets, for instance, are sometimes presented in a particularly grotesque manner), others, more rarely used, were hastily conceived. Figures drawn by laic artists were sometimes highly decorative, influenced by the Turkish or Byzantine style. Other figures were more simply naturalistic. Perspective was often mixed—one set piece in larger proportions than another against the flat plane of the screen—sometimes done consciously as a player's attempt to emphasize pieces of greater interest or psychological importance. Sequential differences were also used artistically to create a sense of relative distance. A figure moving away from a building, for example, would be replaced by a similar figure of a smaller size. Time as well as space was presented in a mixed manner. Simultaneous settings were used to represent, in the same space and at the same time, events that actually took place at a great distance from one another and at different times. Just as it became difficult at times to distinguish between a Gregorian chant and a muezzin's call or between an Islamic complaint and a klephtic ballad in the live songs of the performance, design elements and scenic techniques sometimes became indistinct. Indeed, although they were intended to represent the period and style of the Turkish occupation, the scenery and puppets of most troupes mixed various styles and periods.

Behind the screen, the puppet player is aided by an apprentice who makes sound effects, sets and changes scenes, and works supernumerary puppets. Singers, primarily engaged to sing, sometimes designed and painted puppets, made programs for the performance, or played an accompanying mandolin, bouzouki, or guitar. Affluent players hired a small orchestra using some combination of violin, bouzouki, clarinet, hand drum, trombone or cornet, and santuri. Avraam likens the orchestra of 1939 to a jazz band and adds the piano, flute, and saxophone to the list of possible instruments. In modern times, the player either uses recorded songs and dances or sings himself. Whereas some players, like Andonaros, are naturally gifted singers, others, like Spiros Karambalis, are primarily singers who have resorted to puppeteering as well. Many singers, hired on tour by a player, were simply local favorites chosen from the village in which the performance was held. A few, like Petros Kiriakos who sang for Mollas, went on to become professional cabaret singers.

Sound and light effects in the Karagiozis performance are relatively simple. Clapping one's hands, slapping together two pieces of wood wrapped in a rag, or hitting a piece of tin are used to indicate various kinds of beatings. Thunder is created by shaking a piece of tin or rattling stones in a tall can. The sound of broken glass is simply duplicated with real glass, and gunshots, by means of blanks. The sound of the monster in the *Alexander* play is made by blowing into a bamboo pipe, while the mysterious aura of the monster's cave is created by masking the shelf lights with red crepe paper. Although phosphorous is used for the fire effect when heroes are martyred and sparks of light simulate lightning, effects of night and day are created by masking and unmasking lights. A light in an open-ended can is passed from one side of the screen to the other to create a moon effect.

Special scenic effects are, however, often used. Theodoropulos speaks of a series of special light effects for his performance of *Karagiozis to the Moon* in which he uses a pre-set screen, a moon, a primitive projection of drawings of a moon landscape, and a star effect created with special lights. Beginning in darkness, he shows the moon in all its phases. As Karagiozis's rocket approaches the moon's surface, its landscape comes closer into view until Karagiozis disappears behind it and a flood of light drowns the landscape. Another lighting effect required a funnel-shaped piece, the mouth of which could be gradually narrowed to a pinpoint of light that could finally disappear. Special scenic effects are generally used in the *Karagiozis Shipmaster* play to create a shipwreck: a boat rocks, cut-out waves roll, a can of stones rattle, a light flashes, and a conch shell is blown. In other plays, caves and trees are opened so puppets can pass miraculously through, and set pieces during battles are severed. The smell of charred meat wafts through the audience to suggest the martyred Diakos roasting on a spit, while the crackling of a broken twig replicates the sound of a breaking leg. Imitating silent cinema, a change of place or of the passing of time was sometimes noted on cardboard signs pinned to the screen.

Until 1940, a pistol shot was used to signal that a performance had begun, a vestige of Turkish Ramadan performances when a cannon shot announced sunset and thus the beginning of evening festivities. When *Katsandonis* was performed, a shot signaling the death of Veli Gekas was often met with cheers from nearby taverns. The pistol was ultimately replaced by an iron pipe into which five or six holes were drilled. The holes, stuffed with a light explosive and covered with a round piece of iron, created a great noise when hit with a hammer. With this device, battles could be convincingly fought on screen. Under the German occupation during World War II, however, a plank hit against the floor of the booth had to suffice for pistol shots, while a bell announced the opening of the performance.

A few players consciously experimented with scenic innovation. Among them, Kostas Manos tried performing without a screen, using numerous set pieces and dressing his figures in cloth to increase the effect of performance spectacle. Sotiris Spatharis experimented with an "apotheosis" to end his performance. He simply raised the shadow screen and played a *tableau vivant* with live actors in front of a painted backdrop. Other attempts placed the actors behind a gauze curtain. Such experiments were inspired by the need to compete more effectively with both cinema and live theater in the post–World War I period. To compete with television, one modern player, Nikolas Lekkas, speaks of opening a future theater with ten screens for quick scene changes and a *stefani* or crown of small lamps or candles to create a mysterious flickering effect that will take the audience back to the early days of shadow theater.

APPENDIX C: THE PRINT TEXTS

The first text of a Karagiozis performance to be published was Andonios Mollas's *Karagiozis Engagement*, 26 May 1921, in *Ellas*. In that same year, the French Folklorist Louis Roussel published a dictated text, *A Little of Everything*, by the same player together with twenty-nine synopses of other Mollas performances in his work *Karagheuz ou un théâtre d'ombres à Athènes*. This text was dictated in 1918. Other texts soon followed under the supervision of the players; first, twenty-eight texts of Markos Ksanthos in 1924, then thirty-one texts of Andonios Mollas, 1925, followed by thirteen more by Ksanthos and nineteen by Yanios. Shortly thereafter came six texts by Kostas Manos, five more by Ksanthos, and then two by Manos.

Thus by 1926, at least four players had presented printed versions of their performances. Of those four, Yanios's work appears in the most confused state, and Manos's is the most authentically preserved.

After 1926 publishers rushed into print individual texts by such minor players as Kondos, Yiannopulos, and Peropulos. A few series were published as well, including a series by Manos (seven texts), a series by Dava (fifteen texts), four series by Mustakas (ninety-two texts all together), one by Kostatzis (about ten texts), two by Th. Mimaros (fourteen texts in the first and an unknown number in the second), and one by Dh. Rulias (an unknown number of texts included in Mimaros's second series). All these series were published before 1945. In 1947, a comic periodical entitled *O Karagiozis* published adumbrated versions of eighteen Karagiozis texts by the player Dimitris Basios and a complete text in sixteen parts, *Karagiozis in America*, by Manolopulos.

To absorb widespread public interest between 1926 and 1945, publishers, to use their term, "cut" their own texts, presenting Karagiozis in contemporary adventures and roles: Karagiozis as boy scout, soccer player, cowboy, and tourist. Publishers protected themselves from copyright laws by referring to these "little books" or *vivliorakia* as *Karagiozis-Paramithia* (Karagiozis stories or tales), *Theatron o Karagiozis* (Karagiozis theater), *Parastasis tu Karagiozi* (Karagiozis performance), or *Ikonografimenos Karagiozi* (illustrated Karagiozis), without ascribing the texts to an author or referring to them as the works of a *Karagiozopekti* (Karagiozis player). By contrast, texts by actual players featured the term *Karagiozopekti*, with the player's name immediately following the title: "by the renowned Karagiozis player Markos Ksanthos," "by the famous artist and well-known Karagiozis player Mr. Yiannis Mustakas." In several instances, Karagiozis-style theatrical texts appeared under the name of such theatrical authors as Vasilis Rotas, Fotos Politis, and Th. Sinadinos. In such instances, the edition clearly labeled the texts *Theatrika Erga* (theatrical works) and identified the author as a *singrafeos* (writer). Only in the texts of Nikos Rutsos, an amateur Karagiozis player of the 1960s, does conscious deception appear. Here the texts are introduced as "A performance of the shadow theater of Nikos Rutsos." Even in this instance, however, the term *Karagiozopekti* is not used.

Pirated editions became most common when publishers had no players' texts to print. Even then, publishers' advertisements were aimed at a secondary Karagiozis audience—children. Darima, the largest single distributor of forged texts, indicates in an editorial disclaimer attached to one of its texts the distinctive nature of its publication: "Darima, which has been in operation for some time now, represents the best entertainment for both children and adults. Furthermore, each child is given the opportunity to acquire a beautiful collection of the heroes of the screen."[1]

According to one estimate, some four hundred Karagiozis texts by players were ultimately published, including two sets of texts since 1945—seven of Mihopulos in 1972 and seven of Sotiris Spatharis and his son Evyenios Spatharis in 1979. That number may be exaggerated; only 280 texts can, at present, be verified as the works of players. The Angira publishing house was apparently the largest publisher of texts, as well as the hastiest and least discriminating. Papadimitrios, the second largest, was the players' house that printed the most pirated editions. The most discriminating and, as a result, the least prolific publishers were Deli and Saravanos-Vuniseas.

Players' printed texts have not, unfortunately, been systematically collected, the result of delayed recognition by Greek folklorists of the value of the Karagiozis performance as oral art and a folklore product. A prominent exception, the Greek folklorist Stilpidon Kiriakidis, asserted as early as 1921 on the pages of the prestigious folklore journal *Laografia*[2] that the performance both deserved and would reward serious study. Although he never studied Karagiozis himself, Kiriakidis collected eighty-four print texts from 1924 to 1926, from which the modern folklorist Yiorgos Ioannos republished eleven texts in 1971–1972. Beside Kiriakidis's collection, thirty-two texts have been gathered by the National Library, sixty-six by the Gennadion Library, and twenty-four by the Theatre Museum, all in Athens. Finally, fifty-one performances and dictations and nineteen oral autobiographies were collected in Greece in 1969 by Mario Rinovolucri for the Center for the Study of Oral Literature, Harvard University. Among these tapes are nine performances and eight dictations, representing five players who essentially belong to the period 1910 to 1940 (Kostas Kareklas, Panayiotis Mihopulos, Dinos Theodoropulos, Vangos, and Vasilis Vasilaros). Cedric Whitman collected an additional eleven texts in the 1960s (these, too, are on tape and on deposit at the Center for the Study of Oral Literature), of which six are performances and nine dictations. In 1971, Ms. Braithwaite collected five oral autobiographies, of which three (Vangos, Vasilaros, and Kareklas) were collected from players of the period 1910 to 1940. A sufficient number of texts are thus available from the period of Karagiozis's greatest artistic development and widest popularity to make possible serious study of the form.

In translation, however, very little is available. In fact, only four texts are available in translation, three of Mollas and one of Ksanthos. The first published was Roussel's 1921 translation into French of Mollas's dictated text, *A Little of Everything*. In 1954, in his *Vulgargriechische Scattenspieltexte*, the German folk historian Hans Jensen translated into German two plays from Mollas's published corpus of thirty-one plays.[3] He translated the first of the series, *The Three Pilgrims*, and the twenty-fourth, *Karagiozis Turkish-Judge*. Finally, in 1977 we published in English Ksanthos's *The Seven Beasts and Karagiozis* in the journal *The Charioteer*.[4]

The early printed Karagiozis texts provide the first full opportunity to view a performance only partially documented in eighteenth- and nineteenth-century Greek commentary and reviews in newspapers and journals. Read by young and old, both working and professional classes, these texts reached all levels of the population. Sold for only a few drachmae, they were largely published in a thirty-two page format into which uniform space plots of various lengths had to be fit. The mode of transmission used in the print texts varied. On one end of the spectrum were editions where an editor shaped a player's dialogue, jokes, and particular phraseology into a coherent whole, tying it together with stage directions. The patchwork result of such an approach is comparable to a young player's first performances put together from recollected scraps and memorized bits taken from his master's work. Mustaka's print texts are indicative of such an approach.

Mollas's *A Little of Everything*, transmitted by direct dictation in 1918 to a folklorist, is somewhat more coherent than edited texts. Dictation resulted, in this instance, in a text that would not necessarily have been performed. Made up of stock scenes, formular phrases, and stereotypical figures in lifeless combination, the text is self-conscious and stilted. Without the means of recording live performances, and without written originals to which they could refer, publishers were stymied. Players therefore began individually to oversee and approve the publishing of texts that were transcribed from the performance by the publisher. The texts were then set by publishers into a form with which they were themselves familiar—that of the acts and scenes of live dramatic productions. In performance, breaks were taken after the prologue and midway through the main performance; in the comedies, usually before or after a sequence of scenes introducing the comic characters performing repetitious variations on the same theme; and in the histories, before the scenes in the mountain devoted to the hero's exploits. In the print texts, the number of act breaks varied. While Mollas's texts used as many as six in a single play, his most common format was the four-act play with twenty to thirty scenes. Ksanthos's texts generally used a three-act format with eleven or twelve scenes. Scenes varied from as few as one to as many as eight in a single act. In general, the number of scenes increased as the play proceeded, reflecting the increased pace of action as the performance came to a close. Scene divisions were largely based upon the entrance of a new character, much like the French scenes of live theater. The player's ability to handle the movement and voices of only two or three puppets at a time partially explains the scene divisions.

Act divisions, on the other hand, were largely arbitrary choices based on con-
venient places to break the action. The Karagiozis texts were not, however,
like the plays of live theater other than in their printed format. They were not
intended as standard or final versions of a plot and were not meant to be used
as performance scripts; rather, they were presented as examples of improvised
composition, temporarily frozen in print form.

Taking an alternative view, and speaking from the point of view of one
whose field is the study of "paraliterary" texts, that is, popular fiction, Kiriakos
Kassis[5] claims that Ksanthos and Mollas did not write their texts as they
played them, but instead created a form of laic theater within the tradition of
shadow theater. His view is that they provided a written prescription or laic
formula to develop a popular form of theatrical writing.

Kassis[6] suggests that the commercialized Karagiozis print texts are thus
continuous with the laic *thrili* or adventure stories published as dime novels.
He argues that these dime novels dealing with heroic adventures and topical
themes did not merely corrupt the Karagiozis tradition after the Karagiozis
texts went into print in the 1920s but had influenced the live performance
from the nineteenth century. He cites, for example, an influence on *Katsandonis* by *thrili* as early as 1862—the popular novel by Ramfus. Published by
the dozens, *thrili* have covered Katsandonis's relationship with such figures as
Kira Vasiliki (1914), Veli Gekas (1924), Yiusuf Arapis (1924), and Ali Pasha
(1928–1933).

Cheap fiction appeared as well on the life of Alexander, including T. Evan-
gelidis's *Alexander the Great*, 1893. After Pseudo-Callisthenes's fictionalized
romance on Alexander's life, *The History of Alexander the Great*, passed into
the popular tradition, we also find laic versions of that text. Yiorgos Veludis[7]
dates them as early as the end of the seventeenth century, with the first printed
Greek version in Venice. Kassis cites several such laic texts from the period of
the development and printing of the Karagiozis texts, including versions in
1898 (published by Feksis), 1915 (published by Flamburas), and 1926 (published by Saliveros).

Kassis's argument implies that Karagiozis can be considered within the context of the tradition of these dime adventure novels, both because the latter
influenced the content of the Karagiozis performance and because pirated Karagiozis print texts followed the same path set by the popular novels in ex-
ploiting topical and fantastic themes. Although Kassis's argument has some
merit, and though it may account for commercialized texts of pirated Karagiozis texts, it cannot account for the performance tradition maintained by
Karagiozis players in both their performances and the print texts published by
players (up to the most recent texts of Mihopulos in 1972 and Sotiris and
Evyenios Spatharis in 1979).

Although Karagiozis admits the influence of the dime novel, its oral tradition and its authentic print texts clearly represent an autonomous tradition
that is part of a larger oral tradition rather than the paraliterary tradition of
the novels. Both traditions are, nevertheless, entertainments distinguished by
their appeal to a lower- rather than a middle- or upper-class audience, a dis-

tinction explained by their mutual Romaic qualities. Sharing this ideological orientation made possible the fluid exchange of themes between the two forms.

Hatzipandazis[8] compares the publishing of Karagiozis texts to the recording of another oral tradition—rembetika songs—in record studios. He adds that the publication of Karagiozis texts bring together the cultural traditions of its two audiences: the city or European audience with its written culture and the folk or Anatolian audience with its oral tradition.

The literary critic Velmos in his review of the print texts[9] concluded that, though performances lost something when transferred to print, print texts expressed theatrical merit, truth of content, and creativity. The texts preserved the personality of the player and managed to characterize the living, contemporary world of the performance. Velmos did not find them, in sum, artificial. Giulio Caimi, an early student and critic of the form (and to whom Mollas gave his body of thirty-two printed texts for comment), claims, by contrast, that the texts show a hasty rewriting of the player's performance rather than true art.[10] But he, too, praises what he calls the rich and, significantly, spontaneous humor of the texts. Truly, he claims, they represent the work of genuine talent. If the humor, like the plots, is sometimes exaggerated and childish, Caimi goes on, one can only attribute it to Mollas's continuing desire to serve his simple public. The texts, he implies, are not lifeless; they represent reasonable reflections of performance improvisation and are responsive to Mollas's theater audience, all indications of a performance attitude, even when restricted to print.

In an interview ten years after the publication of his texts, Mollas himself cited his illiteracy in explaining that these "cold comedies"[11] had been set down by others and that the recorded performance improvisations were not repeated the next time the performance was given. It is thus clear that the texts were transcribed from Mollas's performances, performances the player did not consider statically fixed in the form recorded.

The printed Karagiozis texts clearly reflect the live Karagiozis performance. Indeed, a comparison of print texts to live performances and tape recordings shows that performances do not differ from print texts in their construction, themes, or humor. Print texts do not, of course, rival performances in their spontaneity, immediacy, or responsiveness to the audience. If the print texts are deficient, it is because they are limited to the oral performer's ability to adjust to the new medium. Inexperienced in representing performance spectacle in print, the player was reduced either to using long, narrative stage directions or to omitting the spectacle altogether. By the same token, oral techniques used to guide audience understanding in a performance—techniques such as periodic recapitulation of the outline of the play by various characters or through letters and messages—were sometimes adumbrated.

But even though some semiliterate players modified their plays in print and others appear to have specifically composed pieces for publication, and although unauthorized and pirated editions had the effect of corrupting subsequent Karagiozis performances of mediocre players, it is clear that the printed texts produced during the period 1924–1945 have provided students of the Karagiozis performance with a body of invaluable texts that deserve and reward careful study. The print texts, preserved largely as authentic versions of live performances, are thus evidence of the nature of the performances at the height of the popularity and artistic development of the Karagiozis form, as well as, by retrospect, the culminations of the nineteenth-century development of the form. Since live performances were not preserved on tape until late in the history of the form, beginning in 1962, it is all the more important that students of Karagiozis have these texts to work from. Indeed, as the Karagiozis scholar Yiannis Kiurtsakis [12] claims, as a laic performance addressing itself to Greek society, the printed texts of the early period present a more faithful picture of Karagiozis than even today's performances.

NOTES

PREFACE

1. See Walter Puchner, *Das Neugriechische Schattentheater Karagiozis* (Munich: Institut fur Byzantinistik und Neugriechische Philologie, 1975), pp. 221–36; and W. Puchner, "Sintomi analitiki vivliografia tu theatru skion stin Ellada," *Laografia* 31 (1978):294–324 for the holdings of the Gennadion Library, the Theatre Museum, and the National Library in Athens. See Yiorgos Ioannos for the holdings of the private Stilpidon Kiriakidis Collection: "Isagogi," *O Karagiozis*, vol. 1 (Athens: Ermis, 1971), pp. 43–54 and 83–84. Angira Publishing House claims to have published three hundred texts; see Y. K., "Apo ton Brahali os tus simerinus Karagiozopektes," in *O Karagiozis*, ed. Dimitris Siatopulos (Athens: Angira, 1973), p. 18. According to an interview held by the translators with the then head of that publishing house in 1969, Angira still holds copies of these texts. The nature of those texts must, however, remain in doubt. See, in addition, Linda S. Myrsiades, "A Bibliography of Primary Materials for the Study of Karagiozis," *Mantoforos* 21 (April 1983):15–42. In all, it appears that over two hundred verifiable players' texts were published from 1924–1945. Of those texts, the Theatre Museum has eight of Th. Mimaros's, twelve of Mustakas's, and four of Kostatzis's; the National Library has thirty-one of Mollas's; the Gennadion has thirty-one of Mollas's, sixteen of Mustakas's, and eighteen of Davas's; the Kiriakidis Collection has an unknown number of Yanois's, thirty-three of Mollas's, five of Manos's, and forty-six of Ksanthos's.

2. Some notable exceptions should be mentioned here: the work of Kostas I. Biris, "O Karagiozis: Elliniko laiko theatro," *Nea Estia* 52 (1952):846–53, 924–28, 1064–70, 1128–34, 1220–28, 1269–75, 1374–78, 1434–39; Athanasios Fotiadis, *O Karagiozis o prosfigas* (Athens: Gutenberg, 1977); Spiros Kokkinis, *Andikaragiozis* (Athens: Iridos, 1975); Walter Puchner, *I valkanikes diastasis tu Karagiozi* (Athens: Stigmi, 1985); Linda S. Myrsiades, "Historical Source Material for the Karagkiozis Performance," *Theatre Research International* 10 (1986): 213–25; L. S. Myrsiades, "The Karaghiozis Performance in Nineteenth-Century Greece," *Byzantine and Modern Greek Studies* 2 (1976):83–99; and L. S. Myrsiades, "Adaptation and Change: The Origins of Turkish Karagkiozis in Greece," *Turcica* 18 (1986): 119–36.

3. Grigoris M. Sifakis, "I Paradosiaki dramaturgia tu Karagiozi," *Politis* 5 (September 1976):25–39 should be mentioned here, and note made of a thesis by Loring M. Danforth, "Greek Shadow Theatre: A Metasocial Commentary" (Master's thesis, Princeton University, 1974), and dissertations by Katerina Mystiakidou, "Comparison of the Turkish and Greek Shadow Theatre" (Ph.D. diss., New York University, 1978), Walter Puchner, *Das Neugriechische Schattentheater Karagiozis*, Miscellanea Byzantina Monacensia 21 (Munich: Institut fur Byzantinistik und Neugriechische Philologie der Uni-

versitat, 1975), and Linda S. Myrsiades, "The Karagiozis Tradition and Greek Shadow Puppet Theatre: History and Analysis" (Ph.D. diss., Indiana University, 1973). See also, Loring M. Danforth, "Humour and Status Reversal in Greek Shadow Theatre," *Byzantine and Modern Greek Studies* 2 (1976):99–111; L. Danforth, "Tradition and Change in Greek Shadow Theatre," *Journal of American Folklore* 96 (1983):281–309; Katerina Mystiakidou, *Karagoz: To theatro skion stin Ellada ke stin Turkia* (Athens: Ermis, 1982); Yiannis Kiurtsakis, *Proforiki paradosi ke omadiki dimiuryia* (Athens: Kedros, 1983); Yiannis Kiurtsakis, *Karnavali ke Karagiozis: I rizes ke i metamorfosis tu laiku yeliu* (Athens: Kedros, 1985); Linda S. Myrsiades, "Aristophanic Comedy and the Modern Greek Karagkiozis Performance," *Classical and Modern Literature* 7, no. 2 (Winter 1987):99–110; L. S. Myrsiades, "Oral Traditional Form in the Karagiozis Performance," *Ellinika* 36 (1985): 116–52; L. S. Myrsiades, "Traditional History and Reality in the View of the Karaghiozis History Performance," in *Modern Greek Studies Yearbook*, vol. 1, ed. Theofanis G. Stavrou (Minneapolis: University of Minnesota Press, 1985), pp. 96–108; L. S. Myrsiades, "Theatre and Society: Social Content and Effect in the Karaghiozis Performance," *Folia Neohellenica* 4 (1982):145–59; L. S. Myrsiades, "The Female Role in the Karaghiozis Performance," *Southern Folklore Quarterly* 44 (1980):145–63; L. S. Myrsiades, "Oral Composition in the Karaghiozis Performance," *Theatre Research International* 5 (1980):107–21; L. S. Myrsiades, "Nation and Class in the Karaghiozis History Performance," *Theatre Survey* 19, no. 1 (May 1978):49–62; L. S. Myrsiades, "Greek Resistance Theatre in World War II," *The Drama Review* 2, no. 1 (March 1977): 99–107; and L. S. Myrsiades, "Legend in the Theatre: Alexander the Great and the Karaghiozis Text," *Educational Theatre Journal* 27, no. 3 (October 1975): 387–95.

4. See Kostas Myrsiades and L. S. Myrsiades, "Texts and Contexts: A Primer for Translating from the Oral Tradition," *Translation Review*, no. 11 (1983):45–59.

CHAPTER 1

1. For a typical comment, see Giulio Caimi, "Isagogi," in *Ena lambro mathima tou Karagiozi*, by Andonios Mollas (Athens: n.p., 1953), pp. 5–7. For a range of comments see the special issue of *Theatro*, no. 10 (July–August 1963) devoted entirely to Karagiozis, and the special issues devoted partially to Karagiozis of *Zygos*, no. 20 (May–June 1976); *Anti*, 10 January 1976; and *Epitheorisi Tehnis* 22, no. 129 (October 1965). In particular, however, see Leon Kukulas, "I zoi tu theatru," *Piraika Grammata*, no. 6 (June 1943):299.

2. See Hermann Reich, "Karagoz und die alte attische Komodie," *Der Mimus: Ein Litterar-ent-wrickelungs geschichitliche Versur* (Berlin: Weidmannoche Buchhandlung, 1903), pp. 686–93; Cedric Whitman, "Karaghiozes and Aristophanic Comedy," *Aristophanes and the Comic Hero* (Cambridge: Harvard University Press, 1964), pp. 281–93; Athanasios Fotiadis, "Aristofanis ke theatro skion," in *O Karagiozis o prosfigas*, pp. 49–54; Giulio Caimi, "Apo ton Aristofani sto Karagiozi," *Stoa*, no. 3 (October 1971); F. J. Kakridis, "Karagiozis und Aristophanes," *Hellenika* 1 (1972):18–20; "To theatro skion ke i arhea attiki komodia," *Roda* (December 1969); K. Y.

Yiangullis, "Makroskelis leksis ston Aristofani, ston Karagiozi ke stus piitarides," *O Kiklos* 6 (November–December 1980):207–8.

3. See Fotos Politis, "O Karagiozis," *Eklogi apo to ergo tu,* vol. 2 (Athens: n.p., 1938), pp. 143–53 and 107–211.

4. See R. M. Dawkins, "The Modern Carnival in Thrace and the Cult of Dionysus," *The Journal of Hellenic Studies* 26 (1906):191–206; R. M. Dawkins, *Modern Greek Folktales* (Oxford: Clarendon Press, 1953); Yiorgis A. Megas, "I Apokria," *Elliniki Dimiurgia* 13 (1 March 1954):264–6; Y. A. Megas, *Greek Calendar Customs,* 2nd ed. (Athens: Rhodis, 1963); Y. A. Megas, *Folktales of Greece* (Chicago: University of Chicago Press, 1970); A. J. B. Wace, "Mumming Plays in Southern Balkans," *The Annual of the British School in Athens,* NR 19 (1912–1921); A. J. B. Wace, "North Greek Festivals and the Worship of Dionysius," *The Journal of Hellenic Studies* 26 (1906).

5. See Vasilios Kalfantis, "O gamos tu Karagiozis sti Gonusa tis Korinthos," *Laografia* 17 (1901):417–19.

6. On the history of Turkish Karagoz see Sabri Esat Siyavusgil, *Karagoz* (Istanbul: Milli Egitim Basimovi, 1951); Metin And, *A History of Theatre and Popular Entertainment in Turkey* (Ankara: Forum Yayinlari, 1963); Metin And, *Karagoz* (Ankara: Dost Yayinlari, 1975); Ilhan Basgoz, "Earlier references to Koukla and Karagoz," *Turcica* 3 (1971):9–21; Alessio Bombaci, "On Ancient Turkish Dramatic Performances," *Aspects of Altaic Civilization,* 13 (Bloomington, Ind.: Indiana University Press, 1963), pp. 87–117; Talat Sait Halman, "Comic Spirit in the Turkish Theatre," *The Theatre Annual* 31 (1975):16–42; Jacob Landau, *Studies in Arab Theatre and Cinema* (Philadelphia: University of Pennsylvania Press, 1956); Nicholas M. Martinovitch, *The Turkish Theatre* (New York: Theatre Arts, Inc., 1933); Refik Ahmet Sevengil, *Sur l'anciennete de l'art dramatique turc* (Istanbul: Direction Generale de la Presse, 1949).

7. Sevengil, pp. 28–30.

8. See Landau, p. 23; Bombaci, pp. 98–100.

9. See And, *A History,* p. 39; Evliya Chelebi, *Narrative of Travels in Europe, Asia, and Africa in the Seventeenth Century,* vol. 2, trans. Joseph von Hammer (London: Oriental Translation Fund, 1846), p. 243ff.

10. See Allardyce Nicoll, *Masks, Mimes and Miracles* (1931; reprint, New York: Cooper Square Publishing Co., 1963), pp. 37, 167.

11. See Nicoll, pp. 48, 82 for mime figures whose features inescapably resemble those of Karagoz; see also Yannis Vlahoyiannis, "Moros, mavros, mavroidos," *Nea Estia* 24 (1938):920–921; Reich, pp. 616–93.

12. Nicoll, pp. 214–15; Aleksis Solomos, *O Agios vahos i to agnosta hronia tu elliniku theatru: 300 p.h.–166 m.h.* (Athens: Keramikos, 1964), p. 213; see also Takis Dragonas, "Kommendia ke Karagiozis: Enas ellinas zani ston bernde," *Theatro,* no. 22 (July–August 1965):76–79.

13. Michel LeFevre, *Théâtre de la Turquie où sont représentées les choses les plus remarquables, qui s'y passent aujourd'hui* (Paris: Jacques LeFevre, 1688), p. 321.

14. See Chelebi, vols. 1 and 2; Metin And, "Dances of Anatolian Turkey," *Dance Perspectives,* no. 3 (Summer 1959):1–76.

15. In particular, R. Elliott Stout, "An Ottoman Festival," *Ohio State University Theatre Collection Bulletin,* no. 14 (1967):30–42; R. E. Stout, "The

Sur-i-Humayun of Murad III: A Study of Ottoman Pageantry and Entertainment" (Ph.D. diss., Ohio State University, 1966).

16. See Chelebi, vol. 2; also Fredericka Bremer, *Greece and the Greeks: The Narrative of a Winter Residence and Summer Travel in Greece and its Islands*, vol. 1, trans. Mary Howitt (London: Hurst and Blackett, 1863), p. 102ff; Thomas Smart Hughes, *Travels in Sicily, Greece, and Albania*, vol. 1 (London: J. Mawman, 1820), p. 312; John C. Hobhouse, *A Journey Through Albania and Other Provinces of Turkey in Europe and Asia, to Constantinople, during the Years 1809 and 1810*, vol. 1 (Philadelphia: M. Carey and Son, 1817), pp. 72-73.

17. On the location of Doliani, see Fotiadis, pp. 121-25, where he discusses the possibilities at length. Walter Puchner, *I valkanikes diastasis*, p. 17, accepts Fotiadis's identification of Banjsko, northeast of Strumika near the Greek border.

18. As quoted by Kostas I. Biris, "O Karagiozis: Elliniko laiko theatro," *Nea Estia* 52 (1952): 847.

19. Siyavusgil, pp. 5-6.

20. Chelebi, 2:243.

21. And, *Karagoz*, pp. 22-23; see also Bombaci, pp. 93-100.

22. And, *Karagoz*, p. 26; see also Stout, "the Sur-i-Humayun."

23. Landau, p. 25.

24. See And, *Karagoz*, pp. 67-76.

25. Puchner, *I valkanikes diastasis*, pp. 9-10.

26. Giulio Caimi, *Karaghiozi ou la comédie Grecque dans l'âme du théâtre d'ombres* (Athenes: Hellenikes Technes, 1935), p. 2; K. Th. Dimaras, *Istoria tis neoellinikis logotehnias* (Athens, 1968), p. 248; R. Dostalova-Jenistova, "Das neugriechische Schattentheater Karagoz: Einige Bemerkungen zu seiner weiteren Erforschung," *Probleme der Neugriechischen Literatur* 4 (Berlin, 1959):185.

27. Biris, p. 849; H. Jensen, "Das neugriechische Schattenspiel im Zusammenhang mit dem orientalischen Schattentheater," *Probleme der neugriechischen Literatur* 4 (Berlin, 1959):206.

28. The Fanariote (or Phanariote) was a Greek resident of the Fanariote Quarter of Constantinople (so-called for the lighthouse of the Golden Horn); it is a term describing the Greek official class under the Turks and came to mean a Greek aristocrat.

29. Puchner, *I valkanikes diastasis*, pp. 30-31; Th. Vellianitis, "Ta theatra epi Othonos," *Estia Ikonografimeni* (1893):321ff; Thodoros Hatzipandazis, "I isvoli tu Karagiozi stin Athina tu 1890," *O Politis*, no. 49 (March 1982):68.

30. In 1608 in Novi Sad, a Turkish pasha held a performance presented with marionettes that was viewed by Ambassador von Herberstern. K. Nehring, *Adam Freiherr zu Herbersteins Gesandtschaftsreise nach Konstantinopel* (Munich: R. Oldenbourg, 1983), p. 101; Puchner, *I valkanikes diastasis*, p. 16.

31. At a wedding of the Prince of Moldavia's daughter in 1652, Turkish performers presented various plays. N. Iorga, *Acte si fragmente cu privire la istoria Romanilor* (Bucharest: Imprimeria statutui, 1895), p. 211; Puchner, *I valkanikes diastasis*, pp. 16-17.

32. The Turkish traveler Evliya Chelebi noted a shadow theater performance in 1666 in Doliani near the Greek border. See note 17.

33. Puchner, *I valkanikes diastasis,* pp. 17—18; R. Trickovic, "Beogradski pasalik," unpublished manuscript, 132.

34. D. Kantemir, *Geschichte des osmanischen reichs* (Hamburg: C. Herold, 1745), pp. 377ff; Puchner, *I valkanikes diastasis,* p. 18.

35. A. M. del Chiaro, *Istoria delle moderne rivolluzzioni della Valachia* (Venice: A. Bortoli, 1718), p. 3; Puchner, *I valkanikes diastasis,* p. 18; Lazare Sainean, "Les marionnettes en Roumanie et en Turquie," *Revue des Traditions Populaires* 19, nos. 8—9 (August–September 1901):417.

36. Franz Joseph Sulzer, *Geschichte des transalpinischen Daciens* (Vienna: R. Graffer, 1781), pp. 401—2; Puchner, *I valkanikes diastasis,* pp. 1921; Sainean, p. 417.

37. Stefano Raicevich, *Osservazioni storiche naturali e politiche intorno la Valachia e Moldavia* (Naples: G. Raimondi, 1788), p. 244; Puchner, *I valkanikes diastasis,* p. 21.

38. Puchner, *I valkanikes diastasis,* pp. 19—21.

39. N. Batusic, *Povijest Hrvatskoga kazalista* (Zagreb: Skolska knjiga, 1978), p. 155; Puchner, *I valkanikes diastasis,* p. 25.

40. Puchner, "O protos ellinikos Karagiozis," *Nea Estia* 115, no. 1367 (June 1984):792.

41. Z. Muljacic, "Dopune rad N. Beritic," *Prilozi* 22 (1956):84ff; Puchner, *I valkanikes diastasis,* p. 25.

42. E. Popescu-Judetz, "L'influence des spectacles populaires Turcs dans les pays Roumains," *Studia et Acta Orientala* 5—6 (1967):343; Puchner, *I valkanikes diastasis,* p. 18.

43. Puchner, *I valkanikes diastasis,* p. 28; G. Veludis, *Der neugriechische Alexander. Tradition in Bewahrung und Wandel* (Munich: Institut für Byzantinistik und neugriechische Philologie der Universität Munchen, 1968), p. 259; Puchner, "O protos," p. 791. Other supportive, early testimony cited by Puchner includes the following: between 1820 and 1850 performances of shadow theater were common in Belgrade. Puchner, *I valkanikes diastasis,* p. 25; V. T. Stefanovic, "Stari Beograd," *Glasnik* (1911):149. In the beginning of the nineteenth century in a cafe in Bucharest, a comedy called Hagi Ivat (or Hatziavatis) was performed using two protagonists (usually Armenian or Turkish) who told jokes, danced, sang, and played scenes from the life of the laos in Turkish and Romanian. T. T. Burada, *Istoria teatrului in Moldava,* vol. 1 (Jassy, 1915), pp. 79ff; Puchner, *I valkanikes diastasis,* pp. 23—24; in Gimpulin in 1834, puppets of the *berde* (or screen) were presented. G. Opreascu, *Istoria teatrului in Romania* 1 (Bucharest: Editura Academiei Rupublicii Socialiste Romania, 1965):117; Puchner, *I valkanikes diastasis,* p. 23.

44. Puchner, *I valkanikes diastasis,* p. 22.

45. See footnotes 9 and 20 of this chapter.

46. See footnote 35 in this chapter.

47. Karagoz was seen in Sarajevo between 1868 and 1877 by several observers (Z. Ilic, "Jedna zabrana izvocenja 'Karacoz' pozorista u Sarajevu," *Politika,* 1 January 1966, p. 20; *Sarajevski cvjetnik za 1870 godini,* p. 47; F. Kanitz, *Donau-Bulgarien und der Balkan,* vol. 2 (Leipzig: H. Fries, 1877), p. 191ff; Puchner, *I valkanikes diastasis,* pp. 25—26). At the end of the nineteenth century, Turkish Karagoz players from Skopia were seen in the area of Kossifopediu (T. Vukanovic, "Studije iz balkanskog folklora," *Vranjski glasnik* 5 (1969):337ff; Puchner, *I valkanikes diastasis,* p. 25). After 1895, Karagoz appeared in Kostantza and its provinces in Turkish, Armenian, and Greek

(Puchner, *I valkanikes diastasis*, p. 24); and until the twentieth century Karagoz appeared in Ohrid, Bitola, Veles, and Stip (D. Antonijevic, "Karacoz," *Gradska kultura na Balkanu*, XV–XIX vek, Balkanoloskog insituta SANU, no. 21 [Belgrade: The Instituta, 1984], p. 391; Puchner, *I valkanikes diastasis*, p. 25).

48. In the summer of 1695 merchants from Turkey came to Belgrade from Anatolia. Among them were found Karagoz figures, along with the candles used to light the performance. Puchner, *I valkanikes diastasis*, p. 18; Trickovic, p. 132; Antonijevic, p. 390.

49. See Fedonos Kukulis, "Ta laika theamata ke i laiki diaskedasis," pp. 247–69, and "I emboriki paniyiris," pp. 270–83, in *Vyzantinon vios ke politismos*, vol. 3 (Athens: Institut Francais d'Athenes, 1949).

50. Hobhouse, 1:425.

51. M. Guys, *Voyage littéraire de la Grèce, ou lettres sur le Grecs, anciens et modernes, avec un parallèle de leurs moeurs*, vol. 1 (Paris: Veuve Duchesne, 1783), p. 481.

52. See Linda Suny Myrsiades, "Non-Theatrical Entertainments in Greece: Through the Eyes of Foreign Travellers, 1750–1850," *East European Quarterly* 16 (Spring 1982):45–58.

53. See Linda Suny Myrsiades, "The Struggle for Greek Theatre in Post-Independence Greece," *Journal of the Hellenic Diaspora* 7, no. 1 (Spring 1980):33–52.

54. Apostolos E. Vacalopoulos, *The Greek Nation, 1453–1669: The Cultural and Economic Background of Modern Greek Society*, trans. Ian and Phania Moles (New Brunswick, N.J.: Rutgers University Press, 1976), pp. 28–29.

55. Vacalopoulos, p. 30; see also Al. N. Oikonomidis, "Foreword," in *Modern Greek Folklore and Ancient Greek Religion: A Study in Survivals*, by John Cuthbert Lawson (1909; reprint, New York: University Books, 1964), pp. vi–viii. For travelers to Greece see Shirley H. Weber, *Voyages and Travels in Greece, the Near East, and Adjacent Regions, Made Previous to the Year 1801*, 2 vols. (Princeton: American School of Classical Studies at Athens, 1952–1953).

56. Sir Glenville Temple, *Travels in Greece and Turkey Being the Second Part of Excursions in the Mediterranean*, vol. 2 (London: Saunders and Otley, 1836), pp. 218–19; Aubrey Thomas de Vere, *Picturesque Sketches in Greece and Turkey* (Philadelphia: A. Hart, 1850), p. 313.

57. Charles White, *Three Years in Constantinople; or, Domestic Manners of the Turks in 1844*, vol. 3 (London: Henry Coleman, 1845), p. 244.

58. A. Ubicini, *La Turquie actuelle* (Paris: Librairie de l'Hachette et Cie, 1855), p. 318.

59. Francois C. H. L. de Pouqueville, *Voyage en Morée, à Constantinople, en Albanie, et dans plusieurs autres parties de l'empire othoman, pendant les années 1798, 1799, 1800 et 1801*, vol. 1 (Paris: Chez Gabon et Compe, 1805), p. 52.

60. Hobhouse, 1:159–60.

61. Myrsiades, "Struggle for Greek Theatre," pp. 33–52.

62. The theater wars extended to a competition between popular and literary theater in the last quarter of the nineteenth century. The post-liberation distinction between popular and literary theater was, apparently, typical only of Greece. In Turkey, theater and puppetry had continued their Byzantine

partnership to the extent that in a Constantinople cafe of 1850 a theater performance might follow a Karagoz performance (Gerard de Nerval, *Voyage en Orient,* vol. 3 [1850; reprint, Paris: Le Divan, 1927], p. 90). In this Karagoz performance and in one witnessed by Slade in 1829 (Adolphus Slade, *Records of Travels in Turkey, Greece, etc. and of a Cruise in the Black Sea with the Captain Pasha, in the Years 1829, 1830, and 1831,* vol. 1 [Philadelphia: E. L. Carey, 1833], p. 300), actors reportedly supplied the puppet voices.

63. See John Petropoulos, *Politics and Statecraft in the Kingdom of Greece, 1833–1843* (Princeton: Princeton University Press, 1968).

64. de Pouqueville, 1:52.

65. Ibid., 2:134–35.

66. Ibid., 2:134.

67. Ibid., 2:135.

68. de Nerval, pp. 76, 81; Theophile Gautier, *Constantinople* (1856; reprint, Paris: G. Charpentier, 1881), pp. 173, 176–77.

69. Hobhouse, 1:75.

70. Ibid., 1:159–60.

71. de Pouqueville, 2:135.

72. Basgoz, pp. 10–11.

73. Hr. S. Solomonidis, as quoted by Fotiadis, p. 140.

74. M. Michaud and M. Poujoulet, *Correspondance d'Orient: 1830–1831,* vol. 2 (Paris: Ducollet, 1833), p. 197.

75. See Petropoulos, pp. 311–17.

76. Hobhouse, 1:75.

77. Ibid., 1:159–60.

78. Panayiotis Mihopulos, "I Yenisis tu theatru skion ke to prosopo tu Karagiozi," in *Pende komodies ke dio iroike,* ed. Ketis Mazi (Athens: Ermias, 1972), p. 13.

79. Babis Anninos, *Estia* (1888), as quoted by Fotiadis, p. 75.

80. Hatzipandazis, pp. 64–87.

81. *Tahipteros Fimi,* 9 February 1852, p. 3, as quoted by Biris, p. 1066.

82. N. I. Laskaris, *Istoria tou neoelliniku theatru,* vol. 2 (Athens: M. Vasilios and Sons, 1939), p. 249.

83. Even though in the 1802 Turkish performance viewed by Sevin the wedding procession is not even included, it clearly formed a large part of the 1856 performance seen by Gautier (p. 177). Its prominence seems to increase when the performance is censored, under criticism, or performed for a more elite audience. Richard Davey, *The Sultan and His Subjects* (London: Chatto and Windus, 1907), p. 244, provides in 1894 a typical description of another kind of procession, of pilgrims to Mecca, that is clearly used to balance the more risqué elements of a Karagoz performance he viewed. The same situation seems to apply to Athens in 1852.

84. We find the following additional notices of Karagiozis performances during the period: in *Tahipteros Fimi,* no. 130, 18 August 1841, an announcement of a performance in Naflion referring to a debate between Hatziavatis and Kutzuk Memetin (Biris, p. 1066; Puchner, *I valkanikes diastasis,* pp. 32–33). *Stratiotiki zoi en Elladi* (Vrela, 1870) notes that in Halkida in 1856 there was a Karagiozis performance in a cafe every evening (Puchner, *I valkanikes diastasis,* p. 35). In the 1890s, Turkish-style Karagiozis performances were noted in Anafiotika (see *Nea Efimeris,* 15, 16, 17 August 1891; Hatzipanda-

zis, p. 75, footnote 22; Puchner, *I valkanikes diastasis,* p. 41); Kastela (see *Akropolis,* 20 July 1893; Hatzipandazis, p. 76, footnote 29; Puchner, *I val-kanikes diastasis,* p. 41); and in platia Deksameni, to which players came from Constantinople (*Nea Efimeris,* 13 August 1892; Hatzipandazis, p. 76, footnote 28; Puchner, *I valkanikes diastasis,* p. 41). In 1893, Th. Vellianitis, "Ta theatra epi Othonos," *Estia Ikonografimeni,* pp. 321ff., claimed that, after Athens became the capital of Greece, there was no theatrical life there. Only the disgusting Karagiozis was "encamped in a cafe of Vrision in the North still in Turkish possession." It was described as performed with contemporary vulgarities and as satirizing encroaching Western habits (Hatzipandazis, p. 68; Puchner, *I valkanikes diastasis,* p. 30).

Hatzipandazis cites a lack of interest in Karagiozis after 1890 as a result of the popularity of such performances as Fasuli and pantomimes. Puchner ("Erevnitika provlimata stin istoria tu neoelliniku theatru," *Istorika neoelliniku theatru eksi meletimata* [Athens: Rairidi, 1984], pp. 227–28), by contrast, makes the claim that Karagiozis at the end of the nineteenth and the beginning of the twentieth centuries entertained a public larger than all other theatrical performances put together.

85. General Order No. 85, 31 December 1836, as quoted by Fotiadis, pp. 330–32.

86. Ibid., p. 331.

87. *Athinas,* 4 January 1854, in Biris, p. 1069; see also Fotiadis, p. 332.

88. *Athinas,* 8 February 1854, in Biris, p. 1069; see also Fotiadis, p. 332.

89. Yior-gos, "Kalamatianes ikones: Karagiozitis," *Fare,* no. 56, 14 July 1896, as quoted by Spiros Kokkinis, *Andikaragiozis* (Athens: Iridos, 1975), p. 12.

90. *Estia,* 26 July 1894, as quoted by Fotiadis, p. 336. Puchner, *I valkanikes diastasis,* p. 41, makes it clear that both Karagiozis and Fasuli (a puppet performance similar to Punch and Judy) were censored in this instance.

91. *Yeniki Efimerida,* 17 December 1827, as quoted by Fotiadis, p. 73; Puchner, *I valkanikes diastasis,* p. 28.

92. Mavromihalis, *Ellinika Simmikta,* vol. 1, p. 47, Paris, as quoted by Fotiadis, p. 73; see Puchner, *I valkanikes diastasis,* p. 29. We find, as well, a reference by Panayiotis Sofianopulos, *I proodos tu Sofianopulu* (Paris, 1839), to Karagiozis satirizing the four periodicals of this period (see Fotiadis, pp. 73, 206; and Puchner, *I valkanikes diastasis,* p. 29).

93. *Theatis,* 20 July 1837, as quoted by N. I. Laskaris, 1:139.

94. Ibid.

95. J. J. Ampere, *La Grece, Rome et Paris* (Paris: Didier, 1844), as quoted by Fotiadis, p. 206.

96. Ubicini, p. 317.

97. de Pouqueville, 2:135.

98. Hatzipandazis, pp. 64–70.

99. L. S. Myrsiades, "Aristophanic Comedy."

100. See Reich; Nicoll; and Solomos.

101. *Estia,* 1 August 1894, as quoted by Fotiadis, p. 336.

102. Yior-gos, in Kokkinis, pp. 9–13.

103. Ibid., p. 11.

104. See Fotiadis, p. 91.

105. Edmondo de Amicis, *Constantinople,* trans. Caroline Tilton, 4th ed. (1878; reprint, New York: G. P. Putnam, Sons, 1882), p. 139.

106. Adolphe Thalasso, "Molière en Turquie: Étude sur le théâtre de Ka-rageuez," *Le Molièriste*, NS I (1887):262–63.

107. Gustave Flaubert, *Voyage En Orient: Égypte, Palestine, Asie Mineure, Constantinople, Grèce, Italie (1849–1851): Constantine, Tunis et Carthage (1858)*, vol. 2 (Paris: Societé Les Belles Lettres, 1948), p. 552.

108. de Nerval, pp. 84–85.

109. Michaud and Poujoulet, p. 197.

110. Slade, p. 100.

111. Ubicini, pp. 317–18.

112. Ibid., p. 317.

113. Davey, p. 242.

114. Gautier, p. 176.

115. Davey, p. 246.

116. And, *Karagoz*, p. 67.

117. Joseph Pierre Agnes Mery, *Constantinople et a Mer Noire* (Paris: Belin-Leprieur et Morizot, p. 358; see And, *Karagoz*, p. 68.

118. *Fare*, 9 July 1896, p. 2, in Kokkinis, p. 15, footnote 11.

119. *Fare*, 23 June 1896, p. 3, in Kokkinis, p. 16, footnote 11.

120. Filaretos, *Evia*, 1 November 1879, p. 4, in Kokkinis, p. 6.

121. Ibid., p. 7.

122. Fotiadis, p. 91, refers to this as a Karagiozis performance, whereas Puchner (*I valkanikes diastasis*, p. 41) claims it was a performance of Fasuli.

123. See Myrsiades, "Struggle for Greek Theatre," pp. 43–48.

124. Hatzipandazis, p. 69; Karagiozis did not often appear in Athens in the first decade of the rule of George I (1863–1873); it was cultivated almost exclusively in the provinces.

125. Yior-gos, in Kokkinis, p. 12.

126. Filaretos, in Kokkinis, p. 7.

127. Yior-gos, in Kokkinis, pp. 10–11.

128. Ibid., p. 11.

129. Ibid.

130. Ibid., p. 13.

131. Hatzipandazis, p. 87.

132. Ibid., p. 86.

133. Yiro-gos, in Kokkinis, p. 12.

134. G. V. Tsokopulos, "O fasulis," *Parnassos* 15 (1892):215, as quoted by Fotiadis, p. 72.

135. Fotiadis, p. 91.

136. *Estia*, 26 July 1894, as quoted by Fotiadis, p. 336.

137. Hatzipandazis, p. 69. Hatzipandazis examines Karagiozis in the context of a wide range of theatrical performances, from puppet and marionette performances, pantomimes, comic idylls, and improvised comedy to live literary theater. He finds cross-fertilization of Karagiozis, Fasulis, and pantomime in shared heroic, historical, and mythic titles such as *Athanasios Diakos, Katsandonis and Ali Pasha, Napoleon the Great*, and *The Trojan War*. Cross-fertilization of Karagiozis and puppet theater occurs in the following titles: *The Living Dead, The Hero Athanasios Diakos, Paradise and Hell, Genovefa, The Castle of the Demons, The Devil as Best Man, Don Ilias the Pumpkin Head, The Two Brothers, Captain Pasadoros, Armatoles and Klephts*, among others. He cites titles from Greek theater of the period in Rulias's performances of the 1890s: *Faith, Hope, and Charity, The Great*

Jewelry Store and *The Female Thief of Paris,* and *The Eternal Lovers.* From theatrical reviews, he cites Rulias's performance of *The Dreyfus Trial.*

138. Ibid., p. 75.

139. Ibid., pp. 77, 86.

140. Michael Herzfeld, *Ours Once More: Folklore, Ideology, and the Making of Modern Greece* (Austin, TX: University of Texas Press, 1982).

141. Dimitris Tziovas, "The Organic Discourse of Nationistic Demoticism: A Tropological Approach," in Margaret Alexiou and Vassilis Lambropoulos, *The Text and Its Margins: Post-Structuralist Approaches to Twentieth-Century Greek Literature* (New York: Pella, 1985).

142. See Tziovas.

143. See Herzfeld.

144. Puchner, *I valkanikes diastasis,* p. 36.

145. We find in the work of the Karagiozis player Vasilaros, for example, significant influence from popular melodramas and theatrical staples of the live theater in such titles as *The Two Sergeants, The Franco-Austrian War, General Velissaros, The Two Orphans, The Stranger,* and *Genevieve.* See Ap. Yiayiannos, Ar. Yiayiannos, and I. Dinglis, *O kosmos tu Karagiozi,* vol. 2 (Athens: Ermis, 1976), p. 190. Commonly, Greek history plots were directly influenced by poorly constructed patriotic dramas mounted hastily in Athens during the Greco-Turkish War (1897) and the Balkan Wars (1912—1913). Interestingly, Katsandonis was not represented among the heroes presented in those live theater performances. See I. T. Pambukis, "I Turkokratia ke to ikosiena sto repertorio tu theatru skion," *Parnassos* 1 (1968):241—45; Kostas I. Biris, "I leventia tis Rumelis: To Elliniko laiko theatro," *Nea Estia* 61 (1957): 661—68; Dimitris Siatopulos, *To Theatro tu eikosiena* (Athens: Alkeos, 1972); N. I. Laskaris, *Istoria tu Neoelliniku Theatru,* 2 vols. (Athens: M. Vasilios and sons, 1938—1939); and Myrsiades, "Struggle for Greek Theatre," pp. 33—51.

146. Andonios Mollas, O Katsandonis, o Ali Passas, i kira Frosini ke o Karagiozis, in *O Karagiozis tu Molla* (Athens: Deli, [1925]); see also the monster-abduction texts (Ali Pasha, the giant, the Christian-fighter, Captain Gris, forced marriage, Alexander the Great, and the riddle texts), as noted in Linda S. Myrsiades, "Oral Traditional Form in the Karagiozis Performance," *Ellinika* 36 (1985):145—46.

147. Dimitris Manos, *To hani Gravias,* in the Rinovolucri Collection, Center for the Study of Oral Literature, Harvard University (henceforth referred to as Rin.), tape 28—29; Markos Ksanthos, *O Athanasios Diakos,* in Yiorgos Ioannos, *O Karagiozis,* vol. 2 (Athens: Ermis, 1972); Panayiotis Mihopulos, *Astrapoyiannos ke Lambetis,* in *Pende komodies ke dio iroika.*

148. See D. Aleksopulos, *I metania tu listi,* Rin. tape 3; Savvas Yitsaris, *O listarhos Lafuzanis,* Rin. tape 36; Mimis Mollas, *O kapetan Arkudoyiannis,* Rin. tape 30; Sotiris Spatharis, *Astrapoyiannos,* in Sotiris Spatharis and Evyenios Spatharis, *O Karagiozis ton Spatharidon* (Athens: Nefeli, 1979). Distinctions were blurred between the *listes* and the klephts in Karagiozis texts that were influenced by popular lore and the *thrili.* In Sotiris Spatharis's *Fotis Yangulis,* for example (*Apomnimonevmata ke i tehni tu Karagiozi* [Athens, Pergamos, 1960], p. 147), the title figure killed village constables whether they were Turkish or Greek. Yiorgos Haridimos's *Listis Bekiaris* presents a brigand who moves in disguise among the people to learn of their suffering. As Ha-

ridimos explains (interview, January 1987), the brigands were mixed figures who had to die in the end; whatever good they did, they were still murderers and thieves. They were not like the klephts whose purpose was to liberate Greece. The shifting loyalties of the brigands, as well as the confusion expressed in Karagiozis texts between armatoles and brigands, is described in Yiorgos Haridimos's *Davelis*. In this text, the *listi* Megas is pardoned by the queen. Using his experience as a brigand and his knowledge of the mountain hideouts they used, he collaborates with an associate of the brigand Davelis. In an ambush, Megas and Davelis kill each other. While Megas's body is escorted to the palace, Davelis's head is displayed on a pike in the village as a lesson. Other *listi* texts show a similar mix of heroic and antiheroic aspects. Numerous plots are built, for example, around the theme of a pasha who attempts to abduct the daughter of a Greek but is opposed by a popular brigand who, like a godfather, protects the villages in his area (*Twelve on Olympus, The Abduction of Beautiful Helen*).

149. Alkis Kiriakidu-Nestoros, *I theoria tis ellinikis laografias* (Athens: Eteria Spudon, 1978), p. 209.

150. Dimitris S. Lukatos, *Isagogi stin elliniki laografia* (Athens: Morfotiko idrima Ethnikis Trapezis, 1977), pp. 200–1; Fotos Politis, *Eklogi apo to ergo tu ikosi hronia kritikis, II* (Athens: Estias, 1938), p. 147.

151. See Petropoulos.

152. See Tziovas.

153. See Tziovas, p. 270 for his discussion of Dragumis on this issue.

154. See Petropoulos and Vacalopoulos.

155. N. I. Vasiliadis, "To Turkikon theatron o Karagiozis," *Ethnikon Imerologion Skoku* (1895), p. 99, as quoted by Fotiadis, p. 194.

156. Vasiliadis (ibid.) refers to the performance he viewed as made up of three main figures: Karagiozis, Hatziavatis, and the beloved "Vlaha" (a Wallachian type of the rustic) to whom he refers as Babas. In the Turkish performance this Babas was known as Baba Himmet, the woodcutter of Anatolia. Although he is not considered a major figure by either Siyavusgil or Martinovitch, he is given some importance by And, who claims that it is this figure who forms the basis for the highly popular Rumeliote mountaineer, Barba Yiorgos, in the Greek performance. Barba Yiorgos had been presumed by Greek students of Karagiozis to have been created by Mimaros and developed by his student Yiannis Rulias to naturalize the performance as a Greek form in the late 1890s. By And's reasoning, apparently supported by Vasiliadis's notice, the figure did not represent a departure from the Turkish performance. (See And, *Karagoz*, pp. 72–76, in which he refers to an unpublished set of notes by Mario Rinovolucri; both And and Rinovolucri support the position that the Turkish and Greek performances are part of the same cloth.) Vasiliadis speaks, as well, of a "pallikari" or warrior type, about whom plots were fashioned, as the fourth character in the performance he viewed in Constantinople. This figure, called Basimbuzukis, was a brainless hero who stirred up trouble. Rattling his sword, he is said to disentangle and end the plot with one fist. A possible prototype of the hero of the Greek history play (which itself surfaces in the late 1890s in the Greek performance), this figure was probably related to or a form of Tusuz deli Bekir, the drunken and brutal Janissary guard of the serai, and provides yet another tie between the Turkish and Greek forms of this period.

157. Hatzipandazis, p. 75.
158. See I. T. Pambukis, "I Turkokratia ke to ikosiena sto repertorio tu the-atru skion," *Parnassos,* 1, no. 2 (1968):241–45; Kostas I. Biris, "I Leventia tis Rumelis: To Elliniko laiko theatro," *Nea Estia* 61 (1957): 661–68.

159. See Giulio Caimi, whose interviews with players form the basis of his work *Karagiozi ou la comédie grecque;* subsequent publications by players themselves include Sotiris Spatharis, *Apomnimonevmata ke i tehni tu Ka-ragiozi* (Athens: Pergamos, 1960); Panayiotis Mihopulos, "I Yenisis," in *Pende Komodies ke dio iroika;* P. Mihopulos, "O Karagiozis argopetheni," *Rizospastis,* 30 November 1974; Hristos Haridimos, "Ezisa me ton Ka-ragiozi," *Theatro,* no. 10 (July–August 1963):55–58; Andonios Mollas, "O Karagiozis," *To Vima,* 4 January 1949; Mollas, "Isagogi," in *Istoria ke i tehni tu Karagiozi,* by Giulio Caimi (Athens: Kyklos, 1937); Mollas, "O Ka-ragiozis," *Theatro,* no. 10 (July–August 1963):62. For autobiographical tapes collected from twenty-one players in 1969, see L. S. Myrsiades, "A Bibli-ography of Primary Materials for the Study of Karagiozis," *Mantatoforos* 21 (April 1983):15–42. Fotiadis has included materials from interviews in his *O Karagiozis Prosfigas,* pp. 211–62. See also, Sokratis Venardos, *Me ton Sotiri Spathari* (Athens: Rodaki, 1975); Veatrikis Spiliadis, "O Mihopulos mila yia tin tehni tou," *Epitheorisi Tehnis* 22, no. 128 (August 1965):94–97; Aretis Molla-Yiovannos, *O Karagiozopektis Andonis Mollas* (Athens: Kedros, 1981).

160. See Yiannis Kiurtsakis, *Karnavali ke Karagiozis: I rizes ke i metamor-fosis tu laiku yeliu* (Athens: Kedros, 1985).

161. Kiurtsakis, *Karnavali,* p. 375.

162. Rennall Rodd, *The Customs and Lore of Modern Greece* (1892; re-print, Chicago: Argonaut, 1968); John Cuthbert Lawson, *Modern Greek Folklore and Ancient Greek Religion* (1909: reprint, New York: University Books, 1964); C. F. Abbott, *Macedonian Folklore* (1903; reprint, Chicago: Argonaut, 1969).

163. The political role of Karagiozis is treated in the following articles: "O Karagiozis ston polemo ke stin andistasi," *Epitheorisi Tehnis* 22, no. 129 (Oc-tober 1965):270–71; Yiannis Kiurtsakis, "I Kinoniki ke politiki satira tou Karagiozi," *Andi,* 10 Jan. 1976, pp. 25–28; Athanasios Fotiadis, "O Karagio-zis Makronisiotis," *Andi,* 10 January 1976, pp. 28–29; Vangelis Vavanutsos, "O Kinonikopolitikos rolos tu Karagiozi," *Ellinoevropaiki Kinisi Neon* 3 (January 1973):5–14; Vasilis, "O Karagiozis ke i andistasi," *Avgi,* 7 Septem-ber 1975; Mario Vitti, "Compromeso e Ribellione nel' Karagiozis," *Idea* 5, no. 21 (24 May 1953):5; Linda Suny Myrsiades, "Greek Resistance Theatre in World War II," *The Drama Review* 21 (March 1977):99–107; Linda Suny Myrsiades, "Theatre and Society: Social Content and Effect in the Karaghiozis Performance," *Folia Neohellenica* 4 (1982):145–59. [See also a special is-sue on anti-fascist resistance in the arts, *Epitheorisi Tehni* 22, no. 128 (Au-gust 1965).

164. See Kukulas, p. 299, in which he discusses Terzakis's position; see also Lukatos and F. Politis, *Eklogi.*

CHAPTER 2: THE HERO KATSANDONIS

1. John S. Koliopulos, "Military Entrepreneurship in Central Greece Dur-ing the Greek War of National Liberation (1821–1830)," *Journal of Modern*

Greek Studies 2, no. 2 (October 1984):163–87; J. S. Koliopulos, "Shepherds, Brigands, and Irregulars in Nineteenth-Century Greece," *Journal of the Hellenic Diaspora* 8, no. 4 (Winter 1981): 41–53.

2. Social banditry is a widely spread phenomenon in the Mediterranean in Spain, Italy, and Greece. We find it, for example, in the Robin Hood myth in England, with Janosik in Poland and Slovakia, and Diego Corrientes in Andalusia. From the eighteenth to the twentieth centuries it can be documented from Sicily to the Carpatho-Ukraine. See E. J. Hobsbawm, *Primitive Rebels: Studies in Archaic Forms of Social Movement in the 19th and 20th Centuries* (Manchester, England: Manchester University Press, 1959).

3. See Hobsbawm.

4. Yiorgos Haridimos, personal interview, January 1987.

5. Michael Herzfeld, *Ours Once More: Folklore, Ideology, and the Making of Modern Greece* (Austin, TX: University of Texas Press, 1982).

6. Jan Vansina, *Oral Tradition as History: A Study in Historical Methodology* (1965; reprint, Madison, WI: University of Wisconsin Press, 1985).

7. A. Politis, *To dimotiko tragudi* (Athens, 1973).

8. Roderick Beaton, *Folk Poetry of Modern Greece* (Cambridge: Cambridge University Press, 1980), p. 93.

9. We are aware of the debate wherein folklore as a mirror, a reflection, or a projection of culture is disregarded in favor of viewing it as a sphere of interaction in its own right, a social interaction, a communication process, an aesthetic response (Dan Ben-Amos, "Toward a Definition of Folklore in Context," in *Towards New Perspectives in Folklore*, eds. Americo Paredes and Richard Bauman [Austin: University of Texas Press, 1972], pp. 3–15). But folklore is still seen as having a social and cultural base; it is still assumed to carry meaning, to have an intention. We find it, for example, described by Smith (Robert Jerome Smith, "The Structure of Esthetic Response," in *Towards New Perspectives*, pp. 68–79) in terms of both its cognitive aspect (its world view) and its affective aspect (its values), aspects that are central concerns of this study. It has, of course, become less fashionable to accept what Bauman (Richard Bauman, "Differential Identity and the Social Base of Folklore," in *Towards New Perspectives*, pp. 31–41) calls an esoteric perspective, which assumes folklore to be a collective representation of a homogeneous social group, or to discuss folklore as a function of shared identity, a within-group experience. It is now more fashionable to look for direct empirical connections between people and folklore. Moreover, one recognizes that even within the view of folklore as a part of culture, distinctions must be made between folklore that produces guidelines for social action and that which acts as a channel for antisocial motives (Roger D. Abrahams, "Personal Power and Social Restraint in the Definition of Folklore," in *Towards New Perspectives*, pp. 16–30). Nevertheless, there remains in folklore an aspect of shared identity that does contribute to social solidarity and must be studied even though we realize that folklore may be as much an instrument of conflict (Linda S. Myrsiades, "Greek Resistance Theatre in World War II, *The Drama Review* 2, no. 1 [March 1977]:99–107 and "Theatre and Society: Social Content and Effect in the Karaghiozis Performance," *Folia Neohellenica* 4 [1982]:145–59).

10. The intersection of styles that occurred with 150 traveling Karagiozis players criss-crossing the country at the height of popularity of the performance (1910–1940) insured de-localization of the history performance. At the same

time, with apprentices moving freely from player to player, performance texts became mixed, and historical texts that may originally have developed on a regional basis lost their regional characteristics. A hero such as Alexander acted as a magnet attracting material from different historical periods, yet another reinforcement to universalization of the performance, in this instance temporal rather than geographical.

11. See "Katsandonis," *Yeniki pangosmios engiklopedia,* vol. 7 (Athens: Papyros-Larous, 1964), p. 355.

12. Heroes in the Karagiozis performance are treated eponymously rather than personally or truly historically. Indeed, the heroes are so generalized that they are interchangeable with each other from play to play. Thus, Astrapoyiannos is, in one instance, represented as the main figure of an abduction play that incorporates a scene that was always closely identified with the hero—his decapitation by a sub-altern to prevent his being taken alive and his head mutilated and displayed by the enemy, a scene that appears in Mihopulos's *Astrapoyiannos and Lambetis* (in *Pende komodies ke dio iroika* [Athens: Ermis, 1972]). In a second instance, he is presented simply as a monster-slayer (in Andonios Andonaros, *Mavros tis Anatolis,* Rin., tape 42); in a third, he is featured in a romantic triangle that turns into a recognition plot (in Sotiris Spatharis's, *Astrapoyiannos* in *O Karagiozis ton Spatharidon* [Athens: Nefeli, 1979]). The Alexander the Great and Adiohus figures, too, are sometimes interchanged in the main role of the *Riddle* play. (See Yiannis Mustakas, *O Karagiozis ke ta tria enigmata,* in *Dodeka komodies ke to hroniko tu theatru ton skion,* ed. Babis Grammenos [Athens: Angira, 1973]; Vasilis Vasilaros, *Enigmata,* Rin., tape 61; Andonios Mollas, "Antiochus et le lion" in *Karagheuz ou un théâtre d'ombres à Athènes,* vol. 2, ed. Louis Roussel [Athens: Raftanis, 1921]). The most indiscriminately used heroes are the monster-slayers; from Astrapoyiannos, as noted above, to Captain Kissas in Yiorgos Haridimos's play by the same name (Yiorgos Haridimos, *O Karagiozis ke o Kapetan Kissas,* live performance, Athens, 1974) to the klepht Fotis in Spatharis's *Yiangulas Fotis* (in *O Karagiozis Spatharidon*), any number of heroes are considered capable of such a labor.

13. The use of numbers in the history performance illustrates the universalization process as well. Conventional numbers with magical or superstitious significance are, we find, preferred to historical numbers. They are used, for example, in depicting the size of friendly (50 or 100) and enemy (100 to 1000) forces, the disparity between them (10 against 40, 60 against 200), or even the number of times an action is repeated. In Mustakas's *Captain Tromaras* (Athens: Angira), the hero's brother will be hung in two days; Karagiozis has stolen two loaves of bread and claims that he must walk two months to deliver a message to the klepht captain. Sentries in the mountains whistle three times, and three Turks are said to have survived a Greek onslaught. In Mustakas's *Captain Andrutsos,* the battle is begun at 3 A.M. To attack the Greeks in Mihopulos's *Astrapoyiannos and Lambetis* (in *Pende komodies*), the Turks plan to surround the enemy in three concentric circles. Captain Gris is spoken of in both Mustakas's and Ksanthos's *Captain Gris* (in *O Karagiozis,* vol. 3, ed. Yiorgos Ioannos [Athens: Ermis, 1972]) performances as having been in the mountains twenty years; in Mollas's *Katsandonis,* Barba Yiorgos claims he has fought for twenty years, and Yiusuf Arapis applauds Katsandonis as the best he has fought in twenty years.

14. Yiorgos Ioannos's collection of Karagiozis texts uses Ksanthos's version of the first play to represent the whole cycle. See *O Athanasios Diakos ke o Karagiozis kandilanaftis*, in *O Karagiozis*, vol. 2, ed. Ioannos.

15. See Markos Ksanthos, *O Kapetan Gris*, in *O Karagiozis*, vol. 3, ed. Yiorgos Ioannos; Yiannis Mustakas, *O Karagiozis ke o Kapetan Gris*, in *Dodeka komodies*, ed. Babis Grammenos; Markos Ksanthos, *O Karagiozis ke i orfani tis Hiu*, in *Dodeka komodies*, ed. Babis Grammenos; Sotiris Spatharis, *I kakurgos kori*, and *Astrapoyiannos*, in *O Karagiozis ton Spatharidon*.

16. A survey of Karagiozis history plays shows sixty-four different heroes represented in performances. A handful, it appears, are either spurious or so little known that they have importance only as local heroes or as figures through whom some simple, general moral can be illustrated. Of seventy-five heroic texts, twelve are widely performed: *Katsandonis, Athanasio Diakos, Captain Gris, Ali Pasha and Kira Frosini, Alexander the Great and the Cursed Snake, Persecutor of the Christians, The Fall of Patriarch Gregory V, The Black Arab of Anatolia, The Inn of Gravias, The Recognition of Two Brothers, Old Drakos*, and *Astrapoyiannos and Lambetis*. Among the histories performed, unimportant heroes are represented more frequently than major heroes of the period.

Though players from the 1920s–1940s vary in their willingness to list heroic texts in their published repertoires (Andonios Mollas includes two among his thirty-three printed texts, Markos Ksanthos, seven among forty-six, Yiannis Mustakas, seventeen among ninety-two), Yiorgos Haridimos lists in his player's handbook fifty-three heroic performances, almost a third of his total printed texts. Nevertheless, that same player admits to a genuine reluctance to play heroic texts. The heroic cycles, in spite of being reduced in his repertoire to two rather than three evenings, required in his view too much preparation and were too indifferently received by the 1970s to warrant frequent performance. Rather than perform a partial or synopsized version of the longer plays, he prefers the abduction and monster-slaying plays. The most popularly received and widely performed heroic play in both the repertoires of Haridimos and those of his contemporaries is the *Alexander* play. For a more complete list of heroes and heroic titles, see L. S. Myrsiades, "Traditional History and Reality in the View of the Karagiozis History Performance," in *Modern Greek Studies Yearbook*, vol. 1, ed. Theofanis G. Stavrou (Minneapolis: University of Minnesota Press, 1985), pp. 96–108.

17. Yiannis Mustakas, *O Karagiozis, o Ali Pashas ke i Kira Frosini*, in *Nee parastasis Karagiozi* (Athens: Angiras).

18. Andonios Mollas, *O Katsandonis, o Ali Pashas, i Kira Frosini ke o Karagiozis*, 3 vols., in *O Karagiozis tu Molla* (Athens: Deli, [1925]).

19. Yiannis Mustakas, *O Karagiozis ke o Kapetan Andrutsos* in *Nee parastasis Karagiozi*.

20. For the most part, the songs in the heroic texts are not those of specific heroes but are borrowed from a reserve of klephtic songs that are well known and fairly general in their statement and in which generalized incidents, stereotypical personalities, primary emotions, and universal values predominate. Indeed, one alternative to choosing songs from those particularly associated with a given hero in the folk song tradition is for players to maintain their own repertoire of general klephtic songs that they share among themselves.

The pattern of use is not completely consistent from player to player—we find that one song sung by the hero in Manos's and Mollas's *Katsandonis* ("Lads, if brave men and klephts you want to be") is sung as well in Vangos's *Diakos* (Rin., tapes 13, 14, 15). In yet another instance, a poem used in Manos's *Katsandonis* ("Greetings Suliotes") is recited by the hero of Mustakas's *Captain Andrutsos;* indeed, this particular poem is more appropriate to the Karagiozis *Markos Botsaris* play (part of the Suliotes legend) than to either of the former texts. Elsewhere, a song in Ksanthos's *Diakos* ("I started off for Karpenisi") appears, sung by Yero Stamos, in Mihopulos's *Captain Mavrodimos* (in *Pende komodies*). Longas, a klepht in the latter play, sings a song ("The sun came out red") identified in klephtic song collections with Lepeniotis, a more natural addition to a *Katsandonis* rather than a *Mavrodimos* play. (See Arnoldus Passow, ed., *Tragoudia Romaika: Popularia Carmina Graeciae Recentioris* [Athens: Apud Carolum Wilberg, 1860], p. 83.) The song used by Kostas Manos (*O iroas Katsondonis,* vol. 1 [Athens: V. N. Vuniseas], p. 14) for Lepeniotis ("A sea bird") is not specifically identified with Lepeniotis in folk tradition. Certainly, the songs and poems used in the Karagiozis *Katsandonis* text are largely taken from a general store of folk poetry and song and are not specific to the Katsandonis legend.

21. Manos, 1:18.

22. Markos Ksanthos, *I Protomayia tu Karagiozis,* in *Ellinikon Theatron tu Karagiozis* (Athens: Saravanos, Vuniseas ke I. V. Vuniseas, Sia., [1924]), p. 33.

23. Mollas, *O Katsandonis,* 1:18.

24. Panayiotis Mihopulos, *To kafenedaki tu Karagiozi,* in *Pende komodies,* pp. 102–3.

25. Mollas, *Katsandonis,* 1:14.

26. See, for example, the Barba Yiorgos songs in Ksanthos's *O Karagiozis furnaris, O Karagiozis psaras,* and *O Karagiozis stratarhis,* among others (in *Ellinikon theatron*).

27. Studies of interest include Heda Jason, "Concerning the 'Historical' and the 'Local' Legend and Their Relatives," in *Towards New Perspectives in Folklore,* eds. Americo Paredes and Richard Bauman, pp. 134–44; Heda Jason, "A Multidimensional Approach to Oral Literature," *Current Anthropology* 10 (1969):413–26; Alan Dundes, "Folk Ideas as Units of World View," in *Towards New Perspectives in Folklore,* pp. 93–103; J. L. Fischer, "The Sociopsychological Analysis of Folktales," *Current Anthropology* 4 (1963):235–97; Alan Lomax and Joan Halifax, "Folk Songs as Culture Indicators," in *Structural Analysis of Oral Tradition,* ed. Pierre Maranda and Elli Kongas Maranda (Philadelphia: University of Pennsylvania Press, 1971), pp. 235–71; Jan Vansina, *Oral Tradition: A Study in Historical Methodology,* trans. H. M. Wright (Chicago: Aldine Publishing Co., 1965); Vlajko Palavestra, "Tradition, History, and National Feeling," *Journal of the Folklore Institute* 3 (1966):267–76; Kiril Penusliski, "Macedonian Revolutionary Folk Poetry and the National Consciousness of the Macedonian People," *Journal of the Folklore Institute* 3 (1966):250–66; Stavro Skendi, "The Songs of the Klephts and the Hayduks—History or Oral Literature?" in *Serta Slavica in Memoriam Aloisii Schmaus,* ed. Wolfgang Gesemann and Jiri Dankelko (Munich: Rudolf Trofenik, 1971), pp. 660–73.

28. Mustakas, *O Karagiozis ke o Kapetan Andrutsos,* pp. 13–14.

29. Manos, *Katsandonis,* 3:40.

30. A performance viewed in 1918 by Louis Roussel and synopsized in his book, *Karagheuz,* 2:54−55.

31. Conventional scenes from Greek folklore provided the framework for three of the four major events of the play: the capture and murder of Katsandonis's father, the capture and rescue of Katsandonis's supposed wife and son, and the capture and exchange of an invented nephew, Theodore. These scenes expressed common oral traditional compositional principles useful to the Karagiozis player as they capitalized on plot balance (each includes a capture and resolution of that capture), cumulative effect (through the repetition of similar scenes), and variation on a basic theme (each resolves the capture differently, the first by murder, the second by rescue, the third by exchange). Equally important, the scenes represented were already familiar to the Greek audience as scenes common to klephtic ballads, and their universal psychological and cultural truths were generally accessible to that same audience. Other aspects of popular culture also had an influence on the *Katsandonis* text. The general outline of the text is, for example, indebted to the popular novel of Katsandonis's life by Konstantinos Ramfus, *Katsandonis, Klephtic Episodes or a Greek Novel,* published in 1862 (see Yiorgos Ioannos, "Simiomata yia tis komodies pu akoluthun," in *O Karagiozis,* 3:9; and Apostolos Sahinis, "Ta istorika mithistorima tu Steph. Ksenu ke tu K. Ramfu," *Nea Estia* 61 [1957]: 616−19). In this work, Katsandonis kills Veli Gekas and then dissolves the troops of Yiusuf Arapis. He is thereafter captured while sick at a monastery through the cunning of Arapis. A battle of words with Ali Pasha follows, and Katsandonis is martyred. Two particular borrowings of note occur here. First, the figure Kentron in the novel is played in the Katsandonis performance by Karagiozis. Second, a scene in which the hero Katsandonis counsels his young son to go to school and learn his lessons rather than fight in the mountains is adopted for use in the Karagiozis *Katsandonis.*

32. Early performances of the Karagiozis *Katsandonis* text appear in the 1890s by Rulias, in 1901 by Theodorellos, and in 1903 by Levantinos (Thodoros Hatzipandatzis, "I isvoli tu Karagiozi stin Athina tu 1890," *O Politis,* no. 49 (March 1982):81−82.

33. Savvas Yitsaris, *Katsandonis,* Rin., tapes 38, 39, 40.

34. See Helmut Ritter, *Karagos, Turkische Schattenspiele,* vol. 1 (Hanover: Heinz Lafaire, 1941); *Theatro,* no. 10 (July−August 1963); Yiorgos Ioannos, *O Karagiozis,* vol. 1 (Athens: Ermis, 1971); Walter Puchner, *Das Neugriechische Schattentheater Karagiozis* (Munich: Institut fur Byzantinistik und Neugriechische Philologie der Universitat, 1975); W. Puchner, "Sintomi analitiki vivliografia tu theatru skion stin Ellada," *Laografia* 31 (1978):294−324.

35. In a variety of scenes, Mollas explores the pyschology of Vagias as an apostate with a conscience, an intermediary between warring parties, an honest advisor to the pasha, a repentant sinner, and a sympathetic victim of Ali's rage. But Vagias also reverts to type in scenes wherein Mollas capitalizes on the stereotype of a hated apostate, a curse of the Greeks, a shallow, self-seeking character, a fickle lover, ridiculous old man, and a dupe.

36. In his pursuit of Vasiliki, Ali flatters her, appealing to her as a work of art, a piece of white marble. He cajoles, threatens, begs, and makes promises until she is convinced she has no alternative but to marry him. Ali is not here presented as the arbitrary tyrant who took umbrage with Vagias; rather he is a passionate man who, nevertheless, refuses to force the girl he loves into an

involuntary relationship. His great pride requires that she choose him voluntarily, and it is to this end that Ali directs his fullest energies. Here the author provides an ironic comment on the nature of a man who would devote more of his civilized talents to the pursuit of a lovely woman than to the rule of Epirus. In the scenes with Vasiliki, where he is subtle and convincing, Ali is revealed as a man of some depth and much culture. In the scenes dealing with political or military problems, he is typically disloyal, arbitrary, erratic, and headstrong.

37. We find obvious counterpoints and counterbalances missing in scenes involving Karagiozis and Vagias wherein the player seems unaware of the irony when Karagiozis, the Greek agent, is accepted as a trusted Turkish servant, while Vagias, suspect as an apostate, is actually a loyal retainer. In these same scenes, Yitsaris fails to underline parallels and contrasts that occur when Vagias continues to support or recommend vile courses of action, while Karagiozis continues to warn the Greeks; or when Vagias, the cowardly warrior, finds with each new battle a new excuse to avoid service, while Karagiozis with each new Turkish defeat finds an opportunity to recommend that Vagias be thrown into the fray. Although obvious dramatic juxtapositions are maintained (the heroism of Katsandonis, for example, opposed to the brutality of the pasha), those requiring greater depth, motivation, or plotting are obfuscated (for example, religious and psychological differences between Ali, a blasphemer, Vagias, an apostate, and Katsandonis, a true believer, as well as Katsandonis's own brutality as a balance to that of Ali).

38. A number of details, nevertheless, appear to have been borrowed from the text performed by Manos (these same details are absent in Mollas's version), among them the following: Katsandonis is offered soup by the abbot when he begs for water; Katsandonis reveals himself to save the abbot; and Yero Dimos fails to save the hero's wife because he cannot read a warning note. Yitsaris indicates here an awareness of a more developed tradition he might have pursued to profit.

39. The competitiveness of players is apparent throughout players' interviews. D. Mollas, for example, objects to Theodoropulos's failure to integrate his themes in terms of the tradition: "Theodoropulos was never able to tie his themes to tradition. That is to say, he never made his own performances. His work had an individuality. . . . In speech and mimicry he was creative. But, there was something else. He had no connection with his tradition" (Rin., tape 67).

Yitsaris, by contrast, accused Haridimos of being incapable of creating his own works: "His mind doesn't create. Haridimos is seldom sufficient." Haridimos showed the same competitiveness in his comparison of the relative merits of Theodoropulos and his father Hristos Haridimos: "Because Dinos Theodoropulos was educated, he didn't have the power and jokes that my father had. My father had powerful voices. He was powerful and a better mimic than Theodoropulos. . . . Haridimos had life and spirit. Dinos Theodoropulos began free-style Karagiozis. The jokes he spoke were clever but they were heavy. The audience didn't understand them. Haridimos, on the other hand, was one of the people" (Rin., tape 64).

40. *Kefi* is identified in the player's mind with the ability to create *kalamburia* or jokes. The importance to the Karagiozis player of the ability to improvise *kalamburia* can hardly be overstated. Spiropulos sets the tone on this issue:

When I play a scene in which I present the Kolitiria, I use different *kalam-buria* or jokes. You might say one *kalamburi,* whatever it is, whether meant for young or old, and they don't laugh. You deliver others that lean toward love, and they don't like them either. Since they don't laugh with these things, they must like the literary. What can I do, so I gear at least half the work toward the literary. I watch and sneak up on them from behind by placing a phrase, a theft, a duel of frying pans; they like it. So now I prepare again. I pull out something else to create an episode they might laugh at. How about something else? I throw Karagiozis's watering can, the stairs trip the donkey. That's how it's done with the classic pieces. I present something old with various good tricks of my own, various business, so we can laugh. (Rin., tape 68)

Haridimos continues along the same lines in his comments:

I manage the Karagiozis player's exhaustion. This is important from the audience's point of view. Taka, taka, taka, taka, tak, adding the filling, adding the filling, adding the filling, and getting out quickly, players don't last. Deliver the *kalamburia* and bam! I wait for the audience to stop laughing, withdraw, jump into the next one or hold this one with the same words, hit it again, grab the laugh, and lock it up with a golden master-key to get into the theme with gusto. . . . I try to be more brief, to go into the theme and right into the *kalamburia,* because today the audience expects laughs from me and not drama or [themes]. (Rin., tape 64)

41. The ability to develop variants that enrich the tradition is highly prized by Karagiozis players. We found testimony to this effect in an interview with Theodoropulos: "Why did I endure? Why did I create? Why did I do it? How did I manage to stay for six whole months [in one location] . . . and other players couldn't perform? Because I enriched the repertoire. I went to sleep in the evening, and my wife . . . saw me get up at times at 3:00, as soon as something came to my mind, I got up right away to put it down, even if it was only a single letter" (Rin., tape 69).

THE HERO KATSANDONIS: TEXT OF THE PLAY

1. In historical accounts left by eighteenth- and nineteenth-century travelers to Greece, little has survived on Katsandonis. Those that mention him rely to a large extent on folk traditions about the hero; for example, in Claude Charles Fauriel, *Chants populaires de la Grece moderne,* vol. 1 (Paris: Chez Dondy-Dupre, 1824–1825), pp. 161–71; James Emerson, *The History of Modern Greece, From Its Conquest by the Romans B.C. 146, to the Present Time,* vol. 1 (London: Henry Colburn and Richard Bentley, 1830), pp. 438–41; and Eugene Yemeniz, *Scenes et recits des guerres de l'independance Grece moderne* (Paris: Michel Levy Freres, 1869), pp. 25–59. In those accounts that deal rather extensively with the history of Ali Pasha, Katsandonis's nemesis, little or nothing is said of Katsandonis. William Martin Leake in *Travelers in Northern Greece* (1935; reprint, Amsterdam: Adolf M. Hakkert, 1967) discusses Ali in 1:29, 37–50, and in notes from pp. 463–527, but only refers to the death of Katsandonis in 2:551 and Katsandonis's slaying of Veli Gekas in 4:206: "After dinner we have some Klephtic songs, of which the exploits of the Suliote heroes are the subject and those of the celebrated robber Koitz-Andonio, who

slew the no less famous Bolu-bashi Vely Gheghe, sent against him by Aly Pasha." F. C. H. L. Pouqueville (in *Voyage dans la Grece* [Paris: Firmin Didot, 1821]), French counsel to the court of Ali at the height of Katsandonis's career (3:264–460), makes no reference to Katsandonis's exploits in his long description of Ali's career. Thomas Smart Hughes (*Travels in Sicily, Greece and Albania* [London: J. Mawman, 1820]), who devotes almost an entire volume to Epirus and Ali Pasha (in particular 2:121–218), also neglects Katsandonis's career. The same is true of Henry Holland (*Travels in the Ionian Isles, Albania, Thessaly, Macedonia, etc. During the Years 1812 and 1813* [London: Longman, Hurst, Rees, Orme, and Brown, 1815]) who discusses Ali in pp. 103–119 and 175–199, and of John Cam Hobhouse (*A Journey Through Albania and Other Provinces of Turkey in Europe and Asia, to Constantinople, During the Years 1809 and 1810* [London: James Cawthorn, 1813]) who writes extensively on Epirus and Ali's court as Lord Byron's companion on his travels through Greece. Significantly, Katsandonis is not mentioned in either of two important nineteenth-century histories of the Greek revolution: John L. Comstock, *History of the Greek Revolution* (New York: William W. Reed and Co., 1828); and George Finlay, *History of the Greek Revolution* (London: William Blackwood and Sons, 1861). Ali himself is given significant attention in both works as the most prominent Ottoman representative in Greece, second only to the Sultan Mahmud himself (see Comstock, pp. 86–141; Finlay, 1:65–117).

2. The Katsandonis cycle text, according to Karagiozis player Yiorgos Haridimos (1984 interview), is capable of being expanded to as many as five parts, or performances. Haridimos cites the player Vasilaros's expansion of his texts to include a variety of incidents and Manos's elimination and simplification of incidents. Some players, for example, include a battle in Ioannina that Haridimos rejects, citing an encyclopedia to show that Katsandonis was planning such a battle but that he became ill before it could occur. Expansion of the text is possible, Haridimos adds, largely because of the richness of the Ali Pasha figure; he cites here Ali's travels and his contacts with foreigners. Moreover, Haridimos claims that events associated with other heroes (such as the Suliote Markos Botsaris) can be used as if they had occurred to Katsandonis. Finally, Haridimos reveals that besides the traditional text, some players (Mollas and himself among them) maintain a theatricalized version of the Katsandonis performance.

3. Several possibilities exist to explain the origin of Katsandonis's name. (1) It was taken from place names in Epirus: Karakatsanon, Katsanohorion (K. D. Kristallis, "I vlahi tis Pindu, Malakasi," *Evdomas* 4, no. 27 [1891]:5). P. Arravantinos (*Hronografia tis Ipiru*, vol. 2 [Athens: S. K. Vlastos, 1856], p. 77) explains that the Katsanoi (those who came from these villages) probably got their name from the first inhabitants of the area, Katstanu or Katsianu. (2) As E. Frangistas (in *Vios Katsandoni* [Athens: P. I. Vasilios, 1963], p. 11) and Yemeniz (p. 33) claim, he was named after his mother's cry "Kats' Andoni" (which means "sit down, Andonis," or "stay put, Andonis") when, as a boy, he wanted to go into the mountains with the klepht Diplas—by some accounts the godfather who baptized him (see Dimitris Stamelos, *Katsandonis I apotheosi tis palikarias* [Athens: I. K. Kollaros, 1980], p. 61). (3) His name came from *Kitsos* (Hristos) *tu Andoni*, or Kitsos son of Adonis; his father, however, is known to have been called Yiannis (see Evangelos A. Boga, *Ta glossika idiomata tis Ipiru*, vol. 1 [Ioannina: Eterias Ipirotikon Meliton,

1964], p. 168. (4) It comes from *katsizu* from the Vlach *akatsio* meaning "to catch," as he was small and weak as a child (see Stamelos, pp. 41–43. (5)It comes from the Turkish *katzkin*, which means "the hunted one" (Stamelos, pp. 41–43). Yiorgos Haridimos (1984 interview) provides three suggestions from the Karagiozis players. The first repeats the tale of the mother's cry; the second reports that Katsandonis killed an Albanian who stole a goat from his herd and was thus called *Katsiko Andonis* or "Andonis the goat"; the third relates that his name came from the name of his tribe, the Sarakatsani, and that he was thus called *Katsano-Andonis*. The date of Katsandonis's birth is not known. It has been variously estimated from 1770 to 1777; Frangistas's date of 1777 (p. 13) cannot be dismissed easily since he is the son of a member of Katsandonis's band (Katsandonis's first officer Yiannis Frangistas). Petros Spandonidis (*I kleftarmatoli ke ta tragudia tus* [Athens: Difros, 1962], pp. 43–45) claims Katsandonis was born in Piniana of Yiannis Makriyiannis of the Sarakatsaneon clan, who himself was from Vastavetsi (see Stamelos, p. 33), a village sometimes taken as Katsandonis's birthplace. Stamelos (p. 31) has him born in Marathos (Miresi) in Evritanikon Agrafa, a view maintained by Yiorgos Haridimos in a 1984 interview.

4. Katsandonis was not married. Some folk songs do refer to a wife (see note 66), and we find her in a novel on Katsandonis's life by Konstandinos Ramfus, *O Katsandonis, kleftikon episodion i ellinikon mithistorima* (Athens: Koromilas, 1862). Stamelos (p. 276, note 200) denies this information is historical. There is a tradition (reported in Yemeniz, pp. 38–40) of a girl joining Katsandonis's troops to fight beside him, but they were not married; moreover, the songs on which this tradition is supposedly based are not specific to the Katsandonis folk song tradition and do not mention his name (see Arnold Passow, ed., *Tragoudia Romaika: Popularia Carmina Graeciae Recentioris* [Athens: Apud Carolum Wilberg, 1860], pp. 130–32).

5. Yiorgos Haridimos refers to this figure in one place in his 1984 interview as Yiannis Vlahoyiannis (the name traditionally associated with this historical figure) but elsewhere as Yiannis Makriyiannis.

6. The klepht Diplas and not Old Dimas is supposed to have been Katsandonis's godfather.

7. Ali Pasha was born in the mid-eighteenth century between 1741 and 1750 in Tepelini near Ioannina. His family, Albanians of the Hissas clan, had lived there for several centuries (Comstock, p. 94). The milestones of Ali's rise to power would include Ali's collaboration with the Russians in their effort to capitalize on dissension within the Ottoman Empire to facilitate its breakup. At the same time, he was appointed by the Ottoman Sultan to the position of Pasha of Thessaly. He went on to attack and enter Ioannina by deceit and brought the Sultan to accede to his rule over Epirus. Thereafter, he bribed his way into becoming Pasha of Rumeli and annexed Arta.

Ali was reportedly (in an official report to the British Embassy, see Comstock, p. 136) assassinated February 1822 by Mohammed Pasha, governor of Morea. In 1820 Ali had tried to have Pacho Bey assassinated in Constantinople, for which he was excommunicated and Pacho Bey was made Pasha of Ioannina (Comstock, pp. 129–30). Ali joined with Greek and Albanian Christians, Montenegrins, and Serbians to revolt against the Sultan, whereupon the Sultan ordered Ali's assassination (Comstock, pp. 130–37; Finlay, 1:116).

8. Manthos was one of Ali's private secretaries (Comstock, p. 132). The

player Yiorgos Haridimos (interview 1984) refers to him as an advisor to Ali like Psalida (the Kantian schoolmaster and author) and de Pouqueville (the representative of France to Ali's court), an indication of the confusion that occurs between oral and historical traditions. Haridimos further gives him the family name of Ikonomos.

9. Haridimos (interview 1984) says Dionisios, a stock figure of the Karagiozis troupe (the effete dandy from Zakynthos), can be used as Kentron.

10. Leake (1:39) refers to two men Ali kept always near him: "Tatza Bulubashi, a Musulman, and Athanasi Vaia, a Christian, the ready instruments of many an atrocious act of cruelty."

11. Veli Gekas was one of Ali's most well-known officers. His death in battle against Katsandonis is one of the three highlights of Katsandonis's historical career (the other two being his call for a conference of armatoli or armed militia [see note 14] at St. Mavra, in Levkas [Kerkira], and his horrible death by torture).

12. Yiusuf Arapis is referred to by Leake (1:38) as a person in whom Ali placed much trust—"extremely attached to his master, brave, ferocious, active, and cruel." Yemeniz (p. 36) refers to Yiusuf as a man known for his excessive cruelty; Emerson (p. 495) says he was Ali's right hand, "a wretch equal to his master in atrocity."

13. St. John of the Lice: the name of the monastery, Konithari, suggests a refuge for the unclean or ill. Saint John Prodromos, or Forerunner, was himself a physician known for curing fevers. The monastery is located near Paliokatuna in the Agrafa mountains, according to Stamelos, p. 163.

14. According to Comstock (p. 86), the plains of Epirus were sparsely populated for the Christians, departing before the Ottomans, fled into the mountains and armed themselves. Bands of militia or armatoli were organized by Ottoman governors to guard the mountain passes against armed marauders or klephts. Supported by local Greek primates who had much to lose from the klephts, who pilfered from Christians and Turks alike, the armatoli were made up of Greek Christians, who knew the mountains well, as well as Albanian Christians and Muslims.

Finlay (1:29) makes the point that there was a constant interchange of troops between the armatoli and klephts and that the fabled klepht bands of the Ottoman period were less a force of Greek patriotism than a mixed bag of mercenaries, many of whom switched freely from crescent to cross and back again (Comstock, p. 93): "The patriotic brigands of modern Greek poetry are a creation of yesterday. Even at the commencement of the present century, several of the most numerous bands in Macedonia consisted of as many Mussulmans as Christians, and Albanians were always more numerous in their ranks than Greeks." See, on this point, John S. Koliopoulos, "Military Entrepreneurship in Central Greece During the Greek War of National Liberation (1821–1830)," *Journal of Modern Greek Studies* 2, no. 2 (October 1984): 163–87; and J. S. Koliopoulos, "Shepherds, Brigands, and Irregulars in Nineteenth Century Greece," *Journal of the Hellenic Diaspora* 8, no. 4 (Winter 1981):41–53.

15. Andonios Mollas, in a dictated synopsis, states that his performance of the *Katsandonis* text (in Louis Roussel, *Karagheuz ou un théâtre d'ombres à Athènes*, vol. 2 [Athens: Raftanis, 1921], pp. 54–55) opens in Ioannina with Ali Pasha after Veli Gekas has been killed; Haridimos, in a dictated synopsis

(Braithwaite tapes, Center for the Study of Oral Literature [hereafter referred to as Bra.], tapes 1–2), has his text open in a Greek village after Katsandonis's wife and son are taken captive by Veli Gekas.

16. Ali's reputation among foreign travelers varies between Holland's view (p. 118) of him as a protector of his people (" . . . Albania is more happy and prosperous under this single and stern dominion, than when divided among numerous chieftains, and harassed by incessant wars") and Finlay's view (1:29) of him as an opportunist ("Ali was often accused of neglecting to suppress the depredations of the klephts, in order to extend his power as dervendji-pasha"). Leake (4:220–226) claimed he plundered his Muslim neighbors and favored his Christian subjects, while Holland (pp. 195–196) found the Albanians to be his real source of power since he made neither the Turk nor the Greek happy. Comstock (p. 129) borrows the most common, popular view of Ali as a "modern Herod."

17. It is common in Greek to address people by the first name preceded by "kir" (Mr.), as in "kir Manthos" (Mr. Manthos). Since "Mr." is not used in English with first names in this way, it is omitted in the translation.

18. According to Yiorgos Haridimos (1984 interview), Hatziavatis, who plays the Manthos role in the *Katsandonis* text, acts as a chorus. It is important, as Haridimos explains, that he appear in the first substantive scene of the text, for he introduces us to the play and establishes prior events. He acts as an intermediary between the serai (of the Turkish pasha) and the hut (the common Greek's domicile), Haridimos goes on, to bind the opposite aspects of the performance.

19. The repetition of proper names is important in shadow puppet theater so that the audience clearly understands which figure is speaking.

20. Comstock (p. 115) declares that, as Viceroy of Rumeli in 1800, Ali was charged to collect provincial taxes for the Ottoman treasury. He increased the percentage required to a share of three out of every five, or 60 percent, of the goods of the area and kept two-fifths for his own trouble. Hobhouse (1:120) puts the share at one-tenth, of which Ali himself received one-fourth.

21. Yiorgos Haridimos (1984 interview) claims that Karagiozis players needed a historical figure to play the role of a traitor and chose Vagias because he moved and excited audiences. Known for his role in the massacre of the Gardikiotes (see note 46), Vagias would have been a clearly recognizable figure. Nevertheless, Haridimos believes that Vagias was not historically a traitor.

22. Non-Greek-speaking characters are inconsistent in their grammatical usages and are characterized by distinctive verbal tics. Ali's distinctive vocalism is "Damn it."

23. Literally "he can break his back waiting for me."

24. Travelers to Greece and historians of the Greek revolution create the impression that two events held an interest equal to that of the Greek resistance to Ottoman rule. These were the territorial wars between the pashas (Arravantinos, vol. 1), in which Ali played a central role, and the interference of foreign powers, which resulted in a series of realignments of warring forces in the Ottoman Empire (John W. Baggally, *Ali Pasha and Great Britain* [Oxford: Basil Blackwell, 1938]). All three forces contributed to the breakup of the Ottoman Empire. The latter two events are not, however, reflected in the *Katsandonis* text, which deals exclusively with Greek affairs.

25. Stage directions are written in Puristic Greek and were probably provided by publishers based largely on their experience in publishing literary drama. Act and scene divisions are based on the same experience and do not reflect actual performance divisions or conditions.

26. Like Ali, Veli Gekas has a distinctive verbal tic; Veli's is "Phew." These tics were another way audiences could distinguish between characters when they spoke.

27. Yiorgos Haridimos (1984 interview) explains that Ali calling for his pipe is used as a joke to break up the monotony of the scene. Haridimos contrasts this break in his performance with a scene that follows in which Manthos waxes patriotic.

28. Folk tradition attributes Katsandonis's career as a klepht to his desire to revenge his family and tribe, which had been impoverished by Ali Pasha. He sold his flocks, burned his fold and huts (Fauriel, p. 163; Emerson, p. 438), and joined his godfather Diplas in the mountains when he was about twenty-five-years old in 1802 (Stamelos, p. 61). In an alternate version, Katsandonis knew of the klephts from his life as a shepherd and, according to Yemeniz (p. 32), joined them as a result of having been unjustly thrown into jail by the order of a local Turkish ruler. Ransomed and set free, he swore vengence, caught a sentry in a deserted place, and threw the body into a precipice. A third opinion is expressed by the Karagiozis player Yiorgos Haridimos (1984 interview) who claims that Katsandonis, having killed an Albanian who stole a goat from Katsandonis's herd, had to flee from persecution.

29. Raki is a potent drink distilled from leftover grapeskins after the vintage.

30. Angelos Hatzimihalis, *Sarakatsani*, vol. 1 (Athens, 1957), pp. 27–28, cites numerous hideouts for Katsandonis throughout Agrafa and Thessaly, largely on the mountains of Akarnania, Etolia, and Pindos, which make up the territory of the Sarakatsani.

31. Uncle George's (or Barba Yiorgos) first entrance onto the screen in each performance is traditionally handled by an entrance dressing scene that serves as a parodic comment on rites of initiation or dedication, commonly found in oral epics and romances, in which a warrior setting off on a mission of deep significance is dressed in ornamental clothing and arms that signal his role as a hero. In the heroic dressing scene, the arming of the hero has meaning. The dressing may proceed, as does that of Alexandros in Homer's *Iliad,* Book III (*The Iliad of Homer,* trans. Richmond Lattimore, [Chicago: University of Chicago Press, 1961] pp. 330–338), from bottom to top and from clothing to weapons, in order of progressively greater importance, or, as with Basil Akritas in the Byzantine epic *Digenes Akritas* (trans. John Mavrogordato [Oxford: Clarendon Press, 1963] lines 1199–1208), it may proceed from top to bottom, more or less in the order one normally dresses. The point of greatest detail, central focus, or significance culminates the scenes. The dressing of Barba Yiorgos, on the contrary, represents an inversion of the heroic order. The framework for the scene is established when the hero calls his domestic staff, the women of the household (in early instances merely one housekeeper serves him), to gather round him. See L. S. Myrsiades, "Oral Composition in the Karaghiozis Performance," *Theatre Research International* 5 (1980): 113–15.

32. Yiannis Mustakas's *O Karagiozis ke o iroas Katsandonis* (Athens: Papadimitrios [c. 1945]) does not include the scene in which Katsandonis is miss-

ing and his troops are worried. He replaces it with a scene in which Katsandonis and his soldiers wonder why Veli Gekas has not been seen lately and what tricks he is up to.

33. Yiorgos Haridimos (1984 interview) claims that Katsandonis was known as a small child for getting lost in the mountains; he describes this incident as strange and like what happened to Christ (perhaps a reference to Christ in the temple as a child). He compares the child Katsandonis to the classical hero Heracles and the Byzantine hero Digenis Akritas, asserting that he was first in running, first in everything.

34. The wars (1792–1803) between Ali Pasha and the heroes of Suli (Fotos Tzavellas and Kitsos Botsaris) were the central events in Ali's relations with the Greeks, eclipsing the events of Katsandonis's career in travelers' memoirs and Greek histories of the revolution (see Comstock, pp. 118–121; and Finlay, 1:51–63).

35. Yiorgos Haridimos (1984 interview) says he has Katsandonis decide to burn the warehouse and then sing a song to break the monotony.

36. Two different traditions have developed around Katsandonis's rise from Captain Diplas's subaltern to a captain himself. Fauriel reports (pp. 155–156) that Katsandonis masqueraded as Captain Diplas when the latter's troops were surrounded by the enemy. Diplas identified himself and was killed; Katsandonis escaped and became chief of the band. Yemeniz (p. 35), on the contrary, believes that Diplas was so impressed by Katsandonis's skill that he voluntarily relinquished command to Katsandonis. Attacked by the enemy, Diplas claimed he was Katsandonis; his head was cut off and taken to the pasha in Ioannina where the mistake was recognized and the head spoke: "Tremble Ali. Katsandonis fights still in Agrafa" (Yemeniz, pp. 46–47).

37. One folk tradition (reported in D. Lukopulos, *Sta vuna tu Katsandonis* [Athens: I.N. Sideris, 1934], pp. 141–43) gives Katsandonis a sister who was taken to Ioannina by Albanians; unaware that Katsandonis is her brother, she falls in love with him. Lukopulos cites two songs in Passow (Passow, pp. 130–32) here, but neither is in the Katsandonis folk song tradition nor is there any other indication that these songs refer to or are associated with Katsandonis.

38. Both Holland (pp. 195–96) and Leake (4:222) deny the popularly held view that Ali was a zealous Muslim intent on converting Christians; Holland holds, however, that Ali was superstitious. The tale of Vasiliki—reported in de Pouqueville (3:339–340)—of a Christian girl taken into Ali's harem (c.1800) and allowed to keep her faith supports their view.

39. Hughes (3:183) identifies Athanasios Psalidas as a schoolmaster who represented Ali Pasha on a mission to the French representative at Corfu. Hobhouse (1:572–74) refers to him as a schoolmaster in Ioannina and author of several treatises. Emerson (p. 546) adds that Psalidas was a disciple of Kant entrusted by the vizir with what became one of the most eminent schools in Greece.

40. Mukevelis: from the Turkish *mutevelli*, the chief trustee of a vakif.

41. Literally, "damn their parents."

42. Literally, "and next year may God grant both of you a good forty days and boiled wheat."

43. Piastre: original reference is to a *grosi*, a Turkish coin of small value.

44. This is a play on a possible origin of Katsandonis's name: Katsiko-Andonis, or "goat-Andonis," referring to his years as a goatherd.

45. Play on words between *yiauri* "a Greek" and *yaıduri* "a donkey."

46. Comstock (pp. 125–95), Finlay (1:81), Hughes (pp. 191–96), and Holland (p. 104) report that Ali's mother and sister were taken hostage in the Muslim village of Gardiki and were treated brutally; Ali himself, according to Holland (p. 104), escaped. Forty years later, in 1812, Ali massacred the town's eight hundred inhabitants. Muslim troops were reportedly reluctant to participate in the surprise attack on the villagers, who had been invited by Ali to a banquet in an enclosed courtyard. The work was left to Greek and Albanian troops led by Athanasias Vagias (Finlay, 1:82–83).

47. Yiorgos Haridimos (1984 interview) explains that Manthos's overhearing is used to provide Karagiozis with a role as messenger to Katsandonis.

48. Katsandonis is described in Karagiozis texts as a giant and a genie. Originally carried as a motif in classical myths, the view of the hero as a giant was most immediately borrowed from Ramfus's novel (p. 100), which presents Katsandonis as tall, manly faced and agile. Fauriel (p. 135), Emerson (p. 438), and Yemeniz (p. 30), on the contrary, describe Katsandonis as small, thin, and sickly looking but spirited. Yemeniz describes him as "grele et maladif" and claims that his condition defied the prophecy at his baptism by an armatole that he would have "une vie agitee et glorieuse" (Yemeniz, p. 29). The tale is also told (Yemeniz, p. 31) that one night in front of his tent as the sun set, Katsandonis saw a Muslim pilgrim who asked for hospitality. The pilgrim became ill for several weeks and Katsandonis cared for him. When he recovered, he gave Katsandonis a silver amulet with an Arabic inscription on it. Thereafter, Katsandonis was strong and hardy.

As Herzfeld points out, folk tradition held that the ancient Hellenes were a race of mythical giants, very likely the source for the depiction of Katsandonis as a giant (Michael Herzfeld, *Ours Once More: Folklore, Ideology, and the Making of Modern Greece* [Austin, TX: University of Texas Press, 1982], p. 126).

49. Clogs: a reference to *tsaruhia,* the pom-pom-tipped shoes worn by Greek mountain fighters.

50. Wheat refers to the custom of boiling wheat to make *koliva,* a dish provided for guests after the forty-day service in memory of one who has died.

51. Hobhouse (1:109–24) describes Ali's beard as a prominent feature in a description of him: "The Vizir was a short man, about five feet five inches in height, and very fat, though not particularly corpulent. . . . His beard was long and white, and such a one as any other Turk would have been proud of; though he . . . did not continue looking at it, nor smelling and stroking it, as is usually the custom of his countrymen, to fill up the pauses of conversation." We find additional physical descriptions of Ali in Hughes (2:210–18) and Holland (p. 125). The Ali Pasha puppet used in the Karagiozis performance has a long white beard.

52. Hotzas: a Muslim priest.

53. Literally, "damn your ancestors."

54. Literally, "to get drops."

55. Literally, "to your bad time."

56. This is a play on *skales* (stairs) and *stales* (drops).

57. Literally, "May wrath take him."

58. An endearing form of the name Angeliki.

59. Kentron's monologue on his donkey is elaborated in performance through improvisation to constitute a whole scene. Yiorgos Haridimos claims it is important to cater in this way to the audience if a player wishes to perform

histories. He makes clear that the histories, like the comedies, characteristically include and are inspired by improvisation:

> I try to be more brief, to go into the theme and right into the *kalamburia* [jokes], because today the audience expects laughs from me and not drama or [themes]. Yesterday, I played *Yenitsaros* and one scene included drama. It needs art, it needs acting. I showed my public what my art is. . . . I'll keep playing [my heroic plays] because my playing is so fine. . . . [Other players] bring [the figures] out, they kill them, they create battles. Myself, I refine [the performance] so it will emerge more sweetly, more sweetly, to emerge more sweetly. . . . I put on *Yenitsaros* for them with his kilt, I put on *Gris* for them. All this is a try-out to get my bearings. And suddenly, I have it, bam, *Diakos*. Keep in mind that *Diakos* can be a drama, but even while drama must be dramatic, it has plenty of *kalamburia*. (Rin., tape 64)

60. Literally, "Oh, my little mother."

61. This is a play on *fukaras* (sucker) and *sfugaras* (sponge seller).

62. Yiorgos Haridimos (1984 interview) explains that in the folk tradition Veli Gekas and Katsandonis were considered blood brothers.

63. Literally, "What do you mean a stew, it's even a casserole."

64. The theme of sending letters plays a large role in demotic folk songs and was probably borrowed from there by the Karagiozis performance. In one major stream of Katsandonis folk songs, Katsandonis sends a letter to Veli Gekas who is eating at a priest's house; Katsandonis challenges him to fight in single combat at Kiravrisi. A variant on their meeting has Veli scouring the mountains and ravaging villages looking for Katsandonis (reported along with the letter version in Fauriel, p. 165). A third view, presented in D. Lukopulos, "Thimisis apo tu hrisu ton Agrafon," *Imerologion Megalis Ellados* (1932): 155–57, holds that chief shepherd Galanos sent a letter to Veli Gekas betraying Katsandonis's whereabouts. A pretense, the letter was designed to lead Veli Gekas into an ambush. Katsandonis is reported by Yemeniz (pp. 40–41) to have sent a similar letter to Dervenaga Hassan Belussis. They met, but Belussis fled and was wounded.

65. Literally, "blessed one."

66. Yiannis Mustakas in his *Katsandonis*, p. 19, uses an adumbrated song variant here (dated 1807 in Spandonidis, pp. 250–51) in which Katsandonis receives a letter advising him that Veli Gekas has seized his wife and child and taken them hostage to Ali Pasha in Ioannina. Spandonidis dates this song earlier than the novel on Katsandonis's life by Konstandinos Ramfus in 1862. This dating would make the song the source of giving Katsandonis a wife and child and having them kidnapped by Veli Gekas, whereas Yiorgos Ioannos, *O Karagiozis* (Athens: Ermis, 1972), has credited the novel with these additions (3:9).

67. Literally, "I should give you my word who I am?"

68. The song sung here is from a variant of one of the minor folk songs about Katsandonis. There are five different sets of songs about Katsandonis in the demotic tradition. The two major streams of songs follow:

I. A. Opening
       1. The birds sing (or)
       2. Katsandonis has a dream (or)

3. Yiorgos Hasiotis goes for water
B. Katsandonis is discovered by the Turks at a cave
C. Katsandonis's brother Yiorgos fights for their freedom
D. Katsandonis asks that his head be cut off by his brother
E. Muhuntaris, sent by Ali, captures them both

See John W. Baggally, *Greek Historical Folksongs* (Chicago: Argonaut, 1936), p. 72; Stamelos, p. 185; Spandonidis, pp. 14, 254; Passow, pp. 78–81; and Apostolos Melahrinos, *Dimotika tragudia* (Athens: Karavakos, 1946), pp. 36–37.

II. A. Veli Gekas eats at a priest's home
     B. Katsandonis sends a letter challenging him
     C. Veli Gekas is killed with three shots
     D. Veli Gekas asks that his comrades take his head
     E. Ali Pasha bites his beard at the news

See Baggally, *Greek Historical Folksongs*, p. 71; Stamelos, pp. 112, 116; Passow, pp. 76–78; Fauriel, pp. 172–79; Melahrinos, p. 137; and N. G. Politis, *Eklogi apo ta tragudia tu elliniku lau* (Athens: Vagionakis, 1966), pp. 72–74. The three minor streams include the following:

I.   A. Katsandonis is told to stay in Europe and become a captain
     B. He decides to go to Karpenisi (Passow, p. 80)
II. A. Katsandonis raids Christian villages, takes women and money, wastes churches, and makes slaves (see Baggally, *Greek Historical Folksongs*, p. 70; Passow, p. 82)
III. A. Katsandonis is identified as having a wife and child
     B. He asks they be told he has been betrayed; or he receives news they have been taken hostage

See N. G. Politis, p. 74; Spandonidis, pp. 250–51. One additional song occurs in which Katsandonis is featured as a minor player. His chief Diplas is told to flee and take his subaltern Katsandonis with him, for Muhurntaris has been sent with several thousand men (see Passow, pp. 75–76; Fauriel, p. 157). Two songs deal with Ali Pasha (Fauriel, pp. 348–53; Passow, pp. 166–67); in both, Ali speaks well of the Greeks, citing the heroism of the Suliotes, their preference for death over slavery, and their loyalty. He concludes in a version included in both Passow and Fauriel that whoever tries to subjugate them makes a great mistake and that they should receive their freedom. An epic song on Ali Pasha is included in Leake, 1:463–97; this song, however, was composed not in Greek but in Albanian.

69. Katsandonissa: the feminine form of Katsandonis.

70. *Fustanella* is the kilt worn by mountain fighters in Albania and Greece since Byzantine times. This skirt was the costume of the Byzantine border guard.

71. Literally, "when all my blood will have left."

72. Yiorgos Haridimos (1984 interview) explains that Veli Gekas must die in hand to hand combat since he is a warrior (*pallikari*) and no one but his equal (Katsandonis, his blood brother) can kill him. When Katsandonis kills Veli Gekas, Haridimos has him bow and kiss him; Katsandonis's men accompany the body and fire a salute.

73. Stamelos (p. 116) places Veli Gekas's death in the area of Prosiliako between the villages of Miresi and Agrafa. Yiorgos Gazis, *Viografia ton iroon Marku Botsari ke Karaiskaki* (Agina, 1828), p. 17, holds that Karaiskakis, at that time one of Katsandonis's band but later to become a renowned figure himself, killed Veli Gekas: " . . . when Karaiskakis was with Katsandonis he killed . . . Dervenaga Veli Gekas by his own hand." But the same work (p. 67) also refers to "Dervenaga Veli Gekas who was killed by the famous Katsandonis." Leake (4:206) holds to the more traditional view that Katsandonis killed Veli Gekas.

The date of Veli Gekas's death is also in dispute. Folk songs confound the issue by reporting the date as "15 May the twentieth of the month" and "12 May 18 August." Stamelos (pp. 256–58, note 124) holds that it was May 1807, although Hristoforos D. Grammenos, in *Iera moni panagia i Katusiotissa anthiru argitheas karditsis* (Athens, 1976), p. 57, reports that in the Book of Remembrance found in the outer narthex of the Thessalian monastery of the Virgin of Katusiotissa, it reads that in "1806 . . . Veli Gekas was killed. Katsandonis ambushed him; . . . he was killed with four other people."

74. Yemeniz (pp. 35–38) reports that it was the battle with Yiusuf and not with Veli Gekas that took place after Ali's capture and murder of Katsandonis's mother and father (whose bodies, like Katsandonis's, were supposed to have been thrown into the lake at Ioannina). According to Yemeniz (p. 35), Katsandonis sent Ali a blank page "brulee aux quatre coins," an Albanian declaration of war. He then took out his vengeance on the surrounding villages, his prisoners, and hostages. In retaliation, Ali sent Yiusuf to take hostages from the village of Katuna on a forced march to Ioannina. Katsandonis's troops waited in ambush and massacred Yiusuf's troops. This event is probably the model for the capture and forced march of Katsandonis's wife and son and for the massacre of Veli Gekas and his troops in the Karagiozis text.

75. The use of a monk's cassock as a disguise is interesting, considering the ambivalence that appears in Katsandonis folk material over the role of the clergy. In the folk song tradition, we find a priest identified as the possible betrayer of Katsandonis, and we see Veli Gekas eating at a priest's house when he receives Katsandonis's letter of challenge to single combat. Both Mollas (pp. 233–234) and Manos (3:38) use a song in their *Katsandonis* texts in which Katsandonis, following his capture at St. John's monastery, calls for burning the abbot, the monastery, and the traitor monk Karderinis. Although we find in the *Katsandonis* text that a priest is called to read the letter of warning to Yero Dimos, he is barely trusted and is summarily dismissed before any plans are discussed to get the news to Katsandonis. The tradition in which the monk Makarios was supposed to have been an aide to the historical Katsandonis is reflected in a Haridimos synopsis of his *Katsandonis* text (Rin., tape 64) in which a priest is taken prisoner with Katsandonis; he interprets a dream for Ali and is asked to pray for him.

76. The calling together of the armatoli in Agia Mavra, Levkada (Kerkira), is considered, together with Katsandonis's slaying of Veli Gekas, a highlight of Katsandonis's career. Nevertheless, there is little historical evidence of Katsandonis's role in that conference. The conference is reported in the 1 July 1807 issue of *Efimerida tis Agias Mavras* (see Stamelos, p. 133), in which Katsandonis is listed as one of four chiefs (the others were Kitzos Botsaris, Skilodimos, and Kumbaros). He is also registered with the rank of major in a list of

those who attended the conference in the *Arhiofilakio Levkadas* (see K. I. Mahera, *Politiki ke diplomatiki istoria tis Levkadas* [*1797–1810*], vol. 2 [Athens, 1954], p. 559). Stamelos concludes (p. 137) that Katsandonis was recognized as the chief of the klephts at this meeting. Nevertheless, Katsandonis became ill and Emerson (pp. 500–503) reports that the meeting resulted in an insurrection led by Enthimias Vlahavas, which was put down by Ali Pasha.

77. John Anthony Kapodistrias (1776–1823) was born in Corfu. He served for thirteen years in the Russian diplomatic service before being elected president of the Greek Republic in 1827. He was assassinated.

78. Play on words: *afentiko* (master) and *apondiko* (for *Pondiki*, mouse).

79. Dervenagas is a title used for one in authority, a local Turkish ruler.

80. A fictitious figure, representing a Westernized Greek.

81. Katsandonis fought against a number of officers sent by Ali Pasha. Indeed, the tradition grew up that Ali repeatedly sent forces against Katsandonis (Emerson, pp. 438–39). Those forces and the order in which they fought Katsandonis are as follows: Yiusuf Arapis (and his lieutenant Kutzumustafabey), Iliasbey, Hassan Belussis (and his bey Aga Vassiaris), Veli Gekas (and his lieutenant Bekir Giocador), Muhurntaris, and Alios Beratis.

82. The whole issue of force size and losses in battle is tinged with romanticism: Hughes (2:148), for example, reports that Tzavellas with a force of two hundred lost only twenty men, while the three hundred Albanians against him lost five hundred men. The usually reliable Hughes has this to say, however, in his defense: "It is scarcely possible to conceive how the loss on each side could be so disproportionate, nor did I believe it myself until I saw the scenes of action, where numbers must have created confusion instead of being advantage, and where the party attacked had such a superiority from its power of concealment" (Hughes, 2:148). The number of troops sent against Katsandonis varies considerably in period sources. For example, L. Frangistas's source (p. 30) claims that Veli Gekas took eight hundred; Fauriel (p. 165) says it was in the thousands, and Yemeniz (p. 43) estimates the force of twenty-five to thirty-hundred men or ten times greater than the force he credits Katsandonis with. Arravantinos (2:283) is much more moderate in his estimate of the fifty to three hundred man force Muhurntaris took to capture Katsandonis at the cave.

83. Literally, "I became a pilot."

84. Mustakas in his *Katsandonis* text has Theodore sent to Levkada as a monk. He does not, however, return in the text; the scenes of his capture and exchange are thus omitted.

85. Onufrio and Lavrentio are saints after whom monasteries in Platanon, the site at which Katsandonis was martyred, were named. A village grew up around each of these monasteries, heightening their importance.

86. Literally, "My son, Alexander, let me kiss you."

87. Literally, "To your health."

88. Literally, Kostas: "Glory be to God." Kentron: "And from the clever one, amen."

89. A reference to the Thessalian headquarters of the Tsaros family of klephts—an important meeting place.

90. Yiorgos Haridimos (1984 interview) explains that Hatziavatis or a passing shepherd can be used to arrange the trade for Theodore.

91. Literally, "My little mother."

92. Dervens refers specifically to narrow mountain spaces and passages, but also carries the meaning of territories.

93. The church was caught in a peculiar position during both Ottoman rule and the Greek revolution. It provided stability and retained its independence under the millet system of Ottoman rule, whereby national groups in the empire were allowed to govern themselves to a large extent while paying tribute to the Sultan. Nevertheless, it provided during the revolution a number of heroes, including Patriarch Gregory the Fifth and the Deacon Athanasios Diakos; and a monk, Makarios of Osia Lukas from Agia Mavra, is held by Stamelos (p. 241) to have served as an aide to Katsandonis.

94. Katsandonis is reported to have been wounded or to have contracted a "maladie de langueur" (Yemeniz, p. 50) and to have gone to Agia Mavra for therapy (see Stamelos, p. 219) with European doctors in 1806 (Yemeniz says 1808, p. 50). He is reported to have later caught smallpox in Agia Mavra at the convocation of the armatoli in July, 1807. He left for the monastery of St. John near Paliokatuna (Stamelos, p. 163). An important piece of testimony regarding Katsandonis's sickness was preserved in the Codex of the Monastery of the Virgin of Paliokarias near Olympus. It reads, "In the year 1807 . . . one Katsandonis, a Captain of Agrafa, came with 500 troops and struck all the villages of Agrafa as far as Metsovon. And in this year, the Captain was lost; they took him alive as he was ill with smallpox" (D. Lukopulos, "Apo ena kodiko dialimenu monastiriu tu Olimpu," *Imerologion tis megalis Ellados* [1936]:128).

95. The folk song tradition largely reports that Katsandonis left the monastery where he first rested with his sickness, for he was afraid he would be discovered there by Ali's troops (although one song [Spandonidis, p. 14] has Katsandonis caught at the monastery). Lukopulos (*Sta vuna*, pp. 197–99) identifies the cave to which he fled as a well-hidden hole in the little mountain Kedraki. Yemeniz (pp. 51–52) writes of Katsandonis in a cave deep in the mountains of Monastiraki in spring 1809. It was at this cave, Yemeniz tells us (p. 54), that Katsandonis told his comrades he had a dream. Quoting from Yiannis Frangistas, Katsandonis's first officer, Yemeniz reports it was a dream of "un fleuve dont le rivage se derobait sans cesse et qui roulait des touts parts des membres mutites." Katsandonis takes the dream as a forecast of his defeat and death. The same dream is referred to in the folk song tradition: see Passow, pp. 79–81, and Melahrinos, pp. 36–37. Yemeniz (p. 42) reports that Katsandonis's foe Aga Belussis also had a dream prophesying his defeat. A dream figures in the Katsandonis text as well; here Ali has a dream that is interpreted by a priest captured along with Katsandonis (see Yiorgos Haridimos, interview, 1969, Rin., tape 64). Fauriel (pp. 169–70), Emerson (p. 440), and Yemeniz (p. 56) report that at the cave Katsandonis's brother Yiorgos Hasiotis carried Katsandonis on his back and battled his attackers hand to hand.

96. Katsandonis was apparently betrayed at the cave, but by whom and to whom remains in dispute. Arravantinos (2:823) claims it was a priest; a second tradition, reported by Yemeniz (p. 53), has an old woman, a sorceress and an herbalist who searched the mountains for plants for her brews, discover him; a folk song (Passow, pp. 80–81), Lukopulos (*Sta Vuna*, pp. 191–93), and Frangistas (p. 51) have a farmer from Tatarna, Thanasis Gurlias, as the betrayer; the *Yeniki Engiklopedia* (p. 355) reports that he was betrayed by

a girl who brought his food. The folk song tradition details Katsandoniş as being given up to Aga Muhurntaris (as does Frangistas, p. 54). A second prominent candidate is Aga Vassiaris (see Nikolaos K. Kasomulis, *Enthimimata stratiotika tis epanastaseos ton ellinon, 1821–1833*, vol. 1 [Athens, 1940], p. 15). One folk song variant (Yemeniz, pp. 55–56) notes Vassiaris as the officer who captured Katsandonis.

97. The order of Katsandonis's battles puts his meeting with Yiusuf Arapis before that with Veli Gekas. Neither figure is associated with his capture.

The folk variant in the popular tradition of the song Manos uses is cited in Stamelos.

Have you heard what is happening up high at the monastery?
They captured Katsandonis and escort him to his hanging.
One thousand men march in front of him and a thousand march behind.
And he stops short and says to the Agas,
"Turks, reign in the horses so I can look back
and say good-bye to the hills, to the barren retreats.
I want to whistle like a klepht, the way klephts whistle
    in case I might be heard by my lads, Tsongas and Lepeniotis,
    who might be seen on Metsovos coming to my rescue."

(as cited in Stamelos, p. 183)

Manos adopts the song to the needs of the performance. The monk Karderinis of the Karagiozis *Katsandonis* text is identified as Katsandonis's betrayer, replacing a figure identified in one song in the Katsandonis folk song tradition as Paliogurlias (Passow, p. 82). The place of capture, too, is specified as a monastery in Agrafa, again to serve a performance purpose—that of physically locating the place of action. The conventional frame image of developed Katsandonis songs (of a dream that Katsandonis interprets or three birds who appear) drop away in the variant used in the Karagiozis text. Instead, the hero is discovered on horseback attended by Turkish troops to whom he addresses himself. Mollas uses the same song as Manos at this juncture with the addition of the end line, "who went and betrayed me into Ali Pasha's hands" (Mollas, *Katsandonis* in *O Karagiozis*, vol. 3, ed. Yiorgos Ioannos, pp. 223–24).

Unlike other variants on the theme of Katsandonis's capture (see Passow, pp. 76–82), this Karagiozis Katsandonis song no longer expresses the hero's poetic premonition of his capture; it no longer pleads that the hero's head be taken by his own men. At the same time, it continues to rely on some of the same materials: the burning of villages, the loss of the leader, acknowledgement of betrayal and defeat. It is, on its own terms, a dramatic call for revenge that pushes the action forward rather than allowing it to devolve into pathos and pessimism.

99. Kostas Lepeniotis was one of Katsandonis's brothers. A klepht, he was ambushed and killed by Ali Pasha after he submitted to his rule. Lepeniotis's submission occurred after the martyrdom of Katsandonis. Spandonidis (pp. 43–45) and Yemeniz (p. 30) claim there were four brothers in Katsandonis's family (Katsandonis, Yiorgos Hasiotis—born in Hasia—Hristos Kutsikos—"the small one"—and Kostas Lepeniotis—born in Lepenos) but folk tradition, reflected in Emerson (p. 438) and Fauriel (p. 162), cites five brothers. Katsandonis was apparently the oldest of the brothers. A folk song collected by Yemeniz in Agrafa (pp. 55–56) refers to Kutzukis and Lepeniotis in

a refrain traditionally reserved in other Katsandonis songs for Tsongas and Lepeniotis (see Passow, pp. 78–81, and Spandonidis, p. 14). Tsongas might be responsible for the confusion over a fifth brother.

100. Comstock (pp. 87, 90) speaks of distrust of the clergy among the peasants. The klephts, it is clear, made no secret of switching sides from Islamic to Christian forces as their interests dictated. They ravaged Christian as well as Muslim villages and preyed upon rich church lands. The source of anti-church sentiment in the folk tradition is tied to the fact that the church was a large property holder and identified its interests with the Greek primates, many of whom collaborated with the Turks to protect their wealth. Leake (1:48) advises us that "the greater number of Ali's subjects being Christians, he is very watchful over the bishops, often employs them as instruments of extortion, and is careful that every act of theirs shall tend to the stability and extension of his own power . . . [he] shows them favor, so far as to support their authority over the Christians, and sometimes to assist them with a little military force if it should be necessary for the collection of their dues, which consist chiefly in a fixed contribution from every Christian house."

101. The Karagiozis performance in the days of the Greek border wars (late nineteenth, early twentieth centuries) was, according to Yiorgos Haridimos (1984 interview), barbaric and harsh, an approach still reflected but muted in the modern Katsandonis performance. Responding to the information that Mollas in his *Katsandonis* text had the traitor monk Karderinis killed, Haridimos replied that his father, the famous Piraean player Hristos Haridimos, threw the Karderinis puppet figure into the audience, which burned it or tore it to pieces. Elsewhere in the performance, a child was beheaded because he had no gold for Ali. Since World War II, Haridimos has not exacted revenge against the Karderinis figure, for, he explains, to kill him would entail having to kill Vagias as well.

102. In his performance, Yiorgos Haridimos (Rin., tape 64, 1984 interview) adds a scene here in which Ali Pasha hangs Katsandonis's brother Yiorgos Hasiotis (who in the folk song tradition is tortured and martyred along with Katsandonis) to force Katsandonis to convert.

103. Three views grew up in the folk tradition regarding this point in the Katsandonis legend. In the first (Fauriel, p. 170, and Yemeniz, p. 58), the nephew of Veli Gekas is chosen as or volunteers to be Katsandonis's executioner. In the second (Arravantinos, 2:283), Veli Gekas's brother asks Ali to spare Katsandonis, but Ali, seeing the value of Katsandonis's torture as an example, refuses. In the third, (Yemeniz, p. 58), the parents of Veli Gekas bring Ali money and ask for Katsandonis's immediate death, a request to which Ali accedes in spite of his desire to convince Katsandonis to join him and his forces as common enemies of the Sultan.

The second view is picked up in a 1935 synopsis of Manos's *Katsandonis* text (in Guilio Caimi, *La Comedie grecque dans l'âme théâtre d'ombres* [Athens: Hellenikes Technes, 1935], pp. 74–78). Here, Veli Gekas's brother visits Katsandonis in jail and begs Ali for his pardon. In the Mollas text, Veli Gekas's wife plays the same role. Haridimos (Rin., tape 64) has Ali try to enlist Veli Gekas's brother against Katsandonis, but is refused.

104. Fauriel (p. 139) claims Katsandonis cried out under torture since he was ill. His brother Yiorgos derided him for behaving like a woman (Yemeniz, p. 58, and Emerson, p. 440). Leake (3:551), on the contrary, claims that Kat-

sandonis cursed the Turks throughout his torture; Leake learned of Katsandonis's death from villagers in Stamna, near Vrahori, in March 1809. Fauriel's version is much like a song in Passow (p. 79) in which, about to be captured, Katsandonis cries out to his brother to take his head so it won't fall into enemy hands; Yiorgos derides him and says they'll fight instead.

105. Katsandonis's terrible fate is possibly what raises this historical figure in popular appeal above other more accomplished revolutionary heroes. Finlay (1:29), for example, only refers to Katsandonis to note his terrible fate at Ali's hands. Yemeniz (p. 59) cites Katsandonis as not playing as great a role in the history of his country as Tzavellas or Botsaris but "exercent le plus de prestige sur l'imagination du peuple."

The date of Katsandonis's death, like that of his birth, is unclear. Frangistas (p. 56) claims it occurred at Easter, but Stamelos (p. 203) holds it was the end of September, one month after his capture. Kostas Kristallis ("To paniyiri tis Kastritsas," I foni tis Ipiru [October 1892]) claims his death was associated with the celebration of St. John's festival, 23 September, as he learned on a trip to the monastery of Kastritsas near Ioannina (see Kristallis, Apanta [Athens, 1952], p. 629). The year is equally unclear; sources differ, placing it sometimes in 1807 and sometimes in 1808 (Stamelos, p. 203).

It is not clear whether Katsandonis's body was thrown into the lake at Ioannina on the same night he died (Stamelos, p. 280) or if it was given Christian burial, as Ramfus claims (p. 106), in the Proavlion of the Mitropolis in Ioannina. Ramfus's claim that Ali gave the body to two Christians—Stavros Ioannos and Kostas Marinos—is reflected in Mustakas's Katsandonis text in which Karagiozis and Hatziavatis carry off Katsandonis's body to bury it.

106. A popular tradition developed, reflected in the plays, that an eagle (a classical symbol of Zeus) flew down and carried Katsandonis and his brother to heaven (D. Lukopulos, Sta Agrafa ena taksidi [Athens: I.N. Sideris, 192?], p. 171). Yiorgos Haridimos (1984 interview) reports several alternate endings to the Katsandonis text. In one, a devil descends and mounts Ali. In a second, an angel descends to take the soul of Katsandonis in the form of a dove (a Byzantine symbol) as two other angels descend, one carrying the symbol of Greece and the other the Greek flag. In the third version, the Archangel Michael and the devil descend in battle over Katsandonis's soul; Michael wins.

107. Markos Botsaris (1790–1823) was commander in chief in western Greece. He was killed in action. Botsaris was a member of a notable family from Suli that provided a number of important leaders during the revolution.

108. Athanasios Diakos (1788–1821) studied for the priesthood in a monastery, where he killed a Turkish sheriff who tried to seduce him. He served with the famous Odysseus Andrutsos, both as a klepht and, ironically, as Ali Pasha's bodyguard. He opposed Turkish forces most prominently at the Bridge of Alamana. He was roasted to death on a spit.

109. Lambros Katsonis (d. 1804) was an eighteenth-century sea-klepht. He served in mid-career under the Russians and later joined forces with Odysseus Andrutsos.

110. Konstantine Kanaris (1790–1877) of Psara was an admiral famous for destroying the Turkish fleet off Chios.

111. Andreas Miaulis (1769–1835) was an admiral of the Greek navy who later became inspector general of the fleet after King Otho took power in 1832. His most famous act was his mutiny against Capodistria, who had been elected president of the Greek Republic in 1827.

CHAPTER 3: THE SEVEN BEASTS AND KARAGIOZIS

1. Joseph Fontenrose, *Python: A Study of Delphic Myth and its Origins* (Berkeley: University of California Press, 1959), pp. 465–73, 545.

2. The player Yiorgos Haridimos (interview, January 1987), explains the *Alexander* text as being in two versions. The additon or elimination of the murder of the vizir's daughter and the suicide of the hero Alexander distinguish the two texts. He identifies the romance version by the use of the term "seven snakes" in the title rather than merely "the snake"; it represents a longer plot. The shorter heroic version, Haridimos explains, uses Alexander as "the god from the machine" or a "deus ex machina" who simply resolves the plot without playing an extended role. In both versions, Haridimos claims, the player can add or delete a series of scenes in which each one of the figures attempting the feat presents himself to the vizir or pasha at the serai.

3. Yiorgos Haridimos, interview, January 1987.

4. Early testimony of the performance of the Karagiozis *Alexander* text appears in the 1890s with Rulias (*O foveros ofis tu arahniasmenu spilieu*) and in 1900 with Hristos Kondos (*O thanatos tu ofeos ipo tu megalu Aleksandru tis Makedonias*). A related text (*Ta enigmata tis viziropulas*) was performed in the 1890s by Mimaros (Thodoros Hatzipandazis, "I isvoli tu Karagiozi stin Athina tu 1890," *O Politis*, no. 49 [March 1982]:81–82). The first notice of an Alexander performance or its prototype appears in *Evia*, 24 October 1879, in Halkida. The performance occurred in a working-class cafe in a Jewish neighborhood. The notice reports that this performance of *The Beautiful Sirini* created a furor (Walter Puchner, *I Valkanikes diastasis tu Karagiozi* [Athens: Stigmi, 1985], p. 37). Puchner (p. 44) follows Kostas I. Biris's ("O Karagiozis: Elliniko laiko theatro," *Nea Estia* 52 [1952]: 1130) claim that the first performer of Alexander was Liakos Prevezanos and that the Epirote school of players first brought forth the performance (Puchner, p. 50), although not in its present shape. The basic skeleton of the text (the battle with the beast and the hero obtaining Sirini) would have been the same.

5. Published *Alexander* texts include the following: Markos Ksanthos, *Ta epta thiria ke o Karagiozis*, in *O Karagiozis*, vol 2, ed. Yiorgos Ioannos (Athens: Ermis, 1971); Yiannis Mustakas, *O Karagiozis ta epta thiria ke o megas Aleksandros*, in *Dodeka komodies ke to hroniko tu theatru ton skion*, ed. Babis Grammenos (Athens: Angira, 1973); Panayiotis Mihopulos, *O megaleksandros ke to katarameno fidi*, in *Pende komodies ke dio iroika* (Athens: Ermias, 1972; and Sotiris Spatharis, *O megas Aleksandros ke o katiramenos ofis*, in *O Karagiozis ton Spatharidon* (Athens: Nefeli, 1979). A synopsis of a performance by Andonios Mollas was published by Louis Roussel as "Les sept monstres," in *Karagheuz ou un théâtre d'ombres à Athènes*, vol. 2 (Athens: Raftanis, 1921), pp. 32–35.

Taped performances include the following in the Rinovolucri Collection of the Center for the Study of Oral Literature, Harvard University (1969): Avraam, *To fidi*, tape 1; Spiros Karambalis, *To fidi*, tape 19; and Yiorgos Haridimos, *To fidi*, tapes 55–56. A fourth performance, by Haridimos, was taped by us in 1974. A taped dictation by Yiorgos Papanikolaos is also deposited in the Cedric Whitman Collection (hereafter referred to as Whit.) at the center (1962), tapes 2, 3, 4.

A related play, *The Riddles*, in which Alexander is featured as the hero has appeared in the following versions: a print text by Yiannis Mustakas, *O Ka-*

228   NOTES TO PAGES 140–43

ragiozis ke ta tria enigmata, in *Dodeka komodies,* ed. Babis Grammenos; a print synopsis, Andonios Mollas, "Antiochus et le lion," in *Karagheuz,* ed. Roussel, 2:35–37; and two taped dictations, Vasilis Vasilaros, *Ta enigmata,* Rin., tape 61 (1969) and Whit., tape 4 (1971).

6. Puchner, *I Valkanikes diastasis,* p. 51.

7. Yiorgos Veludis, *Diigisis Aleksandru tu Makedonos* (Athens: Ermis, 1977), p. lxxxv.

8. Ibid., p. lxxxvii.

9. Yiorgos Haridimos, interview, January 1987.

10. Veludis, *Diigisis Aleksandru,* pp. lxxxvi–lxxxvii, 92.

11. The ballads are rooted in the thirteenth-century version of the legend; see Jacobus de Varagine, *The Golden legende* (New York: Dauber, 1928).

12. R. M. Dawkins, trans. and ed., *Modern Greek Folktales* (Oxford: Clarendon Press, 1953), pp. 227–43.

13. Fontenrose, *Python: A Study of Delphic Myth,* pp. 466, 515–518; Dawkins, *Modern Greek Folktales,* pp. 123–28; M. I. Manusakas, "Ke pali to tragudi yia to vasilia erriko tes flantras," *Laografia* 15 (1954):355.

14. The player Yiorgos Haridimos (interview, January 1987) refers to the cutting of the tongues as well as the scene with Karagiozis-the-pretend-slayer and the donkey in the serai as *mikri komodies* (or separate, one-act texts used as after-acts with short texts) that found their way into both the *Alexander* and the *Adiohus* texts. Just as they can easily infiltrate a text, they can easily be dropped. On the practical side, Haridimos contends that the Karagiozis and the donkey scene requires two screens (for a change to the interior of the serai and sometimes an additional change to Karagiozis's hut where he asks his family whether his donkey had a head on when he left home). Setting up the screen and making the scene changes require time or a number of helpers. Since the modern player has little help and since the performance is itself difficult and exhausting considering the number of effects, voices, and puppets the player must manage with limited help, Haridimos simply cuts out these scenes.

Haridimos calls these one-act texts *sfines* or *tzurnales* and describes them as twenty- to thirty-minute pieces, half performances, fillers, and epilogues. They can as well be transformed into full-length performance texts. Not only do such small comedies find their way into the performance prologue, but the earliest known prologues (the braying donkey and the Hatziavatis and Karagiozis debate over a wallet) were themselves simply small comedies. It is likely that the fully developed modern prologue may have been generated by putting together such popular filler comedies.

15. See George Pilitsis, "Saint George in Folk Tradition," paper delivered at the Greek-Turkish Conference, Balch Institute, Philadelphia, April 1985.

16. Kostas I. Biris, "Ellinikos o Karagiozis," *Theatro,* no. 10 (July–August 1963):14.

17. Interview with Yiorgos Haridimos, 10 May 1974.

18. See Puchner, *I Valkanikes diastasis.*

19. See Grigoris M. Sifakis, "I paradosiaki dramaturyia tu Karagiozi," *O Politis,* no. 5 (September 1976):25–39.

20. See Veludis, *Diigisis Aleksandru.*

21. Sifakis, p. 67.

22. Veludis, *Diigisis Aleksandru,* p. lxxxvi.

23. Ibid., p. lxx; B. Schmidt, *Griechische Marchen, Sagen und Volkslieder* (Leipzig: Teulner, 1877), pp. 145–48.

24. Veludis, *Diigisis Aleksandru*, p. lxxiii; K. E. Manusos, "To paramithi tu Megalu Aleksandru," *Laografia* 6 (1917):653ff.

25. Veludis, *Diigisis Aleksandru*, pp. lxxvii, lxxxviii; G. K. Spiridakis, "Dimodis paradosis peri tis tomis tu porthmu Vosporu ipo tu Meg. Aleksandru," in *Is mnimin K. Amantu* (Athens, 1960), p. 378ff.

26. Veludis, *Diigisis Aleksandru*, p. lxxix.

27. Ibid., p. lxxx.

28. Ibid., p. lxxxviii; and Sifakis, p. 70.

29. Sifakis (p. 39, footnote 26) claims the evidence provided by Veludis is insufficient to demonstrate the identification of Alexander as a dragon-slayer. Puchner (*I Valkanikes diastasis*, pp. 64–65) takes the position that the legendary form of Alexander was known in the written and oral traditions across the Balkans but that the Greek oral tradition had not made a connection between Alexander and dragon-slaying, although we do not find general tales of dragon-slaying in the Peloponnesos, Thessaly, Epirus, and Macedonia. Whereas, however, the decades after 1821 saw the imprinting of the Alexander *filladia*, folk tales, folk songs, and iconographic traditions on shadow theater in Greece, similar steps incorporating these traditions did not occur in the Balkans. Manusakas, p. 358, points out one song in which an Alexis slays a dragon in its lair, but he makes clear that Alexis is not a name generally associated with Alexander.

30. See George Cary, *The Medieval Alexander* (Cambridge: Cambridge University Press, 1956), p. 11; and William W. Tarn, *Alexander the Great: Sources and Studies,* vol. 1 (Cambridge: Cambridge University Press, 1948), p. 363. References to *The History of Alexander the Great* are taken from Ernest A. Wallis Budge, ed., *The History of Alexander the Great, Being the Syriac Version of the Pseudo-Callisthenes* (Cambridge: Cambridge University Press, 1889).

31. Pseudo-Callisthenes, *The History of Alexander,* 1.34; 2.14.

32. Ibid., 3.3, 3.7, 3.9.

33. Ibid., 3.7.

34. Ibid., 3.17.

35. Biris, "O Karagiozis: Elliniko laiko theatro," *Nea Estia* 52 (1952):1271.

36. See A. P. Pallis, *Greek Miscellany: A Collection of Essays on Mediaeval and Modern Greece* (Athens: Constantinades and Mihalas, 1964).

37. John Mavrogordato, "Introduction," *Digenes Akritas* (Oxford: Clarendon Press, 1956), p. lxxix.

38. Ibid., p. xxix, footnote 2.

39. Ibid.

40. Halil Inalcik, *The Ottoman Empire: The Classical Age 1300–1600,* trans. Norman Itzkowitz and Colin Imber (New York: Praeger Publishers, 1973), pp. 187–88.

41. F. W. Hasluk, *Christianity and Islam Under the Sultans,* vol. 2, ed. Margaret M. Hasluck (1929; reprint, New York: Octagon Books, 1973), pp. 647–55.

42. Veludis, *Diigisis Aleksandru*, p. lxxxvii.

43. Puchner, *I Valkanikes diastasis,* p. 62.

44. Sifakis, p. 39, footnote 29.

45. Synopsized in Metin And, *Karagoz: Théâtre d'ombres turc.* (Ankara: Dost Yayınlari, 1977).

46. Sifakis (p. 65) refers to a folk tale in the tradition of "Snow-White" as a

possible influence on the Alexander text. In this folk tale, a woodcutter, who is supposed to throw the daughter into a fire, vows the girl will not be killed and appears to her father as a dragon-slayer.

47. Puchner, *I Valkanikes diastasis*, p. 61.

48. Ioannos, 2:xii.

49. Spiros Melas, "Mia diaskedastike erevna, O Karagiozis," *Akropolis* (4 November 1952).

50. Sifakis, p. 39, footnote 29.

51. Puchner's survey (*I Valkanikes diastasis*, p. 67) of folk tales shows three forms of the monster. The most frequent is the *thirio* or "beast." The *drakos* or *drakondas* (a winged dragon) frequently occurs. The *fidi* or "snake" is the least frequent. In the folk tales, the *drakos* takes on anthropomorphic qualities. In the Byzantine iconography of Saint George, the monster often appears as an *ofis* (or snake) but also as a winged *drakondas*. Karagiozis, by contrast, uses all these terms in titles of Karagiozis texts, but uses the Turkish-style snake borrowed from the Turkish Karagoz performance as the puppet figure.

52. In some folk-tale versions, Saint George rides away with the girl or finds a noble young man to marry her; see Dawkins, *Modern Greek Folktales*, pp. 126–28.

53. The *Alexander* text has spawned variants capitalizing on both modern and classical themes. Evyenios Spatharis's performance *The Labors of Heracles* features Heracles slaying a seven-headed snake to save a terrorized city. Yiorgos Haridimos (interview, January 1987) cites a modern heroic text performed by Vangos in which the pasha offers the hand of his daughter to whomever can defeat his "secret weapon." After a series of suitors fails, an anonymous hero succeeds. He denies the girl as a reward and accepts money for his band of warriors.

54. Whereas print texts that could act as performance master texts do exist, players regard these as merely one performance of a text, not as an original or authoritative text. More importantly, mature players have little knowledge of these texts and thus could not have learned their performances from them. It is true that players sometimes have their apprentices read passages from heroic poems or patriotic speeches of historical interest during a performance, but these passages are not borrowed from print Karagiozis texts. Educated younger players, on the contrary, have been influenced by chapbooks (pirated popular editions of Karagiozis texts) in their youth. Those who never learn to go much beyond these adumbrated texts are rarely admitted to the Karagiozis Players Association and are thus not licensed as players, an inhibition that does not seem to keep them from performing, nevertheless.

Yiorgos Haridimos speaks to this issue: "Many Karagiozis players perform written [texts], that is, they write their performances from beginning to end in workbooks. They don't have an opportunity to improvise; they lack good memory. . . . I begin systematically. I get into my performance. I complete everything from beginning to end. At this point, I improvise, whereas those who write in books do not. . . . They don't remember, and they perform in a limited way, in a studied way. They depart from the elements of our art . . ." (Bra., tape 1–2).

55. In the player's view, just as creativity must be balanced by tradition, so must improvisation be balanced by respect for the "classical" shape of the performance that, in Yiorgos Haridimos's view, represents both a standard and a

resource for the Karagiozis text. This is not to say that he believes improvisation is constrained by this view: "I can immediately transform one improvisation, two words, or something that might occur in my work, in my improvisation, into an entire performance. The whole performance that results will be correct, classical, that is to say, that which I seek. You see? [The classical performance] is so deeply rooted in me that it emerges by itself. My work gives it birth" (Bra., tape 1–2).

THE SEVEN BEASTS AND KARAGIOZIS: TEXT OF THE PLAY

1. The Greek performance traditionally opens with a prologue, which the players refer to as a *komodia* or comic piece. A curtain-raiser that has its own traditional content and is complete in itself, the prologue is infrequently represented in print texts and for that reason was not included in the original print versions of either Manos's *Katsandonis* text or Ksanthos's *Alexander* text. The Greek prologue differs from that of its Turkish forerunner in which the hunchback's associate, Haciavad, recites a poem, sings a song, and offers prayers. In the Greek performance, a modern prologue typically includes some combination of the following scenes: Karagiozis's opening dance, his marching and quizzing of his sons, a quarrel between the rustic Barba Yiorgos and the palace guard Veli Gekas, an announcement by Karagiozis and his sons of the evening's performance, and an extended stock scene of some type (the supposed death and resurrection of Karagiozis, for example). On the development and history of the prologue, see L. S. Myrsiades, "Oral Composition in the Karaghiozis Performance," *Theatre Research International* 5 (1980):109–13.

2. The whole text in performance, according to player testimony, is essentially a three-part construction of initial, middle, and concluding phases, variously described. Theodoropulos sees his performance as being in three parts: the preliminary Hatziavatis-Bey scenes; the Hatzaivatis-Karagiozis scene where the laughs begin; and a final opportunity. Haridimos's first division is made up of the Hatziavatis-Bey scene and the Hatzaivatis-Karagiozis scene, which for him begin the action; second is a series that constitutes the action; third is the close. M. Mollas discusses his father's divisions: "[Andonios] Mollas devoted the first act of his performance to sketching the psychology of character types. He stereotyped them. . . . His second act was devoted to conflict, and the third to dissolution. (Rin., tape 67).

The *Alexander* text exhibits the three performance divisions noted by players with a pre-action set of scenes, a sequence of repeated actions by different characters, and a post-action set of scenes. The first set includes the announcement scene complex; the second set includes the parade of characters who attempt to slay the beast; and the third includes that part of the text dominated by Alexander, who fulfills and dissolves the main action of the performance. The last part takes place after the performance intermission. For discussion on composition of the *Alexander* text, see Linda S. Myrsiades, "Oral Traditional Form in the Karagiozis Performance," *Ellinika* 36 (1985):125.

3. Bey: a rich Turkish gentleman.

4. Pashina: the feminine form of the title "pasha," or governor of a province.

5. The Alexander figure in the Karagiozis performance penetrates modern Greek history through a surrogate, Captain Astrapoyiannis. A figure created by the modern Greek poet Valaoritis and linked in his epic poem to the Greek Revolution of 1821 (see *I Megali elliniki engiklopedia*, 2nd ed., vol. 5 [Athens:

Finiks, 1964], p. 924), Astropoyiannis appears in a Karagiozis performance similar to *Alexander* (Andonaros's *O mavros tis Anatolis*, Rin., tape 42). True to the ideal hero's role, Astrapoyiannis finds his real reward in preserving his homeland as he destroys the monstrous giant to whom Christian Greeks had been fed.

6. Dervenagas: battalion commander responsible for guarding public roads and mountain passes under the Turkish occupation. The term carries the colloquial meaning of "he-who-does-what-he-wants."

7. The player cultivates a range of tricks and techniques to differentiate characters, based largely on a flexible use of the tongue and fluid breath control. He must be able to control the size and volume of his voices from both the throat and the diaphragm and to express varied tones and colors through the larynx. It is through breath control and control of the larynx that the player changes his voices; the degree of nasality and changes in the morphology of the face hold the voice in place. Since a player's performance relies on his ability to use his voice, Haridimos claims, he must be able to play continuously without tiring. He must keep his tongue from getting twisted, his throat clear and unstuck, his sounds clear and well distinguished, and his ability to mimic dialects undiminished. If the throat tires and projection diminishes, he must be able to maintain a strong laryngeal tone for each character and play without leaving a void, or empty space, in his performance, a trick accomplished with a flexible tongue.

8. The percentage of a performance done in music, both dances and songs, differs from player to player. With live music, it can range from twenty-five percent (Y. Haridimos) to as much as forty percent (A. Andonaros), depending on the player's singing ability and the general richness of his performance text. Most players know the traditional songs and possess at least the minimal ability to sing their own songs. A sample of thirty-five live performances resulted in 124 live songs sung by nineteen different players, indicating that a great many do choose to sing.

9. Dervish: a member of the Muslim clergy vowed to chastity and poverty.

10. The song Hatziavatis sings, the Turkish amane, is a long, drawn-out song with fancy and intricate vocalizations that are improvised in performance. The amane, a song type from Asia Minor that originated possibly as early as the fourteenth century, is spontaneously improvised and is generally sad, lamenting the futility of life, a common theme in songs of the late Ottoman Empire. Hatziavatis's songs in particular are pessimistic and floridly poetic and deal with the pain Hatziavatis feels as an unrequited lover.

11. The bey's song, an *amane* like Hatziavatis's song, has been affected in performance by the disappearance of professional singers, but, unlike the Hatziavatis song, it still continues to be widely sung. The art of *amane* singing, together with the singing of klephtic songs, constituted one of the chief charms of the Karagiozis performance in its most popular period.

12. Roussel describes Hatziavatis's voice as "mielleuse et hypocrite" (1:19).

13. A turkish term for one high in rank or authority.

14. Where the Turkish performance initiated its main action with a battle of wits between Karagoz and Haciavad, the Greek performance differs. The debate—which commonly appears in the Greek form as part of a second scene wherein Hatziavatis calls Karagiozis from his hut—is replaced in the first position by an opening narrative scene in which a bey engages Hatziavatis to sat-

isfy some whim or need, thus providing the initiating spark for the action to follow. Another variant, functioning as a secondary prologue, occurs with limited frequency as an opening scene. In it, Karagiozis plays out a joke at some length; the tricks themselves, irrelevant to the action of the play, function as a comic interlude, sometimes involving arguments between Karagiozis and his wife, Karagiozis's dreams, his desire for food, or his escape from a pursuer.

15. Ksanthos's *Alexander* text provides an example of the typical structure of the announcement scene: Hatziavatis engages to call out the decree for pay and declares he will do so by beginning at the agora, or market place; Hatziavatis announces the decree; Karagiozis is woken and objects to the commotion outside his door; Karagiozis attempts to learn how to call out; off on his own, Karagiozis confuses the decree and is beaten by Veli Gekas. A secondary structure is evident within the scene, for four opportunities arise for a repetition of the message: when Hatziavatis himself reads the decree or is told of its contents; when Hatziavatis actually announces the decree; when Hatziavatis repeats the decree in conversation with Karagiozis; and when Karagiozis distorts the announcement as he calls it out. The announcement itself is viewed in three ways. First, it is seen as a whole, an authoritative formal command. Second, it is seen, as Hatziavatis announces it, in terms of its constituent six parts as a proclamation: asking for attention, naming the ranks of its audience, appealing by nationality, affirming the authority behind the decree, naming the deed to be done, and describing the reward. In the learning sequence, finally, the decree is divided into short phrases, the more easily to be memorized by Karagiozis. The last division provides an intensive opportunity for punning and rapid-fire exchanges. The repetitions and shifts in the way the decree is viewed move us progressively closer and closer to it, as if we were acoustically engaged first from a distance, then on middle ground, and at last in extreme close-up.

16. Roussel describes the voice of Karagiozis as "très stridement traditionnelle" (1:19). It is "agréable dans sa gaîté, renferme mille éléments comiques: le registre est très étendu: la voix est celle d'un baryton, mais susceptible d'une fausset aigu, très amusant" (1:25). For the Karagiozis figure, which is constantly on stage, the player uses largely his natural voice, recognizing that this figure would tire him out too rapidly if it required too contrived a sound. The freedom needed to characterize such a complex character as Karagiozis can only be provided by a voice that requires little artificial control.

17. The player has several scenes available for getting Karagiozis on stage for his traditional opening scene with Hatziavatis. His choice is based on the principle of scene substitution. The player can, for example, use either of the following scenes: Hatziavatis cannot get Karagiozis to come out ot his hut; Hatziavatis wakes Karagiozis from his dream; Karagiozis is chased on screen by an angry crowd and knocks Hatziavatis down. Elsewhere in the performance, when the player needs to send Karagiozis to the cafe (an important social center), he once again has several scenes open to him based on the dictates of the plot: if he is going for food for his master, Karagiozis is beaten by the cafe owner for not paying his bill; if he is going for a job interview, he is interrogated by a bey; if he is a guest of a bey, he orders ridiculous items. Given an opportunity to expand his performance, the player in some cases links several of these scenes together.

18. Although this Ksanthos text does not provide us with an example of a

Karagiozis song, Karagiozis does sing more frequently and with a greater variety of songs in modern performances than any other figure. This phenomenon has, however, only emerged since the post–World War II years. Print texts from 1924–1945 contain significantly fewer Karagiozis songs. Of all the songs of the Karagiozis performance, those of Karagiozis and Stavrakas most reflect the force of events that changed the lives of modern Greeks. The following song illustrates Karagiozis's role as spokesman for the have-nots:

> What is this that we suffer
> all this time;
> all us children are hungry,
> and our bellies dance.
>
> All of us became hungry in a line
> in a moment.
> We cut our hunger in a line.
> I sing to the bread.
>
> High up in the mountains there,
> I see a loaf way up there,
> but I can't get there,
> and here on earth my belly dances.
>
> But apart from the hunger,
> there are other more fearful things;
> whenever winter takes hold,
> I am left without an overcoat.
>
> May you shiver from the cold,
> and I beat you,
> and you return to the road,
> trembling and I sing.
>
> There is no overcoat for me, there is no overcoat.
> There is no overcoat for me
> because he didn't give me a place in line
> so I go around without a coat.
>
> (Aleksopulos, Theodoropulos, Vasilaros)

19. The original play on words here is between *fermani* (decree) and *hurmani* (date).

20. Minion: from the French for "delicate" or "graceful."

21. Delicatsion: from the Italian for "delicately."

22. The play on words is between *beides* (beys) and *dembelides* (loafers).

23. The play on words is between *agades* (agas) and *avgulades* (egg eaters).

24. The play on words is between *pasades* (pashas) and *patsades* (tripe eaters).

25. The play on words is between *dervisades* (dervishes) and *tsurvatzades* (respected, propertied Christians).

26. The play on words is between *kinezi* (Chinese) and *kirkinezi* (a small hawk).

27. The play on words is between *angli, gali, rosi* (Englishmen, Frenchmen, Russians) and *gali, papagali,* and *grosi* (Frenchmen, parrots, and a piastre).

28. The play of words is between *Opios dinithi ke fonevsi* (Whoever finds and kills) and *Sambos evrethi ke honepsi* (Might be found and digest).

29. The play on words is between *Ta epta thiria pu vriskonde sto ka-tarahniasmenon spileon* (the seven beasts of the deserted cave) and *I mirmiria pu vriskete sto yiahnismeno spileon* (the muttering found in the stewed cave).

30. The word used here is *hronos* (time), which rhymes in Greek with *thronos* (throne).

31. The name used by Karagiozis is *Misindzeri*.

32. Pom-pom-tipped shoe: the traditional clogs worn by the Greek mountain warriors, called *tsaruhia*.

33. Karagiozis means here that Demosthenes was also a pimp. Demosthenes (384–322 B.C.) is generally considered to be the greatest of Greek orators.

34. The play on words is between *davanduria* (racket) and *yaiduria* (donkeys).

35. A popular Greek stringed instrument closely related to the mandolin.

36. *Tahini:* a paste of ground sesame seeds.

37. Here the *Alexander* text shifts to a *sira* construction in which a parade of characters enter, each performing essentially the same action. Besides the *Alexander* text, sixteen Karagiozis text types characteristically utilize the *sira* construction to form the central unit of the performance. Not all text types show regularity in the order in which characters appear. When a regular order does appear within a text type, it is not necessarily the same order that appears in other text types; nevertheless, when regularity characterizes a text type, that regularity is maintained even by players with highly individualized playing styles.

Within the Alexander *sira* (where we do find regularity in the order of appearance), for example, the figure Barba Yiorgos tends to be introduced last in the *sira*, the old man tends to be introduced first, Dionisios floats freely throughout the *sira*, appearing in any position, and the figures Stavrakas, Omorfonios, and the Jew generally appear one after the other, as if held together by some "tension of essences" (see A. B. Lord, *The Singer of Tales* [1960, reprint, New York: Atheneum, 1965], from whom this term is borrowed). Thus, when regularity appears, both the position of individual figures in the *sira* of a given text type and the way in which the *sira* is used by individual texts of that text type follows clear and regular patterns.

38. Roussel describes the voice of Kolitiris: "parle . . . du nez, et ne peut prononcer le son 'r' dont il fait une 'l'" (1:25).

39. Roussel describes Dionisio's voice as "le chantonnement monotone du parler de Zanthe" (1:19). According to Yiorgos Haridimos, Dionisios's voice is high and light, requiring little projection; it has a nasal tone and employs quick action in the tongue. Performing such distinctive, regional dialects as Dionisios's, represents, in this player's view, the greatest challenge of the performance. Like a singer, Haridimos relies for his performance of dialects on sounds that rise and fall like musical notes: loud and soft sounds, colors, shades, pitches, tones, and dialectical inflections. The sounds are memorized and retained just as one might learn a musical score. They have for this player the same exact placement and phrasing, the same tonality, as musical notes.

40. Dionisios's song, the Italian cantada of the Ionian islands, is a serenade or lyrical love song usually accompanied by a mandolin. It was highly popular from its first use in the Karagiozis performance in the late nineteenth century. In its most completely developed form, the song combines the love of home

typical of the character, his romantic predilections, and references to the patron saint, Saint Dionisios, of the figure's home island, Zante.

41. *Finamenta:* from the Italian for the "latest news." The play on words
here is between *finamenta* and *tsimenta* (cement).

42. Roussel describes Omorfonios's voice as "nasillarde et stupide," Omorfonios "parle horriblement du nez avec une voix lente et pénible" (1:25).

43. Ksanthos does not provide us with an example of Omorfonio's song,
which typically mixes themes of food and love, often in a meaningless way. A
comic lover, his complaints comment on his lack of success with the female
sex. Like the figure himself, the song he sings, once quite popular, has in modern performances lost its interest; it has been shortened to a single prototypical
verse entirely without melody. Indeed, even in its original form it was a non-
descript tune of little individual quality and no regional location to root it in
the memory of its audience. The song has been retained as an introductory
poem recited by this character when he enters the stage:

> 1. I am called Omorfonios,
> alias golden pride,
> and all the young women go crazy
> over who will have me first. Ouit.

or (lines 2–3)

> I have a secret pride
> all the young women kill themselves

(A. Mollas, Ksanthos, Mihopulos, Y. Haridimos, Yeneralis, Ianaros, Yitsaris)

44. Stadiu Street is a main avenue in Athens.

45. Roussel describes Stavrakas's voice as "un timbre mou et voyoucra-
tique, une malsaine désenvolture de chenapan dans l'articulation et les intona-
tions spécials d'un ivrogne invétéré . . ." (1:25).

46. Stavrakas, like Karagiozis, provides a rich proliferation of songs for the
performance. The rebetika songs he sings are urban folk songs of the rebetes,
marginal people living an underworld existence in the taverns and harbors of
urban Greece. Originally created as a fusion of music, lyrics, and dance, these
songs can be dated as a distinct group from the mid 1800s. They increased in
popularity in the 1920s, peaking during the Greek Civil War years (1946–
1952). The rebetika are characterized by their own special argot of rich expressions whose ultimate sources were jails and opium dens. Typically accompanied by bouzoukia or baglamas (guitarlike instruments of nine and eight
strings, respectively), they were meant to be danced to and thus were highly
rhythmic and responsive to free expression. Many were characterized by a
wailing vocal style.

Yiorgos Haridimos provides an example of a typical Stavrakas song:

> Tonight you make "bam!"
> They see you and take joy in you
> as if they see a trolley.
> You live among my followers
> at the jail's oil lamp.
> May you live like a levendi
> a levendi you become.

> Tonight we make "bam!"
> Relax in the taxi,
> let's go have a good time
> in the back room of the store
> tonight at the tavern.
> Oh, what will happen.
> Make like you're dancing;
> no glass shall remain.
> Tonight we make "bam!"

47. *Aglea:* the word means "shining" or "bright."

48. *Fasiani:* the name is that of a bird, the pheasant. The origin of the word is the river Fasis.

49. Manusos Kretikos is almost completely dependent upon his thick Cretan dialect for his effect. Foreign types (the Englishman, the Frenchman, the German) rely in particular on such depiction. Manusos, another type of braggart warrior, is from Crete, a region known for its uncommonly courageous resistance to foreign invaders, particularly, in modern times, to the Germans in World War II. In addition, the earthy Manusos was known for his vulgarity in the performance. This trait is not, however, always reflected in his songs, which are preoccupied with themes related to women and love. Manusos's bravado and vulgarity were exploited to express sexual and political innuendos under the dictatorships and military rule that have plagued Greece throughout the twentieth century. Manusos's song is a simple, Cretan folk song of rhymed distichs:

> Come, come, come, my maiden,
> come, come, come, for my heart grows small.
>
> Groom, lad, Phaskian, what do you carry in your baggy pants?
> I have two lumps of sugar and a bottle of raki.
>
> Come, come, come, my little, little, little one,
> come, come, for she has possessed my mind.
>
> Come, come, come, my maiden,
> come, come, come, to my embrace.
>
> Come, come, come, and leave again,
> come, come, into my own embrace.
>
> Come, come, come, my maiden,
> from my sadness my hair has whitened.

> > (Mustakas)

50. Styliani: a saint to whom is attributed the power of protecting children from ailments.

51. Napoleons: a French gold coin.

52. Yiorgos Haridimos describes Barba Yiorgos's voice as a thunderous, rumbling sound arising from the larynx; it requires a shift in the morphology of the face and a lumbering use of the tongue.

53. *Tsaruhi.*

54. Barba Yiorgos is associated with various heroic songs in the performance. This association does not affect the frequency of these songs but does

affect their individual definition, ultimately generalizing their lyrics and stereo-typing rather than individualizing their melodies throughout the several gen-erations of the transmission process. The earliest known song for this figure is presented by the player Sotiris Spatharis in his autobiography. The song is in-troduced as one used by Yiannis Rulias, who is credited with having added the Barba Yiorgos figure to the performance.

> Yiorgos passed over yonder
> going to Karpenisi
> for a child in order to
> baptize a child
> and to name him Yiorgos.

Ksanthos provides an example of a Barba Yiorgos song more characteristic of his role as a shepherd:

> I have a thousand sheep,
> five hundred goats,
> and between the two mountains
> six grinding mills.
>
> Three grind with water,
> and the other three with milk;
> on the froth of the milk,
> three girls wash.

55. *Fustanella.*

56. In this scene, Karagiozis players refer to Alexander as a devil in armor (Mustakas), a fisherman with a spear (Mihopulos, Haridimos), and, punning on his name Alexander of Macedonia, Mr. Quince Tree—*Kir Kidonia* (Ha-ridimos, Mihopulos, Karambalis).

57. Drachma: a Greek coin of small value. Presently one drachma is less than one penny.

58. The play on words here is between *thoraka* (breastplate) and *koraka* (crow).

59. *Irini:* a saint from Macedonia and one of three martyred, maiden sis-ters. The name means "peace."

60. We find in our sample of ten *Alexander* texts, five players (Y. Hari-dimos, A. Mollas, Mustakas, Mihopulos, and Papanikolaos) who use a vari-ant in which Alexander cuts out the tongues of the beast and uses them to expose Karagiozis who pretends to be the beast-slayer at the serai.

61. In seven versions of the *Alexander* text (Papanikolaos, Spatharis, Mus-takas, Avraam, A. Mollas, Mihopulos, and Haridimos's 1969 variant), an added scene complex, inspired by a popular folk tale, appears at this point. In the added scene complex, Alexander cuts out the tongues of the beast; Kara-giozis pretends to Hatziavatis to be the slayer and Hatziavatis and Karagiozis carry off the beast; Karagiozis announces himself as the beast-slayer at the serai; and Alexander exposes Karagiozis by means of the tongues. When the addition is not made, the player simply omits the cutting of the tongues and ends with Karagiozis and Hatziavatis carrying off the beast. When a text needs to be cut short, such added scene complexes are among the first units to disappear.

62. The play on words is between *Makedon* (one from Macedonia), *kirkidon* (a play on the word *kidonia*, quince), and *kidonia* (quince).

63. The play on words is between the double meaning of *fortoma*, which can mean "to be a burden upon someone" or to badger, or can refer to the load placed on a donkey.

64. Three players in our sample of ten *Alexander* texts allow Alexander to accept the pasha's daughter as a reward for slaying the beast (Ksanthos, Karambalis, and Haridimos, 1969). One, Spatharis, substitutes a Greek girl as a reward. Two players have Alexander reject the pasha's daughter (Mihopulos and Papanikolaos), and four (Haridimos, 1974, Avraam, Mustakas, and A. Mollas) avoid the issue altogether. The fact that Haridimos in one version has Alexander accept the girl and in another avoids the issue suggests that the theme is losing its relevance in modern Karagiozis performances, both as an erotic motif and as a sign of Alexander as a saintly warrior. We find the same split in versions of the related *riddle text,* a text in which Alexander also appears. His task in the *riddle text* is to answer a riddle rather than to slay a beast (a theme reminiscent of the Oedipus myth). Of three versions of the *riddle text,* one (that of Vasilaros) makes the hero reject the girl; one (that of Mustakas) has him accept her; and one (that of A. Mollas) avoids the issue. A. Mollas uses the Adiohus figure as an Alexander surrogate in his riddle text (*Adiohus and the Lion*); here, the hero both answers the riddle and slays a beast, combining both Alexander functions. Disassociation of these tasks led to later substitutions of modern klephtic heroes in a monster-slaying text called variously *The Persecutor of the Christians* and *The Black of Anatolia,* texts that placed the monster-slaying more directly in the context of Greco-Turkish relations of the Ottoman period.

65. A. Mollas is the only player other than Ksanthos to use the poisoned apples theme in this context. He uses it in the related riddle text in his variant *Adiohus and the Lion.*

66. The play on words here is between *fakello* (envelope) and *faskelo* (a rude gesture).

67. The suicide theme appears only in Ksanthos's version; it apparently is not repeated in any other text in the Karagiozis repertoire.

68. Ksanthos is the only player in this context to use the classical theme of burial as a sacred course of action to prevent humiliation of the corpse and the consequent eternal wandering of the spirit (see the Antigone myth). We do find the theme repeated, however, in two places in the *Katsandonis* text (A. Mollas's variant). The first occurs when Karagiozis rescues the body of the hero Katsandonis's father, Lepeniotis, to prevent the Turks from despoiling it and denying it Christian burial; the second occurs when Karagiozis rescues the body of the hero Katsandonis to save it from the limepit or the lake—the famed lake in which Kira Frosini (Ali Pasha's captive Greek bride) was said to have been drowned (an event reported in the *Ali Pasha* texts of both Mustakas and Ianaros).

69. The endings of the Greek performance are arbitrary, unlike the prescribed format of the Turkish performance in which a debate between Karagoz and Haciavad and a conventional farewell conclude the evening's entertainment. Rather, the Greek performance might close with the pursuit of the fool-hero, a beating, or a celebration. It might end abruptly without tying together any of the plot's loose threads, or it might conclude with confirmation of some

larger moral order. The most completely decisive terminal actions occur in the history plays, which end in acts of bloody revenge, primitive assertions of·justice, or celebrations of the feats of a hero. More common, however, is one last twist of the comic screw in which Karagiozis reduces seeming order to chaos in a supreme assertion of his ability to turn the world topsy-turvy.

APPENDIX C: THE PRINT TEXTS

1. From the inside cover, O Karagiozis ekserevnitis, no. 20, Parastasis aftotelis (Athens: Darima, n.d.).

2. Stilpidon Kiriakidis, "Vivliografia: Roussel, Louis, 'Karagheuz,'" Laografia 1 (1921):280–83. Though he never studied Karagiozis, Kiriakidis collected eighty-four texts from which the modern folklorist Yiorgos Ioannos published eleven in his O Karagiozis, 3 vols. (Athens: Ermis, 1971–1972).

3. Hans Jensen, Vulgargriechische Schattenspieltexte (Berlin: Deutscher verlag der wissenschaften, 1954).

4. Markos Ksanthos, The Seven Beasts and Karagiozis, trans. by Kostas and Linda Myrsiades, The Charioteer, no. 19 (1977):20–49.

5. Kiriakos Kassis, Paralogotehnia stin Ellada 1830–1980: Laika filladia. O graftos Karagiozis (Athens: Ihor, 1985), pp. 32–33.

6. Kassis, p. 81.

7. Yiorgos Veludis, Diigisis Aleksandru tu Makedonos (Athens: Ermis, 1977), pp. 10–14.

8. Thodoros Hatzipandazis, "I isvoli tu Karagiozi stin Athina tu 1890," O Politis, no. 49 (March 1982):67.

9. Velmos, "O Karagiozis tu Molla," Frangelio, 3 December 1927, p. 3; see also, Frangelio, 19 December 1927.

10. Giulio Caimi, "O Mollas," Nea Estia 45 (1949):377. On this question see also, Athanasios Fotiadis, O Karagiozis o prosfigas (Athens: Gutenberg, 1977), pp. 243–52; Yiorgos Ioannos, "Isagogi," O Karagiozis, pp. 39–41; Ilias Petropulos, Ipokosmos ke Karagiozis (Athens: Grammata, 1978), p. 92.

11. Mollas from Politia, 31 July 1932, as quoted by Fotiadis, O Karagiozis o prosfigas p. 252.

12. Yiannis Kiurtsakis, Karnavali ke Karagiozis: I rizes ke i metamorfosis tu laiku yeliu (Athens: Kedros, 1985), p. 48.

INDEX

DATE DUE